280 delicious recipes for every meal

weightwatchers
50th anniversary cookbook

ST. MARTINS GRIFFIN ✦ NEW YORK

Note: Many recipes in this book were previously released in *Greatest Hits,* a Weight Watchers meeting room cookbook.

Editorial and art produced by W/W Twentyfirst Corp., 675 Avenue of the Americas, New York, N.Y. 10010

On the cover: The Iconic Weight Watchers Burger, page 104

www.stmartins.com

ISBN 978-1-250-03640-7 (hardcover)
ISBN 978-1-250-03641-4 (e-book)

First Edition: April 2013

10 9 8 7 6 5 4 3 2 1

about weight watchers

Weight Watchers International, Inc. is the world's leading provider of weight-management services, operating globally through a network of company-owned and franchise operations. Weight Watchers holds nearly 45,000 meetings each week worldwide, at which members receive group support and education about healthful eating patterns, behavior modification, and physical activity. Weight-loss and weight-management results vary by individual. We recommend that you attend Weight Watchers meetings to benefit from the supportive environment and follow the comprehensive Weight Watchers program, which includes a food plan, an activity plan, and a behavioral component. **WeightWatchers .com** provides subscription weight-management products, such as eTools and Weight Watchers Mobile, and is the leading internet-based weight-management provider in the world. In addition, Weight Watchers offers a wide range of products, publications (including **Weight Watchers Magazine**, which is available on newsstands and in Weight Watchers meeting rooms), and programs for people interested in weight loss and control. For the Weight Watchers meeting nearest you, call **1-800-651-6000**. For information about bringing Weight Watchers to your workplace, call **1-800-8AT-WORK**.

PUBLISHING GROUP

VP, Editorial Director
Nancy Gagliardi

Creative Director
Ed Melnitsky

Photo Director
Deborah Hardt

Managing Editor
Diane Pavia

Assistant Editor
Katerina Gkionis

Food Editor
Eileen Runyan

Editor
Jackie Mills, R.D.

Nutrition Consultant
U. Beate Krinke

Production Manager
Alan Biederman

Photographers
Rita Maas
Romulo Yanes (cover)

Food Stylists
Michael Pederson
Anne Disrude (cover)

Prop Stylists
Cathy Cook
Lynda White
Amy Elise Wilson (cover)

contents

about weight watchers *iii*
foreword *vi*
about our recipes *vii*
timeless tools for healthy cooking *ix*
cooking foods to safe temperatures *xi*
the leanest cuts *xii*
dry and liquid measurement equivalents *xiii*
metric equivalents *xiv*
a brief history of weight watchers *xv*

breakfast all day 1
omelettes, frittatas, smoothies, and more

midday meals 23
soups, salads, sandwiches, and breads

classic starters 81
tasty light bites and dips

family entrées 103
hearty meats, poultry, and seafood

meatless mainstays 183
satisfying vegetarian entrées

italian favorites 207
blue-ribbon pizza and pasta dishes

side stories 241
celebrated veggies and sides

best-in-show 281
delicious desserts and sweet treats

PointsPlus value *index* *322*
index *325*

foreword

Fifty, without question, is a milestone. Whether it's five decades spent committed to the same partner, toiling away in the same profession, or simply living on earth, 50 warrants appreciation—and respect. Frankly, in a world of instant everything (texts, tweets, gratification), anyone or anything that stays relevant for 50 years has earned the right to celebrate.

We've embraced that celebratory spirit with *Weight Watchers 50th Anniversary Cookbook,* a collection of favorite recipes that have been updated with two goals in mind: staying true to our past while reflecting how Americans are eating (and living) today. As we started compiling the recipes and information for this manuscript, the significance of this book representing one aspect of our golden anniversary became daunting, a task much more challenging than I had expected: How do you truly reflect (through food information and recipes) the role Weight Watchers has played in so many peoples' lives?

I needed a little historical perspective, so I turned to the numerous cookbooks that have been released under the Weight Watchers name since the company was founded in 1963. I spent time paging through those early books; many of them outlined the updates to the recipes as well as the stories of individuals who found success on the latest plan. Those cookbooks truly captured the excitement that surrounded the organization in its earliest days. At the start I turned to them to be reminded of just how far we've come and how much things had changed, yet what I came away with was the opposite.

Consider this introduction, written by one of the company's founders, Jean Nidetch, in the *Weight Watchers Program Cookbook* of 1972:

> *The Weight Watchers Program, introduced in 1963, was a boon to the overweight, helping hundreds of thousands of people lose millions of unhealthy, unsightly pounds. In 1972 a revised program was introduced, which incorporated the latest findings in nutritional information . . . We have branched out . . . in other ways too. In 1968 we introduced the* Weight Watchers Magazine . . . *Another innovation was the licensing of food companies to produce pre-portioned foods. Thus, you will find in your supermarket freezer fish luncheons and dinners galore, plus turkey, veal, chopped sirloin, and other foods . . . For me, personally, there have been many changes too . . . But above all, my life seems truly significant when I remember that through the Weight Watchers Program so many fat, unhappy people have been born again into thin, happy people. Maybe, this time, it will happen to you . . .*

Ultimately, while everything has changed since the '60s, so much has stayed the same. I recently spoke with a woman who began working at the company in the mid-1970s as a recipe developer, tester, and editor and stills works on various projects. She echoed Jean's words, describing how being a part of Weight Watchers was (and still is) "magical." That's when the mission of this new cookbook became clear to me: provide delicious recipes that will become tools to help people now, and perhaps in the future, find success. The "magic" now and then is also the same: It's about the people—Weight Watchers Members, Leaders, and Receptionists—all committed to helping others lose weight and reach their goals.

—Nancy Gagliardi
VP, Editorial Director

about our recipes

While losing weight isn't only about what you eat, Weight Watchers realizes the critical role it plays in your success and overall good health. That's why our philosophy is to offer great-tasting, easy recipes that are nutritious as well as delicious. We make every attempt to use wholesome ingredients and to ensure that our recipes fall within the recommendations of the U.S. Dietary Guidelines for Americans for a diet that promotes health and reduces the risk for disease. If you have special dietary needs, consult with your health-care professional for advice on a diet that is best for you, then adapt these recipes to meet your specific nutritional needs.

To achieve these good-health goals and get the maximum satisfaction from the foods you eat, we suggest you keep the following information in mind while preparing our recipes:

WEIGHT WATCHERS 360° AND GOOD NUTRITION

- Recipes in this book have been developed for Weight Watchers members who are following Weight Watchers 360°. ***PointsPlus***® values are given for each recipe. They're assigned based on the amount of protein, carbohydrates, fat, and fiber contained in a single serving of a recipe.
- Recipes include approximate nutritional information: they are analyzed for Calories (Cal), Total Fat, Saturated Fat (Sat Fat), Cholesterol (Chol), Sodium (Sod), Carbohydrates (Carb), Dietary Fiber (Fib), Protein (Prot), and Calcium (Calc). The nutritional values are calculated by registered dietitians, using nutrition analysis software.
- Substitutions made to the ingredients will alter the nutritional information and may affect the ***PointsPlus*** value.
- Our recipes meet Weight Watchers Good Health Guidelines for eating lean proteins and fiber-rich whole grains and for having at least five servings of vegetables and fruits and two servings of low-fat or fat-free dairy products a day, while limiting your intake of saturated fat, sugar, and sodium.
- Health agencies recommend limiting sodium intake. To stay in line with this recommendation, we keep sodium levels in our recipes reasonably low; to boost flavor, we often include fresh herbs or a squeeze of citrus instead of salt. If you don't have to restrict your sodium, feel free to add a touch more salt as desired.
- For information about the science behind lasting weight loss and more, please visit WeightWatchers.com/science.

CALCULATIONS NOT WHAT YOU EXPECTED?

- You might expect some of the ***PointsPlus*** values in this book to be lower when some of the foods they're made from, such as fruits and vegetables, have no ***PointsPlus*** values. Most fruits and veggies have no ***PointsPlus*** values when served as a snack or part of a meal, like a cup of berries with a sandwich. But if these foods are part of a recipe, their fiber and nutrient content are incorporated into the recipe calculations. These nutrients can affect the ***PointsPlus*** value.

- Alcohol is included in our ***PointsPlus*** calculations. Because alcohol information is generally not included on nutrition labels, it's not an option to include when using the hand calculator or the online calculator. But since we include alcohol information that we get from our nutritionists, you might notice discrepancies between the ***PointsPlus*** values you see in our recipes, and the values you get using the calculator. The ***PointsPlus*** values listed for our recipes are the most accurate values.

SHOPPING FOR INGREDIENTS

As you learn to eat healthier, remember these tips for choosing foods wisely:

LEAN MEATS AND POULTRY Purchase lean meats and poultry, and trim them of all visible fat before cooking. When poultry is cooked with the skin on, we recommend removing the skin before eating. Nutritional information for recipes that include meat, poultry, and fish is based on cooked, skinless boneless portions (unless otherwise stated), with the fat trimmed.

SEAFOOD Whenever possible, our recipes call for seafood that is sustainable and deemed the most healthful for human consumption so that your choice of seafood is not only good for the oceans but also good for you. For more information about the best seafood choices and to download a pocket guide, go to environmentaldefensefund.org or montereybayaquarium.org. For information about mercury and seafood go to weightwatchers.com.

PRODUCE For best flavor, maximum nutrient content, and the lowest prices, buy fresh local produce, such as vegetables, leafy greens, and fruits, in season. Rinse them thoroughly before using, and keep a supply of cut-up vegetables and fruits in your refrigerator for convenient healthy snacks.

WHOLE GRAINS Explore your market for whole-grain products such as whole wheat and whole-grain breads and pastas, brown rice, bulgur, barley, cornmeal, whole wheat couscous, oats, and quinoa to enjoy with your meals.

PREPARATION AND MEASURING

Before you start cooking any recipe, consider the following advice:

READ THE RECIPE Take a couple of minutes to read through the ingredients and directions before you start to prepare a recipe. This will prevent you from discovering midway through that you don't have an important ingredient or that a recipe requires several hours of marinating. And it's also a good idea to assemble all ingredients and utensils within easy reach before you begin a recipe.

WEIGHING AND MEASURING The success of any recipe depends on accurate weighing and measuring. The effectiveness of the Weight Watchers Program and the accuracy of the nutritional analysis depend on correct measuring as well. Use the following techniques:

- Weigh foods such as meat, poultry, and fish on a food scale.
- To measure liquids, use a standard glass or plastic measuring cup placed on a level surface. For amounts less than ¼ cup, use standard measuring spoons.
- To measure dry ingredients, use metal or plastic measuring cups that come in ¼-, ⅓-, ½-, and 1-cup sizes. Fill the appropriate cup, and level it with the flat edge of a knife or spatula. For amounts less than ¼ cup, use standard measuring spoons.

timeless tools for healthy cooking

With the right tools, any job is easier. Here are the everyday essentials that will help you get healthy meals on the table fast, plus our best advice for choosing the ones that are best for you.

THE RIGHT CUTTING BOARD

A large, sturdy board will make chopping fruits, veggies, and meats easier, and will also help you mince ingredients like fresh herbs and garlic that add flavor to your food without increasing calories. **How to choose:** Your board should fit comfortably on your primary work surface and accommodate the entire blade of your biggest knife with at least an inch or two to spare at top and bottom. Choose wood or plastic: Both materials are durable and will absorb the impact of your knife, making it easier to chop and protecting your blade. Some cooks opt for two boards and designate one specifically for meat and poultry; this can help prevent meat juices from contaminating other foods.

THE THREE MOST IMPORTANT KNIVES

These are the essentials: A small paring knife with a blade 3 to 4 inches long for peeling and slicing small foods; a cook's knife with a 8- or 9-inch blade for all basic chopping, dicing, and slicing; and a long serrated knife for neatly slicing bread. You'll also need a good sharpener since even the best knives will dull over time. **How to choose:** Your budget will be a major factor in your selection, but do buy the best you can afford—a good-quality knife properly cared for should last you a lifetime. If you can, hold the knives before purchasing; their handles and weight should feel comfortable and the grip should be secure in your hand.

A GOOD GRATER

Shredding and grating fruits, vegetables, and cheeses to add flavor and nutrition to your meals is made infinitely easier with a sturdy grater. Our recommendation is a box grater that has four sides with fine, medium, coarse, and slicing blades and a handle on top. Although box models can zest citrus and finely grate small items like fresh ginger, we recommend you also purchase a rasp grater (Microplane) for these more delicate tasks. **How to choose:** Heavy stainless steel will give you the best results and wear well. You can opt for a durable rubber handle on top for comfort and a rubber-rimmed bottom for extra stability if you like.

SPRING-LOADED TONGS

Tongs are vitally important for lifting, flipping, and moving food quickly and gently; a spatula is often too big to fit in a tight pan or may damage delicate foods, and jabbing a fork into meats to turn will allow juices to leak out. **How to choose:** Tongs should be 12 inches or more long to keep your hand comfortably away from hot cooking surfaces. Spring-loaded models can be locked shut for easy storage. Silicone-tipped tongs are a necessity for use on nonstick cookware to prevent scratching; select heat-resistant tips and you will be able to use them over open grill flames as well.

VERSATILE KITCHEN SHEARS

These heavy-duty scissors can do delicate jobs like cutting parchment paper to line pans or snipping herbs for a tasty last-minute garnish, but they're also strong enough for splitting poultry, cutting crustacean shells, opening tough food packages, and many other kitchen tasks. **How to choose:** Shears should be stainless steel to prevent rusting, and the handles should be large enough to fit your hand comfortably and offer protection against slipping. Straight (not curved) blades are the best for most jobs, and a bolt between the blades that can be removed to separate them will allow for easy cleaning. Left-handed people should look for shears designed specifically for them.

AN ACCURATE THERMOMETER

A good meat thermometer is the best way to ensure that your foods are cooked to the proper temperature for safety and peak flavor. **How to choose:** We recommend that you use an instant-read thermometer; not only will it give you a reading in a matter of seconds, most models are small enough to fit in your pocket for quick access. Select a model that is specifically designed for meat and poultry (not candy or oil) and has an easy-to-read dial or digital readout.

cooking foods to safe temperatures

Over the years Weight Watchers has always been concerned with producing recipes that keep in mind food safety. To this end we have followed guidelines from the USDA on cooking foods to safe temperatures. Remember, you can't tell whether meat is safely cooked or a casserole is sufficiently heated through by just looking at it.

Use the latest temperature chart below to ensure that cooked foods reach a safe minimum internal temperature. Here are some techniques to follow:

- Use an instant-read thermometer.
- Insert the thermometer into the center of the food (without touching a bone on roasts or poultry) to get an accurate reading.
- For steaks, chops, and burgers or patties, insert the thermometer into the side of the meat.
- If a recipe calls for letting the meat rest for a specified amount of time, do so before slicing or serving it, since the temperature will continue to rise during this time and destroy harmful bacteria.
- Wash the stem of the thermometer with hot soapy water after each use.

Type of Food	Temperature
Ground beef, pork, and lamb	160°F
Beef, pork, and lamb steaks, chops, or roasts	145°F with 3 minutes standing time
Fresh ham	145°F
Fully cooked ham (to reheat)	140°F
Chicken or turkey, whole, parts, or ground	165°F
Egg dishes	160°F
Leftovers and casseroles	165°F

the leanest cuts

Choosing lean cuts of meats and poultry means you'll have healthier meals with less saturated fat and cholesterol, *and* fewer ***PointsPlus*** values. Use this chart when you shop to make it easy to make the best selections for you and your family.

Most Weight Watchers recipes use cuts from the "leaner" and "leanest" categories and we always recommend trimming away any visible fat before cooking.

Type of Meat or Poultry	Lean	Leaner	Leanest
BEEF	T-bone steak, brisket, filet mignon, flank steak, bottom round steak	Top loin (strip steak), top sirloin steak, chuck shoulder steak	Bottom round roast, eye round top roast, round roast or steak
GROUND BEEF	90% lean	93% lean	95% lean
PORK	Sirloin roast, rib chop	Center loin chop, top loin chop or roast	Tenderloin, ham, Canadian bacon
LAMB	Shank, leg	Loin chop, rack of lamb	Shoulder chop or roast, rib chop or roast
POULTRY	Skinless chicken thighs	Skinless chicken breast	Skinless turkey breast
GROUND POULTRY	Ground chicken or turkey	Skinless ground chicken or turkey	Skinless ground chicken breast or turkey breast

dry and liquid measurement equivalents

Teaspoons	Tablespoons	Cups	Fluid Ounces
3 teaspoons	1 tablespoon		½ fluid ounce
6 teaspoons	2 tablespoons	⅛ cup	1 fluid ounce
8 teaspoons	2 tablespoons plus 2 teaspoons	⅙ cup	
12 teaspoons	4 tablespoons	¼ cup	2 fluid ounces
15 teaspoons	5 tablespoons	⅓ cup minus 1 teaspoon	
16 teaspoons	5 tablespoons plus 1 teaspoon	⅓ cup	
18 teaspoons	6 tablespoons	¼ cup plus 2 tablespoons	3 fluid ounces
24 teaspoons	8 tablespoons	½ cup	4 fluid ounces
30 teaspoons	10 tablespoons	½ cup plus 2 tablespoons	5 fluid ounces
32 teaspoons	10 tablespoons plus 2 teaspoons	⅔ cup	
36 teaspoons	12 tablespoons	¾ cup	6 fluid ounces
42 teaspoons	14 tablespoons	1 cup minus 2 tablespoons	7 fluid ounces
45 teaspoons	15 tablespoons	1 cup minus 1 tablespoon	
48 teaspoons	16 tablespoons	1 cup	8 fluid ounces

Note: Measurement of less than ⅛ teaspoon is considered a dash or a pinch.

metric equivalents

If you are converting the recipes in this book to metric measurements, use the following chart as a guide.

Volume

¼ teaspoon	1 milliliter
½ teaspoon	2 milliliters
1 teaspoon	5 milliliters
1 tablespoon	15 milliliters
2 tablespoons	30 milliliters
3 tablespoons	45 milliliters
¼ cup	60 milliliters
⅓ cup	80 milliliters
½ cup	120 milliliters
⅔ cup	160 milliliters
¾ cup	175 milliliters
1 cup	240 milliliters
1 quart	950 milliliters

Length

1 inch	2.5 millimeters
1 inch	2.5 centimeters

Weight

1 ounce	30 grams
¼ pound	120 grams
½ pound	240 grams
1 pound	480 grams

Oven Temperature

250°F	120°C
275°F	140°C
300°F	150°C
325°F	160°C
350°F	180°C
375°F	190°C
400°F	200°C
425°F	220°C
450°F	230°C
475°F	250°C
500°F	260°C
525°F	270°C

Note: Metric volume measurements are approximate.

a brief history of weight watchers

In 1961, when Jean Nidetch, a housewife from Queens, New York, invited a small circle of overweight friends to her home and conducted what would become the blueprint for Weight Watchers meetings worldwide, she had no idea she was onto something big. Desperate to lose weight after years of fad diets, the thirty-eight-year-old was armed with only the New York City Department of Health guidelines for losing weight and her conviction that sharing support and information was the key to lasting weight loss. Within two months her group had expanded to forty members and the format of getting together weekly to discuss eating and nutrition challenges had proven to be a winner.

How successful was Jean's formula? Two short years after that first meeting, she partnered with friends and business associates Al and Felice Lippert (both of whom had also found success on the Weight Watchers plan) and incorporated the name Weight Watchers International. By 1966 there were two hundred branches worldwide, and Jean published the first Weight Watchers cookbook to great acclaim. The flourishing company went public in 1968. The stock opened at $11.25 per share, and by the end of its first day of trading the value had soared to $30. That same year Jean estimated that her company had helped members lose a staggering 17 million pounds since its inception.

Within a decade of its founding, the Weight Watchers Program had received the acclaim of both the medical community and health organizations across the country. Jean had appeared on every major radio and television talk show and established a magazine, and Weight Watchers secured its place as a part of American culture. Many things about the Program's Food Plan evolved in the 1970s and 80s as it adapted to new scientific research and responded to consumer needs, a trait that would become one of the company's hallmarks. In 1972, foods like bananas and spaghetti became "legal" for the first time, and members were allowed to add alcohol to their meals. An exercise component was added in 1978, making it one of the first weight loss companies to do so.

In 1977, the ***POINTS*** Food System was introduced and became the model for the current program in which no foods are "off-limits" and members are encouraged to make food and behavior choices in line with proven nutritional science. Today the Program draws an estimated 1 million members to weekly meetings worldwide, and countless others participate in an online community at WeightWatchers.com. Former NBA star Charles Barkley became the first male spokesperson for the company in 2011, the same year that the Food Plan highlighted the importance of fruits and vegetables as part of a healthy lifestyle.

While the plan may have changed through the years, the one element that has always remained constant is Jean's philosophy that support from, and sharing success with, a group of likeminded individuals is the key to healthy weight loss—a core belief that continues to this day in Weight Watchers meetings held around the globe.

breakfast all day

omelettes, frittatas, smoothies, and more

omelettes for two

SERVES 2

20 Min or Less
Vegetarian

2 large eggs
3 egg whites
1 tablespoon water
¼ teaspoon salt
¼ teaspoon ground pepper
½ teaspoon olive oil

Fat-free omelettes were a staple in the old days of Weight Watchers. The one caveat was that eggs could only be eaten at breakfast or lunch. Break those long-gone rules deliciously with these foolproof omelettes; they make a great impromptu supper.

1 Beat together the eggs, egg whites, water, salt, and pepper in medium bowl until slightly frothy.

2 Heat ¼ teaspoon of the oil in a large nonstick skillet over medium heat. Add half of the egg mixture and cook, occasionally lifting the edges of the egg and tilting the pan to allow the uncooked mixture to flow underneath, 2 minutes. When almost set, loosen edges of the omelette with a spatula and fold into a half-moon shape. Reduce heat to low and cook 1 minute more, or until set. Repeat with the remaining egg mixture.

PER SERVING (1 omelette): 110 Cal, 6 g Total Fat, 2 g Sat Fat, 213 mg Chol, 436 mg Sod, 1 g Carb, 0 g Fib, 12 g Prot, 29 mg Calc. *PointsPlus value: 3.*

mushroom-swiss omelettes

SERVES 2

20 Min or Less
Vegetarian

1½ cups sliced mushrooms
2 large eggs
3 egg whites
1 tablespoon water
¼ teaspoon salt
¼ teaspoon ground pepper
½ teaspoon olive oil
4 tablespoons shredded reduced-fat Swiss cheese

Instead of mushrooms and cheese, you can fill the omelettes with any variety of cooked meats, vegetables, or poultry. If cholesterol is a concern, substitute 1 cup of fat-free egg substitute for the eggs and egg whites.

1 Spray a large nonstick skillet with nonstick spray and place over medium heat. Add the mushrooms, spreading them in a single layer. Cover and cook until golden, 3 minutes, stirring halfway through cooking. Set aside the mushrooms and wipe out the skillet with paper towels.

2 Prepare the omelette as directed in Omelettes for Two (page 2), up to Step 2. Before folding the omelette, sprinkle on 2 tablespoons of the cheese and half of the mushrooms. Continue with Step 2 as directed, adding the remaining cheese and mushrooms.

PER SERVING (1 omelette): 157 Cal, 8 g Total Fat, 3 g Sat Fat, 217 mg Chol, 455 mg Sod, 4 g Carb, 1 g Fib, 17 g Prot, 198 mg Calc.
PointsPlus value: 4.

For a hearty brunch, serve the omelettes with a fresh fruit salad made with cubed cantaloupe and honeydew tossed with fresh sliced mint.

---

red potato and fontina frittata

SERVES 4

Vegetarian

4 large eggs
4 large egg whites
½ cup low-fat (1%) milk
¼ cup shredded fontina cheese
2 teaspoons minced fresh thyme, or ½ teaspoon dried
3 small red potatoes, thinly sliced
½ teaspoon salt
¼ teaspoon ground pepper
1 tablespoon unsalted butter
4 scallions, thinly sliced

A frittata is a delicious cross between an omelette and a quiche with some unique advantages over both. Although you can cut a single frittata into wedges to feed a family, it cooks much more quickly than a quiche, and doesn't require a fat-laden crust. And unlike an omelette, it requires no turning or folding—just a stress-free trip under the broiler to firm and brown its top.

1 Preheat the broiler.

2 Whisk the eggs, egg whites, and milk together in a large bowl until blended. Stir in the cheese and thyme. Set aside.

3 Spray a 10-inch ovenproof nonstick skillet with nonstick spray and set over medium heat. Add the potatoes, salt, and pepper and cook, stirring occasionally, until the potatoes begin to soften and brown, 6–8 minutes. Transfer to a plate.

4 Return the skillet to the heat. Melt the butter in the same skillet. Add the scallions and cook, stirring frequently, until softened, 3 minutes. Return the potatoes to the skillet. Add the egg mixture; reduce the heat to medium-low and cook, undisturbed, until the bottom of the frittata is firm, 8–10 minutes.

5 Place the skillet under the broiler and broil 5 inches from the heat until the frittata is set in the center, 5 minutes. Cut into 4 wedges and serve at once.

PER SERVING (¼ of frittata): 273 Cal, 11 g Total Fat, 5 g Sat Fat, 203 mg Chol, 491 mg Sod, 30 g Carb, 5 g Fib, 16 g Prot, 172 mg Calc. ***PointsPlus value: 7.***

hash browns, egg, and cheese casserole

SERVES 6

6 strips turkey bacon, sliced crosswise into ¼-inch strips
3 cups (12 ounces) frozen hash brown potatoes
4 scallions, sliced
3 large eggs
3 egg whites
¾ cup low-fat (1%) small-curd cottage cheese
⅔ cup shredded reduced-fat cheddar cheese
3 tablespoons freshly grated Parmesan cheese
3 tablespoons all-purpose flour
¾ teaspoon poultry seasoning or ground sage
½ teaspoon baking powder
¼ teaspoon salt
¼ teaspoon ground pepper

This homey, hearty casserole is a great addition to a brunch buffet. The turkey bacon gives it a rich, smoky flavor without adding a lot of fat. If you find yourself with any leftovers, you can refrigerate them for up to two days and reheat individual portions in the microwave.

1 Place the oven rack in the center of the oven; preheat oven to 375°F. Spray a 1½-quart shallow baking dish with nonstick spray.

2 Spray a nonstick skillet with nonstick spray and set over medium heat. Add the bacon and cook until nearly crisp, stirring occasionally, 4 minutes. Add the potatoes and scallions; continue cooking and stirring until tender, about 7 minutes. Remove from the heat and let cool slightly.

3 Beat together the eggs and egg whites in a large bowl until blended. Beat in the cottage cheese, ⅓ cup of the cheddar cheese, the Parmesan cheese, flour, poultry seasoning or sage, baking powder, salt, and pepper until combined. Stir in the cooled potato mixture and spread evenly into the baking dish. Bake until golden and set in the center, about 30 minutes. Sprinkle evenly with the remaining ⅓ cup cheddar cheese. Let stand until the cheese is melted, about 10 minutes, and serve hot or warm.

PER SERVING (⅙ of casserole): 235 Cal, 8 g Total Fat, 4 g Sat Fat, 129 mg Chol, 665 mg Sod, 22 g Carb, 2 g Fib, 18 g Prot, 205 mg Calc. ***PointsPlus value: 6.***

canadian bacon–cheddar frittata

SERVES 4

1 medium onion, chopped
1 small red bell pepper, thinly sliced
3 large eggs
3 large egg whites
1 cup fat-free milk
1/8 teaspoon ground pepper
4 slices Canadian bacon, chopped
1 large tomato, chopped
1 cup shredded reduced-fat sharp cheddar cheese

This hearty frittata is a natural for breakfast or brunch, but it also makes a wonderful family dinner. Try dressing it up with fresh herbs (chopped chives or fresh oregano would be particularly good) and serving it with a salad of baby lettuces and halved grape tomatoes tossed with an oil and vinegar mix.

1 Spray a 10-inch ovenproof nonstick skillet with nonstick spray and set over medium heat. Add the onion and bell pepper; cook, stirring occasionally, until softened, 5 minutes. Transfer to a small bowl.

2 Preheat the broiler.

3 Whisk the eggs, egg whites, milk, and pepper in a large bowl until blended. Stir in the onion mixture, bacon, tomato, and cheese.

4 Wipe out the skillet; spray with nonstick spray and set over medium heat. Add the egg mixture. Reduce the heat to medium-low and cook, undisturbed, until the bottom of the frittata is firm, 8–10 minutes.

5 Place the skillet under the broiler and broil 5 inches from the heat until the frittata is set in the center, 5 minutes. Cut into 4 wedges and serve at once.

PER SERVING (1/4 of frittata): 233 Cal, 11 g Total Fat, 4 g Sat Fat, 165 mg Chol, 612 mg Sod, 10 g Carb, 1 g Fib, 23 g Prot, 308 mg Calc. *PointsPlus value: 6.*

Instead of the red bell pepper, you can use another vegetable that you might have on hand. Try chopped zucchini, broccoli florets, or fresh fennel.

Canadian Bacon-Cheddar Fritatta

swiss cheese strata

SERVES 6

Vegetarian

- 5 slices whole-wheat bread, quartered
- ¾ cup diced bottled roasted red peppers
- ½ cup shredded reduced-fat Swiss cheese
- 3 scallions, thinly sliced
- 2 cups low-fat (1%) milk
- 2 large eggs
- 3 egg whites
- 2 tablespoons freshly grated Parmesan cheese
- 1 tablespoon Dijon mustard
- ¼ teaspoon salt
- ¼ teaspoon ground pepper

Stratas—a layered casserole of bread, flavorings, and egg custard—are a great way to use slightly stale bread. Another delicious way to use bread past its prime is our Tuscan Panzanella (page 55), an easy bread salad. Try serving this strata for a Sunday buffet or an easy weekend breakfast.

1 Spray a 2-quart baking dish with nonstick spray. Arrange the bread pieces in the bottom of the baking dish, overlapping them slightly. Scatter the red peppers, Swiss cheese, and scallions on top.

2 Whisk together the milk, eggs, egg whites, Parmesan cheese, mustard, salt, and pepper in a medium bowl. Pour over the bread and let stand for at least 20 minutes, or cover and refrigerate for up to 12 hours.

3 Place the oven rack in the center of the oven; preheat the oven to 350°F. Bake the strata until golden and a knife inserted in the center comes out clean, 40–45 minutes. Let stand 10 minutes, then serve hot.

PER SERVING (⅙ of casserole): 166 Cal, 6 g Total Fat, 3 g Sat Fat, 79 mg Chol, 395 mg Sod, 17 g Carb, 2 g Fib, 13 g Prot, 276 mg Calc. *PointsPlus value: 4.*

Stratas make morning entertaining easy—you can assemble them the night before, giving the bread time to soak up the eggs. There's nothing for you to do before your guests arrive but pop the strata in the oven and mix the Bloody Marys.

broccoli-and-bacon egg cups

SERVES 4

6 slices turkey bacon, sliced crosswise into ¼-inch strips
2 cups frozen chopped broccoli
1 small red onion, chopped
1½ teaspoons bottled roasted or minced garlic
2 teaspoons Italian seasoning
2 tablespoons all-purpose flour
1 cup low-fat buttermilk
3 large eggs
3 egg whites
¼ cup freshly grated Parmesan cheese
½ teaspoon salt
½ teaspoon ground pepper

These savory bites look like muffins but taste like little omelettes. They're perfect to serve for a Sunday brunch, and if you have leftovers, they reheat beautifully in the microwave. You can make the vegetable mixture and the egg mixture (minus the buttermilk) up to a day in advance; store them in separate containers in the refrigerator. Whisk in the buttermilk right before cooking.

1 Place the oven rack in the center of the oven; preheat the oven to 350°F. Heavily spray a 12-cup muffin pan with nonstick spray.

2 Spray a nonstick skillet with nonstick spray; place over medium heat. Add the bacon and sauté until crispy, 6 minutes. Transfer to a plate.

3 Return the skillet to the heat. Add the broccoli, onion, garlic, and Italian seasoning; cook until the vegetables are just tender, 7 minutes. Remove from the heat; stir in the flour and the cooked bacon. Set aside to cool.

4 Whisk together the buttermilk, eggs, egg whites, cheese, salt, and pepper in a large bowl until blended. Stir in the cooled vegetable mixture, then spoon evenly into the muffin cups. Bake until set in the center, about 20 minutes. To remove, run a narrow rubber spatula or knife around the edge of each muffin cup.

PER SERVING (3 egg cups): 206 Cal, 10 g Total Fat, 4 g Sat Fat, 185 mg Chol, 882 mg Sod, 12 g Carb, 2 g Fib, 18 g Prot, 216 mg Calc.
PointsPlus value: 5.

For a breakfast on-the-go, bake the egg cups in paper muffin liners. Let them cool, then place in a resealable plastic bag and freeze for up to three months. Reheat in the microwave for a hearty homemade breakfast in a flash.

Spinach, Caramelized Onion, and Tomato Quiche

spinach, caramelized onion, and tomato quiche

SERVES 6

Vegetarian

2 teaspoons extra-virgin olive oil
3 medium onions, chopped
2 garlic cloves, minced
1 teaspoon sugar
1 (10-ounce) package frozen chopped spinach, thawed and squeezed dry
1 (10-ounce) package refrigerated pizza dough
¾ cup evaporated fat-free milk
2 large eggs, lightly beaten
¼ cup light sour cream
1 egg white, lightly beaten
½ teaspoon salt
⅛ teaspoon nutmeg
⅛ teaspoon freshly ground pepper
½ cup shredded reduced-fat Monterey Jack cheese
12 cherry tomatoes, halved

Quiche, a staple of the Alsace-Lorraine region of France, was so popular in the United States in the early eighties that it spawned a 1982 satirical book called Real Men Don't Eat Quiche. *Yet few men—or women, for that matter—can resist this savory tart, flavorful and with a fraction of the fat of the original. Enjoy it hot, cold, or at room temperature.*

1 Heat a large nonstick skillet over medium heat. Swirl in the oil, then add the onions, garlic, and sugar. Cook, stirring occasionally, until the onions are lightly golden, about 10 minutes. Add the spinach and cook 2 minutes longer; remove from the heat and let cool 10 minutes.

2 Preheat the oven to 350°F. Spray a 9-inch pie plate with nonstick spray.

3 Place the dough on a lightly floured work surface and shape it into a 4-inch circle. Cover lightly with plastic wrap and let rest 10 minutes. Roll the dough into an 11-inch circle; fit the dough into the pie plate, and flute the edges.

4 Combine the milk, eggs, sour cream, egg white, salt, nutmeg, and pepper in a medium bowl. Sprinkle the cheese over the bottom of the pie crust. Top evenly with the spinach mixture, then pour in the egg mixture. Arrange the tomato halves, cut-side up, on top of the quiche, in a circular pattern. Place on a baking sheet and bake until quiche is just set, about 45 minutes. Remove from the oven and let stand 10 minutes before cutting. Serve immediately or at room temperature.

PER SERVING (⅙ of quiche): 279 Cal, 9 g Total Fat, 3 g Sat Fat, 80 mg Chol, 571 mg Sod, 38 g Carb, 3 g Fib, 14 g Prot, 250 mg Calc. ***PointsPlus value: 7.***

The quiche makes a great party appetizer, too. Simply cut it into very thin wedges and arrange on a serving platter.

ham-and-mushroom crêpes

SERVES 6

Crêpes

½ cup all-purpose flour
¼ teaspoon salt
¾ cup low-fat (1%) milk
2 large eggs

Filling

¾ cup low-fat (1%) milk
¾ cup reduced-sodium chicken broth
3 tablespoons all-purpose flour
5 tablespoons dry sherry
⅛ teaspoon nutmeg
⅛ teaspoon cayenne
Freshly ground pepper
½ cup freshly grated Parmesan cheese (preferably Parmigiano-Reggiano)
2 tablespoons chopped parsley
8 ounces sliced cremini mushrooms (about 2 cups)
3 cloves garlic, minced
¼ teaspoon salt
6 slices deli-sliced cooked lean ham (about 6 ounces)

Any devoted watcher of Julia Child's cooking show in the seventies would have attempted making these thin French-style pancakes. The technique takes a little practice to master but is deliciously worth the effort.

1 To prepare crêpes, combine the flour and salt in a medium bowl. Whisk the milk and eggs in a separate bowl. Slowly whisk the milk mixture into flour mixture until smooth. Let stand 15 minutes.

2 Spray a small nonstick skillet or crêpe pan with nonstick spray and set over medium heat. Stir the batter, then pour a scant ¼ cup into the skillet, tilting in all directions to form a thin, even layer. Cook until top is set and bottom is golden, 1–1½ minutes. Flip and cook until the second side is lightly browned, 15–20 seconds. Transfer to a plate and repeat with remaining batter to make 6 crêpes. Cover loosely with plastic wrap and reserve.

3 To prepare the filling, whisk together the milk, broth, flour, 3 tablespoons of the sherry, the nutmeg, cayenne, and pepper in a medium saucepan until smooth. Cook over medium heat, whisking constantly, until thickened, 6–7 minutes. Remove from heat and stir in the cheese and 1 tablespoon of parsley; cover and keep warm.

4 Spray a large nonstick skillet with nonstick spray and set over medium heat. Add the mushrooms, garlic, and salt; cook, stirring occasionally, until mushrooms soften, about 6 minutes. Stir in the remaining 2 tablespoons sherry and cook until the liquid evaporates, 1–2 minutes. Remove from the heat and stir in the remaining 1 tablespoon parsley. Let cool slightly.

5 Preheat the oven to 450°F. Spray a 7×11-inch baking dish with nonstick spray. Arrange the crêpes side-by-side on a work surface. Lay one slice of the ham across the center of each crêpe. Spread each with 1 tablespoon of the sauce, then top with one-sixth (about 2 tablespoons) of the mushrooms. Roll up the crêpes jelly-roll style and transfer to the baking dish. Spoon the remaining sauce over the crêpes to cover. Bake until the sauce is bubbly and lightly browned, about 15 minutes.

PER SERVING (1 filled crêpe): 203 Cal, 7 g Total Fat, 3 g Sat Fat, 87 mg Chol, 743 mg Sod, 19 g Carb, 1 g Fib, 16 g Prot, 216 mg Calc.
PointsPlus value: 5.

cheese blintzes

SERVES 8

Vegetarian

1/3 cup fat-free cream cheese, room temperature
1/4 cup sugar
1 1/2 teaspoons grated lemon zest
1/2 teaspoon vanilla extract
1 3/4 cups whipped low-fat (1%) cottage cheese
1 cup low-fat (1%) milk
1 cup all-purpose flour
2 large eggs
2 egg whites
1 tablespoon melted butter
1/4 teaspoon salt

To make the creamy filling for these paper-thin pancakes, we used whipped cottage cheese, a smoother version of regular found in some supermarkets. If you can't find it, simply puree the same amount of dry-curd cottage cheese in a food processor or blender until smooth.

1 To prepare the filling, stir together the cream cheese, sugar, lemon zest, and vanilla in a medium bowl until smooth. Stir in the cottage cheese until combined; cover and refrigerate.

2 To prepare the pancakes, blend together the milk, flour, eggs, egg whites, butter, and salt in a blender or food processor until smooth. Pour into a bowl and let stand 20 minutes.

3 Place the oven rack in the center of the oven; preheat the oven to 350°F. Line a jelly-roll pan with foil and spray lightly with nonstick spray.

4 Spray a small nonstick skillet with nonstick spray; place over medium heat until hot. Pour about 3 tablespoons of the pancake batter into the pan, tilting the pan quickly to evenly coat the bottom. Cook until lightly browned underneath and dry on the top, about 30 seconds. Flip and cook 5 seconds. Remove to a plate and place a piece of wax paper on top. Repeat with the remaining batter (stirring occasionally) to make 16 pancakes, stacking the cooked pancakes between sheets of wax paper.

5 To assemble the blintzes, spoon 2 tablespoons of the cheese mixture on the lower third of the pale side of each pancake. Fold the right and left sides over the filling, then roll up to seal. Place, seam-side down, in the prepared pan and tent loosely with foil. Bake until the filling is hot, 10 minutes.

PER SERVING (2 blintzes): 166 Cal, 3 g Total Fat, 2 g Sat Fat, 61 mg Chol, 181 mg Sod, 21 g Carb, 0 g Fib, 12 g Prot, 68 mg Calc.
PointsPlus value: 4.

huevos rancheros in tortilla cups

SERVES 4

Vegetarian

4 (6-inch) corn tortillas
1 (14½-ounce) can diced tomatoes with green pepper, celery, and onion
1 (15-ounce) can black beans, rinsed and drained
½ cup canned diced mild green chiles, drained
2–3 tablespoons mild pepper sauce, such as Frank's Red Hot
¾ teaspoon ground cumin
3 tablespoons chopped cilantro
4 large eggs
¼ cup shredded reduced-fat cheddar cheese

These ranch-style eggs were the first wave of the Mexican food craze that took off in the seventies and early eighties. Today, they taste better than ever, especially in this pretty presentation, where the eggs are spooned into free-form crisp tortillas.

1 Place the oven rack in the center of the oven; preheat the oven to 425°F. Lightly spray both sides of the tortillas with nonstick spray. Place 4 inverted custard cups on a baking sheet, and drape a tortilla over each to give it a bowl shape. (You may also use an inverted 12-cup muffin pan, placing the tortillas over alternate cups.) Bake until the tortillas are crisped and lightly golden around the edges, 10 minutes. Remove the tortillas and set them on a rack to cool.

2 Combine the diced tomatoes, beans, chiles, pepper sauce, cumin, and 2 tablespoons of the cilantro in an ovenproof skillet. Bring to a boil over medium heat, reduce the heat to low, and simmer until the flavors are blended, 4 minutes. Break the eggs one at a time, on top of the sauce, spacing them evenly apart.

3 Immediately place the pan in the oven and bake until the eggs are almost set, 6–8 minutes. Sprinkle the cheese on top of the eggs and bake until melted, 1 minute. To serve, place the tortilla cups on serving plates and spoon the eggs and sauce into the tortilla cups. Garnish with the remaining tablespoon of chopped cilantro and serve immediately.

PER SERVING (1 filled tortilla cup): 289 Cal, 8 g Total Fat, 3 g Sat Fat, 216 mg Chol, 840 mg Sod, 40 g Carb, 8 g Fib, 17 g Prot, 200 mg Calc.
PointsPlus value: 7.

Make the tortilla cups up to two days ahead; just store them in a zip-close freezer bag at room temperature. Recrisp them in a 425°F oven for 2 minutes before using.

Huevos Rancheros
in Tortilla Cups

Fruit-and-Nut Granola, Ambrosia, page 282, and French Toast, page 18 (clockwise from top)

fruit-and-nut granola

SERVES 12

Vegetarian

4 cups old-fashioned rolled oats
½ cup slivered almonds
¼ cup sesame seeds
1 teaspoon cinnamon
¼ teaspoon salt
⅛ teaspoon nutmeg
6 tablespoons maple syrup
⅓ cup honey
2 tablespoons warm water
2 tablespoons canola oil
1 teaspoon vanilla extract
1 cup golden raisins
1 cup dried cranberries

Though it has always had a California-hippie provenance, granola was served to thousands of concertgoers at the famed 1969 Woodstock Music and Arts Festival in upstate New York. For many, it was their first introduction to the now-ubiquitous crunchy cereal or snack.

1 Preheat oven to 300°F. Spray a jelly-roll pan with nonstick spray.

2 Combine the oats, almonds, sesame seeds, cinnamon, salt, and nutmeg in a large bowl. Combine the syrup, honey, water, oil, and vanilla in a separate bowl. Pour the syrup mixture over the oats mixture and toss to combine. Evenly spread into the pan and bake, stirring and breaking up the clumps every 10 minutes, until lightly toasted, 45–55 minutes.

3 Remove from the oven, and stir in the raisins and cranberries; let cool completely. Store in an airtight container for up to 5 days or up to 1 month in the refrigerator.

PER SERVING (½ cup): 296 Cal, 8 g Total Fat, 1 g Sat Fat, 0 mg Chol, 54 mg Sod, 52 g Carb, 5 g Fib, 7 g Prot, 48 mg Calc.
PointsPlus value: 8.

Packed with almonds, sesame seeds, raisins, and dried cranberries *and* sweetened with real maple syrup and honey, this breakfast cereal is better than anything you'll find on the supermarket shelf. For an additional ***1 PointsPlus*** value, enjoy it with ⅓ cup plain fat-free yogurt.

---

french toast

SERVES 2

20 Min or Less
Vegetarian

1 large egg
2 egg whites
2 tablespoons fat-free milk
¼ teaspoon vanilla extract
Pinch cinnamon
2 slices firm or day-old
whole-wheat bread

The sixties-era Weight Watchers French Toast recipe was simple: plain white bread, dipped in a beaten egg, then "fried" in a dry skillet. No need to miss out on all the goodness and flavor of real French toast today. Double the recipe, if you like.

1 Beat the egg, egg whites, milk, vanilla, and cinnamon until frothy in a shallow dish. Dip the bread into the egg mixture, soaking well. Repeat with the remaining bread slice.

2 Spray a large nonstick skillet with butter-flavored nonstick spray. Place over medium heat until a drop of water sizzles. Add the bread and cook, turning once, until golden brown on both sides, 2–3 minutes.

PER SERVING (1 slice): 131 Cal, 4 g Total Fat, 1 g Sat Fat, 107 mg Chol, 244 mg Sod, 15 g Carb, 2 g Fib, 10 g Prot, 55 mg Calc.
PointsPlus value: 3.

Make the French Toast a full breakfast by serving it topped with fresh strawberries and 1 tablespoon of maple syrup (1 tablespoon of maple syrup will increase the per-serving ***PointsPlus*** value by ***1***). Special day? Add a 1-ounce slice of Canadian bacon to each serving for just ***1 PointsPlus*** value.

“danish” pastry

SERVES 1

20 Min or Less
Vegetarian

¼ cup low-fat ricotta
1 teaspoon packed dark brown sugar
¼ teaspoon vanilla extract
1 slice cinnamon raisin bread, lightly toasted
Pinch cinnamon

This Weight Watchers classic, once made with cottage cheese and white bread, has long been in need of an update. Here's our newer take, with calcium-packed ricotta and flavorful cinnamon raisin bread.

Combine the ricotta, brown sugar, and vanilla in a small bowl. Spread the ricotta mixture on the toasted bread and sprinkle with the cinnamon. Bake in the toaster oven until hot and bubbly, 3–5 minutes.

PER SERVING: 177 Cal, 6 g Total Fat, 3 g Sat Fat, 19 mg Chol, 180 mg Sod, 22 g Carb, 1 g Fib, 9 g Prot, 192 mg Calc.
PointsPlus value: 5.

If ricotta is not your favorite, you can make this with ¼ cup regular creamed cottage cheese instead. The *PointsPlus* value will remain the same.

best-loved breakfasts

These super-fast breakfasts are some of Weight Watchers members' most delicious ways to get going in the morning. Now you have no excuse for skipping the most important meal of the day. Each recipe makes one serving.

tomato scramble

Heat 1½ teaspoons oil in pan. Add ½ chopped tomato and ½ sliced shallot; cook 4 minutes. Put in bowl. Clean pan; heat 2 teaspoon oil. Add ⅔ cup egg substitute and 2 teaspoons chopped basil; scramble. Top with tomatoes. ***PointsPlus*** value: *5*.

berry quinoa

Bring ½ cup unsweetened almond milk and ¼ cup quinoa to boil in pan. Cover and simmer 15 minutes. Let stand 5 minutes. Stir in ½ cup mixed berries and pinch cinnamon. Top with 1 tablespoon blueberry syrup. ***PointsPlus*** value: *5*.

veggie cup scramble

Spray 12-ounce microwavable cup with nonstick spray. Whisk in 1 egg, 1 tablespoon milk, ¼ cup cut-up asparagus, and ¼ cup quartered mushrooms. Microwave on High 30 seconds; stir. Repeat. Add 1 tablespoon goat cheese. ***PointsPlus*** value: *3*.

pepper-cheese muffin

Heat skillet with nonstick spray. Add 2 slices Canadian bacon; cook 1 minute per side. Top ½ toasted English muffin with bacon, ¼ cup low-fat cottage cheese, and ½ sliced piece pepperoncini. ***PointsPlus*** value: *5*.

a.m. banana split

Put 1 split small banana in bowl. Top with ⅓ cup fat-free plain Greek yogurt, 1 teaspoon seedless raspberry jam, ½ cup Cocoa Puffs cereal, 1 teaspoon sunflower seeds, and 1 maraschino cherry. ***PointsPlus*** value: *6*.

strawberry crêpe

Mix 2 tablespoons part-skim ricotta and 1 teaspoon confectioners' sugar; spread onto 1 crêpe. Top with 1 cup sliced strawberries; fold in quarters. Add ¼ cup sliced strawberries, 2 teaspoons sliced almonds and ½ teaspoon confectioners' sugar. ***PointsPlus*** value: *6*.

polenta hotcakes

Cut ¼ pound prepared fat-free polenta (from 1-pound tube) into 4 rounds. Heat 1 teaspoon oil in skillet. Add polenta and cook 3 minutes per side. Top with ⅓ cup unsweetened applesauce and 1½ teaspoons raspberry syrup. ***PointsPlus*** value: *6*.

bacon-egg pita

Microwave ⅓ cup egg substitute in microwavable bowl on High 1 minute, stirring after 30 seconds. Stir in 2 tablespoons cooked winter squash puree and 1 slice crumbled cooked turkey bacon. Spoon into 1 split small pita. ***PointsPlus*** value: *5*.

multigrain cereal

Mix 2 tablespoons quick-cooking barley, 2 tablespoons bulgur, 2 tablespoons oats, and ⅔ cup water in 1-quart microwavable bowl. Microwave on High 2 minutes. Stir in 1 tablespoon raisins and pinch cinnamon; microwave 3 minutes. Top with 1 tablespoon chopped almonds. ***PointsPlus*** value: *6*.

mango-soy smoothie

SERVES 4

20 Min or Less
Vegetarian

1 cup ice cubes
1 small mango, cubed (about 1 cup)
1 cup vanilla-flavored soy drink, well chilled
¾ cup mango nectar
1 tablespoon sugar
1 tablespoon sweetened lime juice, such as Rose's Lime

The nineties soy craze meets Weight Watchers members' penchant for fruity frozen shakes: It's a healthy match made in heaven. This refreshing drink is equally delicious made with ripe peaches.

Crush the ice cubes in a blender (or place them in a zip-close freezer bag, crush them with back of heavy skillet, and place in the blender). Add the mango, soy drink, nectar, sugar, and lime juice; puree until smooth.

PER SERVING (1 cup): 101 Cal, 0 g Total Fat, 0 g Sat Fat, 0 mg Chol, 8 mg Sod, 25 g Carb, 2 g Fib, 2 g Prot, 110 mg Calc.
PointsPlus value: 3.

piña colada smoothie

SERVES 4

Vegetarian

1 cup ice cubes
1 cup crushed pineapple in juice, drained
1 cup frozen low-fat vanilla yogurt
1 cup coconut water
½ cup pineapple juice

The creaminess of this refreshing whip comes from freezing the pineapple first. When poured, the smoothie is reminiscent of a Caribbean umbrella drink—your cue to kick back, relax, and sip!

1 Freeze the pineapple in a freezer container or zip-close freezer bag until solid, at least 3 hours. Let stand at room temperature 10 minutes to thaw slightly.

2 Crush the ice cubes in a blender (or place them in a zip-close freezer bag, crush them with back of heavy skillet, and place in the blender). Add the frozen yogurt, the pineapple, coconut water, and pineapple juice; puree until smooth.

PER SERVING (1 cup): 115 Cal, 2 g Total Fat, 1 g Sat Fat, 2 mg Chol, 93 mg Sod, 24 g Carb, 1 g Fib, 3 g Prot, 90 mg Calc.
PointsPlus value: 3.

peanut butter–banana smoothie

SERVES 4

Vegetarian

1 medium banana, cut into chunks
1 cup ice cubes
2 cups fat-free chocolate milk
2 tablespoons creamy peanut butter

Nuts and peanut butter used to be off limits. Today, we know a variety of nuts (eaten in moderation!) can be positively heart healthy.

1 Freeze the banana chunks in a freezer container or zip-close freezer bag until firm, at least 2 hours.

2 Crush the ice cubes in a blender (or place them in a zip-close freezer bag, crush them with back of heavy skillet, and place in the blender). Add the banana chunks, chocolate milk, and peanut butter; puree until smooth.

PER SERVING (1 cup): 153 Cal, 6 g Total Fat, 2 g Sat Fat, 4 mg Chol, 114 mg Sod, 21 g Carb, 3 g Fib, 6 g Prot, 149 mg Calc. *PointsPlus value: 4.*

Got kids who refuse to eat breakfast? Try this healthy smoothie—made with kid-friendly ingredients—to start their day. Tell them it's delicious, but don't tell them it's good for them!

midday meals

soups, salads, sandwiches, and breads

french onion soup gratinée

SERVES 4

- 1 tablespoon + 1 teaspoon olive oil
- 2 pounds onions, thinly sliced
- 1 (32-ounce) carton reduced-sodium chicken broth
- 1½ teaspoons Worcestershire sauce
- Freshly ground pepper
- 4 (1-ounce) slices French bread, toasted
- 1 cup shredded reduced-fat Swiss or Jarlsberg cheese

A soup (like this one) whose main ingredient was a "limited" vegetable like onions no doubt challenged early Weight Watchers cooks. The versions they created tended to be more broth than onion and bereft of the cheese crouton traditionally served on top. This modern, savory version makes peace with the past, reinventing the French-bistro staple.

1 Heat a large nonstick skillet. Swirl in the oil, then add the onions. Cook, stirring frequently, until golden, about 15 minutes.

2 Preheat the oven to 450°F.

3 Bring the broth to a simmer in a large saucepan; add the cooked onions, Worcestershire sauce, and pepper. Reduce the heat to low and simmer, stirring occasionally, until the onions are tender, about 15 minutes.

4 Place 4 ovenproof soup bowls on a baking sheet. Ladle the soup into the bowls; top each with a slice of bread and ¼ cup of cheese. Bake until the cheese melts, about 5 minutes.

PER SERVING (1 bowl): 299 Cal, 11 g Total Fat, 4 g Sat Fat, 9 mg Chol, 689 mg Sod, 34 g Carb, 5 g Fib, 18 g Prot, 410 mg Calc.
PointsPlus value: 8.

Double this recipe and freeze half for another time. When ready to serve, just thaw the soup in the refrigerator overnight, and reheat it on the stovetop or in the microwave. Then all you have to do at the last minute is toast the bread and shred the cheese. Voilà!

---

asian noodle soup with tofu and shrimp

SERVES 8

2 (32-ounce) cartons reduced-sodium chicken broth
1 (8-ounce) head bok choy, trimmed and sliced (4 cups)
¾ pound snow peas, trimmed and cut into 1-inch pieces
¼ pound small fresh or frozen shrimp, peeled and deveined
2 teaspoons reduced-sodium soy sauce
2 teaspoons sesame oil
1 bunch scallions, trimmed and sliced
8 ounces firm tofu, sliced ¼-inch thick, then into 1-inch squares
1 (8-ounce) can sliced water chestnuts, drained
4 ounces capellini
1 teaspoon rice or white-wine vinegar
Freshly ground white pepper

This delicately flavored soup is a meal in a bowl and a great way to enjoy heart-healthy tofu. In the early days of Weight Watchers, some of the ingredients would have required a trip to an Asian grocery. Today, they're easy to find in almost any supermarket.

1 Bring the broth to a boil in a large saucepan or Dutch oven. Add the bok choy, snow peas, shrimp, soy sauce, and oil. Return to a boil, reduce the heat, and simmer until the bok choy and snow peas are tender but still crunchy and the shrimp are pink but still opaque, about 5 minutes.

2 Add the scallions, tofu, water chestnuts, capellini, vinegar, and pepper. Cook until the capellini is barely tender and the soup is heated through, about 5 minutes.

PER SERVING (1¾ cups): 196 Cal, 6 g Total Fat, 1 g Sat Fat, 28 mg Chol, 576 mg Sod, 21 g Carb, 4 g Fib, 16 g Prot, 139 mg Calc.
PointsPlus value: 5.

mediterranean clam chowder

SERVES 4

4 teaspoons olive oil
1½ cups chopped fennel
1 onion, chopped
1 carrot, chopped
1 celery stalk, chopped
2½–3½ cups hot water
1 (14½-ounce) can stewed tomatoes, coarsely chopped, with their juice
1 cup bottled clam juice or fish broth
1 medium potato, peeled and chopped
1½ teaspoons chopped thyme, or ½ teaspoon dried
1½ teaspoons chopped oregano, or ½ teaspoon dried
Freshly ground pepper
1 (6 ½-ounce) can minced clams
6 large or 10 small black olives, pitted and chopped
2 tablespoons capers, drained
½ teaspoon grated lemon zest
1 teaspoon fresh lemon juice

Here are all the flavors of the classic Manhattan clam chowder, but with the added Mediterranean flavors of fennel, olives, capers, and lemon. You'll love this version's chunky texture and hearty taste.

1 Heat a large nonstick saucepan. Swirl in the oil, then add the fennel, onion, carrot, and celery. Sauté until slightly wilted, about 5 minutes.

2 Add 2½ cups of the hot water, the tomatoes, clam juice or fish broth, potato, thyme, oregano, and pepper; simmer, adding more hot water ½ cup at a time, until the potatoes and vegetables are tender but not mushy, about 15 minutes. Stir in the clams with their juice, the olives, capers, lemon zest, and lemon juice. Cook until heated through (do not boil); serve at once.

PER SERVING (1½ cups): 156 Cal, 6 g Total Fat, 1 g Sat Fat, 16 mg Chol, 520 mg Sod, 19 g Carb, 4 g Fib, 8 g Prot, 86 mg Calc. ***PointsPlus value: 4.***

creamy fish chowder

SERVES 4

1 cup water
2 medium potatoes, peeled and chopped
1 onion, chopped
1 cup chopped mushrooms
1 celery stalk, chopped
1 tablespoon + 1 teaspoon unsalted butter
1 tablespoon all-purpose flour
1 cup fat-free milk
1 cup evaporated fat-free milk
8 ounces firm-fleshed white fish fillets (cod, catfish, tilapia, or barramundi), cut into 1-inch pieces
½ cup fish broth or bottled clam juice
½ tablespoon chopped thyme, or ½ teaspoon dried
Freshly ground white pepper
2 teaspoons chopped thyme (optional)

Thank goodness, times have changed, and there's no need to use cottage cheese purees or dehydrated onion flakes to create a creamy soup like this one. Chunky with fish and potatoes and full of briny flavors, our chowder is the perfect showcase for the freshest fish available at the market.

1 Combine the water, potatoes, onion, mushrooms, celery, and butter in a large saucepan or Dutch oven. Bring to a boil; reduce the heat and simmer, covered, until the potatoes are tender, about 20 minutes.

2 Place the flour in a medium bowl; whisk in the milk and evaporated milk. Stir into the potato mixture in the saucepan. Add the fish, broth or clam juice, thyme, and pepper. Cook, stirring frequently, over medium heat, until the fish is no longer opaque and the chowder has thickened slightly, about 15 minutes (do not boil). Sprinkle with the additional thyme, if using.

PER SERVING (1¼ cups): 215 Cal, 8 g Total Fat, 3 g Sat Fat, 45 mg Chol, 136 mg Sod, 21 g Carb, 2 g Fib, 16 g Prot, 106 mg Calc. ***PointsPlus value: 6.***

Serve this New England classic with a simple salad of romaine, cucumber, and grated carrot tossed with lemon for an ideal soup-and-salad combo.

Split Pea Soup with
Ham and Cheese

split pea soup with ham and cheese

SERVES 8

1 pound split peas, picked over, rinsed, and drained
4 teaspoons vegetable oil
2 carrots, chopped
1 large onion, chopped
1 celery stalk, chopped
1 (32-ounce) carton reduced-sodium chicken broth
2 cups water
¼ pound lean ham, cut into matchstick-size pieces
Freshly ground pepper
2 ounces reduced-fat cheddar cheese, cut into ½-inch cubes

Back in the day, when legumes were considered fattening, Weight Watchers created Mock Split Pea Soup. Made from pureed green beans, asparagus, celery, and a few other ingredients, it only resembled the dish in color. Our updated version of split pea soup is not only made with the real stuff, it's laced with delicious morsels of ham and cheese. Change is good!

1 Place the peas in a large saucepan; add enough water to cover them by 2 inches and bring to a boil. Remove from the heat, then cover and let soak 1 hour. Drain.

2 Heat a large nonstick saucepan or Dutch oven. Swirl in the oil, then add the carrots, onion, and celery. Sauté until wilted, about 5 minutes. Add the peas, broth, water, ham, and pepper. Bring to a boil; reduce the heat and simmer, covered, stirring occasionally, until the peas are tender, about 1 hour. Top with the cheese and serve immediately, or set aside to cool to room temperature, then refrigerate up to 3 days.

3 To reheat, thin the soup with a little water, as needed (it will thicken as it stands); place over medium heat and cook, stirring until warmed through. Top with the cheese and serve.

PER SERVING (1 cup): 288 Cal, 6 g Total Fat, 2 g Sat Fat, 11 mg Chol, 455 mg Sod, 39 g Carb, 15 g Fib, 21 g Prot, 93 mg Calc.
PointsPlus value: 6.

gumbo

SERVES 4

4 teaspoons vegetable oil
1 green bell pepper, chopped
8 scallions, sliced
1 celery stalk, chopped
1 garlic clove, minced
1 (14-ounce) can diced tomatoes, with their juice
1 (14-ounce) can reduced-sodium chicken broth
1 (10-ounce) box frozen okra, thawed
1½ teaspoons chopped thyme, or 1 teaspoon dried
1 bay leaf
¼ teaspoon crushed red pepper
½ cup long-grain rice
12 medium shrimp, peeled and deveined
2 ounces skinless boneless chicken breast, cut into ½-inch chunks
2 ounces kielbasa, sliced
1 cup cooked crabmeat, picked over

Long before the Creole craze in the eighties, Weight Watchers members were stirring up their own (vegetarian) version of gumbo, the famous Louisiana stew packed with okra, green peppers, and tomatoes. Our twenty-first-century recipe is all that and more, with shrimp, chicken, sausage, and crabmeat swimming in a savory broth.

1 Heat a large nonstick saucepan. Swirl in the oil, then add the bell pepper, scallions, celery, and garlic. Sauté until slightly wilted, 5 minutes. Add the tomatoes, broth, okra, thyme, bay leaf, and red pepper. Bring to a boil; reduce the heat and simmer, covered, until the vegetables are soft, about 15 minutes.

2 Stir in the rice and continue cooking until the rice is soft on the outside but still hard in the center, 15–20 minutes. Add the shrimp, chicken, and kielbasa; simmer, covered, until the shrimp is pink and opaque, the chicken is cooked through, and the rice is completely tender, 5–10 minutes more. Add the crabmeat; cook until just heated through. Remove the bay leaf before serving.

PER SERVING (2¼ cups): 311 Cal, 11 g Total Fat, 3 g Sat Fat, 79 mg Chol, 660 mg Sod, 32 g Carb, 4 g Fib, 22 g Prot, 166 mg Calc.
PointsPlus value: 8.

Keeping resealable plastic bags of chopped onions, bell pepper, celery, and other vegetables in the freezer makes preparing soups like this a cinch; they'll last about a month in the freezer.

---

lentil soup

SERVES 8

10 cups reduced-sodium beef broth
1 pound dried lentils, picked over, rinsed, and drained
4 carrots, chopped
2 large onions, peeled and chopped
1 celery stalk, chopped
1 bay leaf
3 canned whole plum tomatoes, drained and chopped
1 cup tomato juice
1 tablespoon red-wine or cider vinegar
Freshly ground pepper
1–2 cups hot water
Chopped scallion (optional)

Lentils were only allowed once a week on a prior version of the Weight Watchers program, but today we know how healthful (and deliciously filling) they are. We've transformed this classic soup into a virtually fat-free, hearty meal. More good news: It's a cinch to prepare, and even tastier a day or two after you make it.

Combine the broth, lentils, carrots, onions, celery, and bay leaf in a large saucepan or Dutch oven. Bring to a boil, reduce the heat, and simmer, covered, stirring occasionally, until the lentils and vegetables are tender, about 30 minutes. Add the tomatoes, tomato juice, vinegar, and pepper; add the water 1 cup at a time until desired thickness is reached. Cover and cook, stirring occasionally, until the flavors have blended, 10 minutes. Sprinkle with the chopped scallion, if using.

PER SERVING (1¾ cups): 261 Cal, 2 g Total Fat, 0 g Sat Fat, 0 mg Chol, 364 mg Sod, 44 g Carb, 15 g Fib, 19 g Prot, 72 mg Calc.
PointsPlus value: 6.

You can store the soup in the refrigerator for up to five days or freeze it for up to three months. It will thicken slightly with time; just thin it with a little water when you reheat it on the stove or in the microwave.

mushroom-barley soup

SERVES 8

2 tablespoons olive oil
2 onions, chopped
3 carrots, chopped
3 celery stalks, chopped
½ cup dry white wine
9 cups reduced-sodium beef broth
⅓ cup pearl barley
2 (10-ounce) packages mushrooms
½ cup minced flat-leaf parsley
Freshly ground pepper
2–3 tablespoons minced flat-leaf parsley (optional)

"Mushrooms, an unlimited vegetable, are a mainstay of the W.W. Program," notes the mushroom-recipe section in the first Weight Watchers Cookbook. And we're still in love with these meaty, flavorful, and fat-free gems. This warming soup is a worthy homage—and a perfect choice on a blustery winter day.

1 Heat a large nonstick saucepan or Dutch oven. Swirl in the oil, then add the onions, carrots, and celery. Sauté until wilted, about 5 minutes. Add the wine; simmer until the liquid is reduced by one-fourth. Add the broth; bring to a steady simmer. Stir in the barley; cover and cook, stirring occasionally, until the barley is tender, about 45 minutes.

2 Meanwhile, clean and trim the mushrooms; separate the stems from the caps. Chop the stems and one-third of the caps; slice the remaining caps.

3 Transfer 1½ cups of the vegetables and barley and ½ cup of the liquid to a food processor; puree. Return the mixture to the saucepan.

4 Add the mushrooms, parsley, and pepper; stir and bring to a gentle boil. Simmer, covered, until the mushrooms are cooked, 15 minutes. Garnish with the additional parsley, if using.

PER SERVING (1½ cups): 123 Cal, 4 g Total Fat, 1 g Sat Fat, 0 mg Chol, 531 mg Sod, 15 g Carb, 3 g Fib, 7 g Prot, 47 mg Calc.
PointsPlus value: 3.

The small amount of wine in this soup adds a great deal of flavor. However, if you'd like to leave it out, substitute ½ cup water and a tablespoon of white-wine vinegar instead.

the beloved weight watchers vegetable soup

In the early days of Weight Watchers members swore by the famous Garden Vegetable Soup for filling you up and not having to count it. We've revisited this classic dish (it now has a ***PointsPlus*** value of ***1***), along with two other delicious original versions that are also low in ***PointsPlus*** value, but big on flavor.

the classic garden vegetable soup

SERVES 6

***PointsPlus* value: *1* per serving (about 1 cup)**

½ cup sliced carrot
¼ cup diced onion
2 minced garlic cloves
3 cups fat-free beef, chicken, or vegetable broth
1 cup diced green cabbage
1 cup chopped spinach
1 tablespoon tomato paste
½ teaspoon dried basil
¼ teaspoon dried oregano
¼ teaspoon salt
1 cup diced zucchini

Spray a large saucepan with nonstick spray and set over low heat. Add the carrot, onion, and garlic and cook, stirring often, until softened, about 5 minutes. Add the broth, cabbage, spinach, tomato paste, basil, oregano, and salt; bring to boil. Reduce the heat; simmer, covered, about 15 minutes. Stir in the zucchini; cook 3-4 minutes more.

vegetable soup circa 1980

SERVES 2

***PointsPlus* value: *2* per serving (about ¾ cup)**

¼ cup diced onion
1 garlic clove, minced
2 cups water
1 cup each thinly sliced carrots and zucchini
¼ teaspoon each thyme leaves and salt
⅛ teaspoon black pepper
2 teaspoons chopped fresh parsley

Spray a small saucepan with nonstick spray and set over medium heat. Add the onion and garlic and cook stirring often until onion is softened, 5 minutes. Add the water, carrots, zucchini, thyme, salt, and pepper. Cover and cook over low heat, stirring occasionally, until vegetables are tender, about 10 minutes. Stir in the parsley.

microwave chickpea and vegetable soup circa 1990

SERVES 4

***PointsPlus* value: *3* per serving (about 1 cup)**

½ cup each chopped onion, diced celery, and diced carrot
1 large garlic clove, minced
1 teaspoon olive oil
1 cup each canned diced tomatoes and reduced-sodium chicken broth
1 cup canned chickpeas, rinsed and drained
1 tablespoon grated Parmesan cheese
1 tablespoon each chopped fresh parsley and chopped fresh basil or ½ teaspoon dried basil leaves
Dash black pepper

Stir together the onion, celery, carrot, garlic, and oil in a large microwave-safe bowl. Cover with wax paper and microwave on High for 3 minutes, stirring once. Stir in the tomatoes, broth, and chickpeas. Cover with wax paper and microwave on High until the vegetables are tender, 5 minutes. Stir in the cheese, parsley, basil, and pepper.

Note: All ***PointsPlus*** values were calculated using the Weight Watchers online recipe builder.

southwestern chicken-vegetable soup

SERVES 4

3 cups reduced-sodium chicken broth
2 cups frozen mixed vegetables (broccoli, cauliflower, carrots, corn, and red bell pepper)
1 (14½-ounce) can diced tomatoes
2 teaspoons chili powder
2 teaspoons ground cumin
1 cup chopped skinless cooked chicken breast
3 tablespoons chopped fresh cilantro
1 tablespoon fresh lime juice
12 baked tortilla chips, crumbled

Rich chicken soup, flavored with tomatoes and chiles and topped with strips of crisp tortillas, is a Mexican classic that first became popular north of the border in the 1980s. Our speedy version is loaded with vegetables and flavored with chili powder, cumin, and plenty of fresh cilantro.

1 Combine the broth, vegetables, tomatoes, chili powder, and cumin in a large saucepan. Bring to a boil; reduce the heat and simmer, covered, until the vegetables are tender, 10 minutes.

2 Stir in the chicken and cook until heated through, 2 minutes. Stir in the cilantro and lime juice. Top each serving with 3 of the tortilla chips.

PER SERVING (1¼ cups soup with 3 tortilla chips): 142 Cal, 3 g Total Fat, 1 g Sat Fat, 29 mg Chol, 719 mg Sod, 15 g Carb, 4 g Fib, 16 g Prot, 79 mg Calc.
PointsPlus value: 4.

Southwestern Chicken-Vegetable Soup

spicy sausage, white bean, and greens soup

SERVES 4

2 teaspoons olive oil
2 links (7 ounces) hot Italian-style turkey sausage, casings removed
1 small onion, chopped
1 carrot, chopped
2 garlic cloves, minced
3 cups low-sodium chicken broth
1 (15½-ounce) can cannellini (white kidney) beans, rinsed and drained
½ head escarole, cut into 2-inch pieces (4 cups)

The very first Weight Watchers cookbook had a recipe for escarole soup calling for little more than broth, tomato juice, and shredded escarole. We're delighted to offer an updated version that's a meal in a bowl, packed with flavorful ingredients, including spicy turkey sausage and creamy cannellini beans.

1 Heat a large saucepan over medium-high heat until hot. Swirl in the oil, then add the sausage, onion, and carrot. Cook, stirring to break up the sausage, until the sausage is no longer pink, 8 minutes. Stir in the garlic and cook for 1 minute.

2 Add the broth and beans. Bring to a boil; reduce the heat and simmer, covered, for 10 minutes. Stir in the escarole and simmer, covered, until the escarole is tender, 15 minutes. Serve at once.

PER SERVING (1¼ cups soup): 270 Cal, 9 g Total Fat, 2 g Sat Fat, 46 mg Chol, 620 mg Sod, 25 g Carb, 6 g Fib, 24 g Prot, 112 mg Calc. *PointsPlus value: 7.*

Enjoy this hearty soup with a slice of our crusty Multigrain Loaf with Flaxseeds, page 73.

creamy white bean–parmesan soup

SERVES 4

Vegetarian

2 (15½-ounce) can cannellini (white kidney) beans, rinsed and drained
3 cups reduced-sodium vegetable broth
2 teaspoons olive oil
1 onion, chopped
2 garlic cloves, minced
½ cup fat-free half-and-half
¼ cup grated Parmesan cheese
⅛ teaspoon ground pepper

Pureeing beans is a classic technique for adding richness and a silky texture to soups without the excess fat. Canned beans were once considered a no-no for those watching their sodium intake, but now, thanks to a number of brands offering no-salt-added varieties, everyone can enjoy them.

1 Combine the cannellini beans and ½ cup of the broth in a food processor or blender and puree.

2 Heat a large saucepan over medium heat until hot. Swirl in the oil, then add the onion and garlic. Cook, stirring frequently, until the onion is softened, about 5 minutes. Add the remaining 2½ cups broth and the bean puree. Bring to a boil; reduce the heat and simmer, stirring occasionally, about 2 minutes. Stir in the half-and-half, cheese, and pepper; cook just until heated through, about 1 minute.

PER SERVING (1 generous cup): 296 Cal, 5 g Total Fat, 2 g Sat Fat, 6 mg Chol, 919 mg Sod, 46 g Carb, 10 g Fib, 18 g Prot, 261 mg Calc. *PointsPlus value: 7.*

Minestrone and Bubble Bread with
Herbs and Sun-Dried Tomatoes, page 74

minestrone

SERVES 4

6 ounces cannellini (white kidney) beans, picked over, rinsed, and drained
8 cups reduced-sodium beef broth
¼ teaspoon salt
Freshly ground pepper
4 teaspoons olive oil
2 onions, chopped
2 carrots, chopped
2 celery stalks, chopped
1 garlic clove, minced
1 (28-ounce) can whole plum tomatoes, drained and chopped (reserve 1 cup juice)
1 small (1-pound) cabbage, cleaned and shredded
3 medium (8-ounce) zucchini, chopped
½ cup chopped flat-leaf parsley
2 tablespoons chopped sage, or 2 teaspoons dried
3 ounces tubetti or other small pasta
¼ cup freshly grated Parmesan cheese

To honor The Weight Watchers vegetable soup tradition, we've updated the ultimate vegetable soup, Italian-style. Loaded with veggies, beans, and pasta, and topped with grated Parmesan cheese, it is a meal in itself.

1 Place the beans in a large saucepan or Dutch oven; add enough cold water to cover them by 2 inches and bring to a boil. Remove from the heat; cover and let soak until the beans have swelled to at least twice their size, about 1½ hours. Drain.

2 Place the saucepan over medium heat; add the broth, salt, and pepper. Bring to a simmer; reduce the heat and simmer, covered, until the beans are barely tender, about 1 hour.

3 Meanwhile, heat a large nonstick skillet. Swirl in the oil, then add the onions, carrots, celery, and garlic. Cook, stirring frequently, until wilted.

4 Stir the vegetable mixture into the bean mixture; add the tomatoes and their reserved juice, the cabbage, zucchini, parsley, and sage. Simmer, stirring occasionally, until the vegetables are tender, about 20 minutes. Stir in the tubetti; continue cooking until they are barely tender, about 10 minutes. Remove from the heat; cover and let stand 10 minutes. Sprinkle with the cheese.

PER SERVING (1½ cups): 221 Cal, 5 g Total Fat, 1 g Sat Fat, 2 mg Chol, 481 mg Sod, 34 g Carb, 8 g Fib, 12 g Prot, 143 mg Calc.
PointsPlus value: 5.

smoky black bean and corn soup

SERVES 4

Vegetarian

1 teaspoon canola oil
1 large onion, chopped
2 garlic cloves, minced
2 cups fresh or frozen corn kernels
1 (14½-ounce) can reduced-sodium vegetable broth
1 (15-ounce) can black beans, rinsed and drained
1 (14½-ounce) can diced tomatoes
1 teaspoon ground cumin
½ teaspoon minced chipotles en adobo
1 teaspoon fresh lime juice
4 tablespoons fat-free sour cream
Chopped fresh cilantro
Thinly sliced scallion

Black beans are one of the most popular bean varieties and one of the healthiest: Their dark pigment is a sign of abundant antioxidants that are linked to a reduced risk for a number of diseases. In this recipe we've paired the beans with sweet corn and robust chipotle en adobo (smoked jalapeños) for a protein-packed vegetarian treat.

1 Heat a large saucepan over medium heat until hot. Swirl in the oil, then add the onion and garlic. Cook, stirring occasionally, until golden, about 8 minutes.

2 Add the corn, broth, beans, tomatoes, cumin, and chipotles. Bring to a boil; reduce the heat and simmer, covered, 10 minutes. Remove from the heat and stir in the lime juice. Top each serving with a tablespoon of the sour cream, and sprinkle with the cilantro and scallion.

PER SERVING (1¾ cups soup with 1 tablespoon sour cream): 229 Cal, 3 g Total Fat, 0 g Sat Fat, 1 mg Chol, 637 mg Sod, 45 g Carb, 11 g Fib, 10 g Prot, 121 mg Calc.
PointsPlus value: 6.

gazpacho with cilantro croutons

SERVES 4

Vegetarian

4 large plum tomatoes, peeled and chopped
1 medium cucumber, peeled and chopped
1 green bell pepper, chopped
4 scallions, sliced
2 cups tomato juice
3 tablespoons chopped cilantro
1 tablespoon white-wine or cider vinegar
1 tablespoon fresh lemon juice
¼ teaspoon hot pepper sauce
4 teaspoons olive oil
1 garlic clove, bruised
2 slices white or whole-wheat bread, cut in 1-inch cubes

In the swinging seventies, no sophisticated summer dinner party was complete without gazpacho on the menu. The refreshing cold soup—an import from sunny Spain—is basically liquefied salad and makes a great light lunch or late-afternoon pick-me-up. Why not pack some in a thermos and sip it throughout the day?

1 Puree the tomatoes, cucumber, pepper, and scallions in a food processor. Pour into a large bowl. Stir in the tomato juice, 1 tablespoon of the cilantro, the vinegar, lemon juice, and pepper sauce. Cover tightly and refrigerate until well chilled, at least 2 hours and up to 2 days.

2 Just before serving, heat a medium nonstick skillet. Swirl in the oil, then add the garlic. Cook, stirring, until fragrant, about 30 seconds. Discard the garlic; add the bread cubes and cook, stirring frequently, until the bread just starts to brown. Transfer to a medium bowl. Toss to coat with the remaining 2 tablespoons cilantro. Serve the soup with the warm croutons.

PER SERVING (1¼ cups): 125 Cal, 5 g Total Fat, 1 g Sat Fat, 0 mg Chol, 517 mg Sod, 18 g Carb, 3 g Fib, 3 g Prot, 49 mg Calc.
PointsPlus value: 3.

To easily peel the tomatoes, immerse them in boiling water for 1 minute; quickly transfer them with a slotted spoon to a bowl of ice water. As soon as they're cool enough to handle, just slip off the skins with your fingers.

butternut squash soup with sage

SERVES 4

2 teaspoons olive oil
1 onion, chopped
1 medium (2-pound) butternut squash, peeled, seeded, and coarsely chopped
1 (32-ounce) carton reduced-sodium chicken broth
2 tablespoons chopped sage
1–1½ cups water
¼ cup fat-free sour cream
2 tablespoons chopped sage (optional)

Two of autumn's best flavors, sweet winter squash and earthy sage, make this colorful soup a wonderful way to welcome the season. For a different flavor, sprinkle on a bit of cinammon instead of the sage for a tasty finish.

1 Heat a large nonstick saucepan. Swirl in the oil, then add the onion. Sauté until translucent, about 5 minutes. Add the squash, broth, and sage; bring to a boil. Reduce the heat and simmer, adding the water ½ cup at a time, until the squash is very soft, about 20 minutes. Remove from the heat and let cool 30 minutes.

2 Pour the mixture through a strainer; reserve the liquid. Transfer the squash mixture remaining in the strainer to a food processor; pulse to a very smooth puree. Add 1–1½ cups of the strained liquid, ½ cup at a time, until the soup has a fluid but creamy consistency. (Refrigerate or freeze any leftover strained liquid for another use.)

3 Transfer the soup back to the saucepan and cook, stirring frequently, until just heated through. Garnish each serving with a tablespoon of the sour cream and a sprinkle of the additional sage, if using.

PER SERVING (1 cup): 184 Cal, 4 g Total Fat, 1 g Sat Fat, 0 mg Chol, 489 mg Sod, 33 g Carb, 7 g Fib, 8 g Prot, 136 mg Calc.
PointsPlus value: 5.

If you have any strained liquid leftover in Step 2, save it for flavoring soups and stews. It will last up to three days in the refrigerator or two months in the freezer.

---

potato-leek soup

SERVES 8

2 (32-ounce) cartons reduced-sodium chicken broth
8 medium (5-ounce) potatoes, peeled and chopped
3 leeks, cleaned and thinly sliced
Freshly ground pepper
2 tablespoons minced chives (optional)

Made with just potatoes, leeks, and chicken broth, this hearty potage has all the robust taste of the traditional one made with cream—minus the fat. It can be completely or partially pureed and served hot or cold. (If you serve it cold, be sure to call it vichyssoise, as sophisticated chefs did in the sixties.)

1 Combine the broth, potatoes, leeks, and pepper in a large saucepan or Dutch oven; cover and simmer until the vegetables are very soft, about 30 minutes. Uncover and let cool slightly.

2 Puree at least 2 cups or up to all of the potatoes and leeks (depending on the texture you want), with 1–2 cups of the broth in a food processor; pour the mixture back into the remaining soup, stir, and reheat. Serve hot, or cover and refrigerate and serve cold; hot or cold, garnish with the minced chives, if using.

PER SERVING (1½ cups): 153 Cal, 1 g Total Fat, 0 g Sat Fat, 0 mg Chol, 477 mg Sod, 28 g Carb, 3 g Fib, 7 g Prot, 44 mg Calc.
PointsPlus value: 4.

To clean the leeks, trim the roots, leaving the root ends intact to hold the layers together. Slice them lengthwise, fan open the layers, and swish them in a large bowl of cool water. Let them stand a few minutes to allow the grit to fall to the bottom, then lift them out.

borscht with sour cream

SERVES 4

¾ pound beets, shredded (2 cups)
1 (14-ounce) can reduced-sodium beef broth
1½ cups water
½ red onion, finely chopped
½ cup finely shredded red cabbage
½ teaspoon packed dark brown sugar
2 tablespoons chopped dill
2 tablespoons fresh lemon juice
¼ teaspoon salt
Freshly ground pepper
¼ cup fat-free sour cream
2 tablespoons chopped dill (optional)

Once upon a Weight Watchers time, borscht was an occasional treat only to be eaten at dinner, because it was made with beets—a "limited" vegetable. Today we can enjoy it anytime and with a dollop of fat-free sour cream, to boot.

1 In a large nonreactive saucepan, combine the beets, broth, water, onion, cabbage, and sugar. Bring to a boil; reduce the heat and simmer, covered, until the cabbage is tender, about 20 minutes. Add the dill; simmer 5 minutes. Remove from the heat.

2 Stir in the lemon juice, salt, and pepper. Pour into a 1-quart storage container and refrigerate until chilled, at least 2 hours and up to 3 days. Garnish each serving with a tablespoon of the sour cream and a sprinkle of the additional dill, if using.

PER SERVING (1 cup): 68 Cal, 1 g Total Fat, 0 g Sat Fat, 0 mg Chol, 294 mg Sod, 13 g Carb, 2 g Fib, 4 g Prot, 62 mg Calc.
PointsPlus value: 2.

chilled broccoli soup with lemon and herbs

SERVES 4

2 (32-ounce) cartons reduced-sodium chicken broth
1 bunch broccoli, trimmed and broken into florets; stalks peeled and chopped
1 onion, chopped
2 garlic cloves, finely chopped
2 tablespoons fresh lemon juice
2 tablespoons chopped flat-leaf parsley
1 tablespoon chopped mint
¼ cup fat-free sour cream or plain fat-free Greek yogurt (optional)

This tasty, healthy soup is the epitome of a low-fat recipe: It's just broccoli, broth, and flavorings, all cooked together and then pureed in a food processor. What could be easier?

1 Combine the broth, broccoli, onion, and garlic in a large saucepan. Bring to a boil; reduce the heat and simmer, covered, until the broccoli is very tender, about 20 minutes.

2 Pour the mixture through a strainer; reserve the broth. Transfer the broccoli mixture remaining in the strainer to a food processor. Add the lemon juice, parsley, and mint; puree, adding the reserved broth ¼ cup at a time, until the mixture is liquid but creamy. Let cool to room temperature, then cover tightly and refrigerate until chilled, at least 2 hours and up to 1 day. (Refrigerate or freeze any remaining broth for another use.) Garnish each serving with 1 tablespoon of the sour cream or yogurt, if using.

PER SERVING (1 cup): 119 Cal, 3 g Total Fat, 1 g Sat Fat, 0 mg Chol, 965 mg Sod, 11 g Carb, 4 g Fib, 13 g Prot, 85 mg Calc.
PointsPlus value: 3.

If you don't have fresh herbs, omit them altogether rather than substituting with dried ones.

chilled zucchini-basil soup with tomatoes

SERVES 4

3 (14½-ounce) cans reduced-sodium chicken broth
½ cup water
3 medium zucchini, chopped
1 onion, chopped
1 garlic clove, minced
2 tablespoons fresh lemon juice
¼ cup chopped fresh basil
2 plum tomatoes, chopped
4 tablespoons plain fat-free Greek yogurt

This refreshing soup is filled with the flavors of summer, but don't hesitate to make it year-round. Mint is a terrific substitute if fresh basil isn't at its peak, and reliably flavorful grape tomatoes can be chopped and used in place of plum tomatoes if the latter aren't super ripe.

1 Combine the broth, water, zucchini, onion, and garlic in a large saucepan. Bring to a boil; reduce the heat and simmer, covered, until the zucchini is very tender, about 15 minutes. Remove the saucepan from the heat. Uncover and let cool about 5 minutes.

2 Strain the zucchini mixture through a strainer set over a medium bowl; reserve the liquid. Transfer the zucchini mixture to a food processor. Add the lemon juice and basil; puree until smooth. With the machine running, add the reserved liquid, ¼ cup at a time, until the soup has the consistency of cream. Let cool to room temperature, then cover and refrigerate until well chilled, at least 3 hours or up to 1 day. Sprinkle each serving with the tomatoes and top with a tablespoon of the yogurt.

PER SERVING (1½ cups soup with 1 tablespoon yogurt): 74 Cal, 1 g Total Fat, 0 g Sat Fat, 0 mg Chol, 735 mg Sod, 11 g Carb, 2 g Fib, 8 g Prot, 82 mg Calc.
PointsPlus value: 2.

vegetable salad with dijon vinaigrette

SERVES 4

1 (10-ounce) box frozen artichoke hearts
1 (10-ounce) box frozen green beans
1 (10-ounce) box frozen asparagus spears
2 tablespoons reduced-sodium chicken broth
4 teaspoons olive oil
1 tablespoon chopped thyme
1 tablespoon white-wine or cider vinegar
2 garlic cloves, minced
1 tablespoon Dijon mustard
1 teaspoon dry mustard
¼ teaspoon salt
Freshly ground pepper
1 hard-cooked egg, finely chopped
1 tablespoon minced flat-leaf parsley

What a pity that glamorously delicious, fiber-rich, and nearly fat-free artichoke hearts were once considered "limited" vegetables on the Weight Watchers eating plan. This elegant and savory salad makes amends, celebrating them with style. Since the vegetables are prepared, dressed, and marinated for hours, it's a good do-ahead dish for company.

1 Cook the artichoke hearts, green beans, and asparagus according to package directions. Drain, then arrange the vegetables on a platter in an attractive pattern.

2 Puree the broth, oil, thyme, vinegar, garlic, Dijon mustard, dry mustard, salt, and pepper in a blender or food processor. Drizzle the dressing evenly over the vegetables; sprinkle with the egg and parsley. Cover tightly with plastic wrap; refrigerate up to 8 hours or overnight. Let stand at room temperature 30 minutes before serving.

PER SERVING (1 cup): 138 Cal, 7 g Total Fat, 1 g Sat Fat, 53 mg Chol, 242 mg Sod, 16 g Carb, 7 g Fib, 7 g Prot, 94 mg Calc.
PointsPlus value: 4.

If you have the time, substitute fresh, trimmed green beans and asparagus spears for the frozen ones; you'll need about 2 cups of each. Steam them until tender-crisp before using. You can also use canned quartered artichoke hearts instead of frozen; a 14-ounce can will work nicely.

arugula-pear salad with gorgonzola dressing

SERVES 4

20 Min or Less
Vegetarian

1 pear, thinly sliced
1 tablespoon fresh lemon juice
1 bunch arugula, cleaned
⅓ cup crumbled Gorgonzola cheese
¼ cup reduced-sodium vegetable broth
4 teaspoons olive oil
1 tablespoon white-wine or cider vinegar
1 garlic clove, bruised
Freshly ground pepper

Pears and Gorgonzola cheese are a favorite duo in Italian cuisine, especially after a meal. Why not serve this elegant salad as a last course at a dinner party? The salad and the dressing can be made ahead of time, refrigerated for up to eight hours, then combined just before serving.

1 Combine the pear with the lemon juice in a small bowl; toss to coat. Arrange the arugula and pear slices on a platter.

2 To prepare the dressing, combine the cheese, broth, oil, vinegar, garlic, and pepper in a small bowl; let stand at least 5 minutes to allow the flavors to blend, then remove the garlic.

3 Drizzle the dressing over the salad just before serving.

PER SERVING (1½ cups): 115 Cal, 8 g Total Fat, 3 g Sat Fat, 11 mg Chol, 182 mg Sod, 8 g Carb, 1 g Fib, 3 g Prot, 97 mg Calc.
PointsPlus value: 3.

Bruising garlic helps release its flavor. Here's how: Place a peeled clove on a cutting board and flatten it slightly with the side of a large knife.

fennel, orange, and red cabbage salad with citrus vinaigrette

SERVES 4

20 Min or Less
Vegetarian

- 2 tablespoons reduced-sodium vegetable broth or dry white wine
- 1 teaspoon grated orange zest
- 2 tablespoons fresh orange juice
- 4 teaspoons olive oil
- 1 tablespoon honey
- 1 teaspoon lemon juice
- 1 teaspoon red-wine or cider vinegar
- 1 teaspoon raspberry vinegar
- 1 teaspoon balsamic vinegar
- ¼ teaspoon salt
- Freshly ground pepper
- 1 small (1-pound) red cabbage, shredded (4 cups)
- 1 fennel bulb, trimmed and thinly sliced
- 2 oranges, peeled, sliced, and cut into bite-size pieces

Designer vinegars such as raspberry and balsamic were a hallmark of the go-go eighties, and Weight Watchers used them to wonderful effect in this delicious salad. The sweet-and-sour combination of vinegars, lemon juice, orange, and honey is a perfect complement to the licorice-y taste of the fennel—and the cabbage pulls it all together.

Whisk together the broth or wine, orange zest, orange juice, oil, honey, lemon juice, red-wine or cider vinegar, raspberry vinegar, balsamic vinegar, salt, and pepper in a large salad bowl. Add the cabbage, fennel, and oranges to the bowl; toss to coat evenly. Serve at once.

PER SERVING (2 cups): 133 Cal, 5 g Total Fat, 1 g Sat Fat, 0 mg Chol, 201 mg Sod, 23 g Carb, 5 g Fib, 3 g Prot, 100 mg Calc.
PointsPlus value: 4.

field greens with roasted beets, goat cheese croutons, and dijon vinaigrette

SERVES 4

Vegetarian

- 2 beets, peeled, trimmed, and cubed
- 1 teaspoon chopped thyme, or ¼ teaspoon dried
- 4 (1-ounce) slices toasted French or Italian bread
- 2 ounces goat cheese
- 2 tablespoons chopped flat-leaf parsley
- 3 tablespoons dry white wine or reduced-sodium vegetable broth
- 4 teaspoons olive oil
- 2 teaspoons white- or red-wine vinegar, or cider vinegar
- 1 teaspoon Dijon mustard
- 1 garlic clove, bruised
- ¼ teaspoon salt
- Freshly ground pepper
- 8 ounces mixed baby greens

Field greens, microgreens, mesclun, baby greens—fancy salad buzzwords in upscale nineties restaurants—are ubiquitous today, available at farmers' markets, supermarkets, and even in prebagged salad kits. Paired with those other nineties staples, beets, goat cheese, and Dijon vinaigrette, they make an elegant but easy salad.

1 Preheat the oven to 400°F.

2 Spray a small baking pan with nonstick spray. Combine the beets and thyme in the pan; toss to coat and spray again with nonstick spray. Roast, stirring occasionally, until tender, about 25 minutes. Set aside to cool.

3 To prepare the croutons, spread the toasted bread slices with the goat cheese; sprinkle with the parsley and set aside.

4 To prepare the dressing, combine the wine or chicken broth, oil, vinegar, mustard, garlic, salt, and pepper in a large bowl; let stand 2 minutes, then discard the garlic. Whisk until smooth.

5 To assemble the salad, drizzle a teaspoon of the dressing over the beets in the pan and toss to coat evenly. Add the greens to the bowl with the remaining dressing; toss to coat evenly. Divide the greens among 4 salad plates. Top each with one-fourth of the beets, then with a crouton.

PER SERVING (2 cups with 1 crouton): 200 Cal, 9 g Total Fat, 35 g Sat Fat, 7 mg Chol, 427 mg Sod, 23 g Carb, 3 g Fib, 8 g Prot, 73 mg Calc.
PointsPlus value: 5.

Creamy goat cheese makes this salad a hearty meal. The good news is that the assertive, nutty flavor of a good goat cheese goes quite a long way so, as in this salad, you only need a little to make a big impact.

Field Greens with Roasted Beets, Goat Cheese Croutons, and Dijon Vinaigrette

arugula, radicchio, and belgian endive salad with creamy garlic dressing

SERVES 4

20 Min or Less
Vegetarian

½ cup plain fat-free yogurt
4 teaspoons vegetable oil
1 tablespoon white-wine or cider vinegar
½ tablespoon light corn syrup
1 garlic clove, minced
½ teaspoon salt
Freshly ground pepper
1 bunch arugula, cleaned
1 head radicchio, cleaned
1 head Belgian endive, cleaned
1 tablespoon minced chives (optional)

Inspired by the Salad Bouquet recipe featured in the first Weight Watchers Cookbook, this colorful trio of salad greens boasts a creamy garlic dressing you'll want to drizzle on everything. Make it ahead, if you like; the dressing will keep in a tightly sealed container in the refrigerator for up to three days.

1 To prepare the dressing, pulse the yogurt, oil, vinegar, corn syrup, garlic, salt, and pepper in a food processor or blender until smooth. Cover and refrigerate until ready to serve.

2 Arrange the arugula, radicchio, and endive leaves on a platter. Just before serving, drizzle the dressing over the salad. Sprinkle with the chives, if using.

PER SERVING (2 cups): 100 Cal, 5 g Total Fat, 1 g Sat Fat, 1 mg Chol, 356 mg Sod, 11 g Carb, 4 g Fib, 4 g Prot, 158 mg Calc.
PointsPlus value: 3.

caesar salad

SERVES 4

20 Min or Less

- 1 large garlic clove, bruised
- ¼ cup reduced-sodium chicken broth
- 4 teaspoons olive oil
- 1 tablespoon fresh lemon juice
- ¾ teaspoon anchovy paste
- ½ teaspoon dry mustard
- Freshly ground pepper
- 1 head romaine lettuce, torn into bite-size pieces (6 cups)
- 1 cup fat-free croutons
- 2 tablespoons freshly grated Parmesan cheese

Caesar salad had its heyday in the sixties, when it was prepared tableside at better restaurants. Chefs rediscovered it in the nineties, and we've gone one better eliminating the raw egg, including a dollop of anchovy paste (rather than fillets), and dusting the salad with grated Parmesan.

Rub a large salad bowl with the garlic clove, then combine the garlic with the broth, oil, lemon juice, anchovy paste, mustard, and pepper in the bowl. Let stand 5 minutes, then discard the garlic. Add the lettuce to the bowl; toss to coat evenly. Sprinkle with the croutons and cheese.

PER SERVING (2 cups): 94 Cal, 6 g Total Fat, 1 g Sat Fat, 4 mg Chol, 184 mg Sod, 6 g Carb, 2 g Fib, 4 g Prot, 83 mg Calc.
PointsPlus value: 2.

Tuscan Panzanella

tuscan panzanella

SERVES 4

Vegetarian

1½ tablespoons red-wine vinegar
1 tablespoon extra-virgin olive oil
¼ teaspoon salt
¼ teaspoon ground pepper
1 (4-ounce) day-old multigrain baguette, cut into ½-inch cubes
2 cups grape tomatoes, halved
1 medium cucumber, thinly sliced
1 small red onion, thinly sliced
¼ cup fresh basil leaves, thinly sliced

A traditional salad of day-old bread dressed with olive oil and vinegar and mixed with garden vegetables has been served in Italian households for hundreds of years. Known as panzanella, it has now become very popular Stateside, partly due to an increased interest in Italian regional cuisine, but also for a very practical reason: It's one of the most delicious ways to use up stale bread.

Whisk together the vinegar, oil, salt, and pepper in a large bowl. Add the bread, tomatoes, cucumber, onion, and basil; toss well. Let stand 15 minutes, tossing occasionally.

PER SERVING (1½ cups): 131 Cal, 5 g Total Fat, 1 g Sat Fat, 0 mg Chol, 288 mg Sod, 18 g Carb, 4 g Fib, 5 g Prot, 56 mg Calc.
PointsPlus value: 3.

pickled beet and onion salad

SERVES 4

Vegetarian

3 tablespoons red-wine or cider vinegar
2 tablespoons dry red wine or reduced-sodium vegetable broth
1 tablespoon balsamic vinegar
2 teaspoons sugar
2 teaspoons olive oil
¼ teaspoon salt
Freshly ground pepper
4 cups cooked sliced beets
1 red onion, chopped

Back in the Weight Watchers day when beets and onions were "limited" vegetables, a recipe for Beet Relish combined canned cooked beets, dehydrated onion flakes, artificial sweetener, and vinegar. Compare that with this twenty-first-century version that makes delicious use of fresh beets, onion, a little oil, balsamic vinegar, and, yes, a bit of sugar to balance the sharp onion flavor.

Combine the wine or cider vinegar, wine, balsamic vinegar, sugar, oil, salt, and pepper in a large bowl. Add the beets and onion; toss to coat. Cover tightly and refrigerate to blend the flavors, at least 30 minutes and up to 1 day before serving.

PER SERVING (¾ cup): 126 Cal, 3 g Total Fat, 0 g Sat Fat, 0 mg Chol, 282 mg Sod, 22 g Carb, 4 g Fib, 3 g Prot, 36 mg Calc.
PointsPlus value: 3.

Save time by making this salad with vacuum-packed precooked beets. Their flavor and texture are usually superb, and they're available in the produce section of most large supermarkets.

---

barley waldorf salad

SERVES 6

Vegetarian

3 cups water
2/3 cup pearl barley
3/4 teaspoon salt
1/4 cup plain low-fat yogurt
3 tablespoons diced sweet onion
2 tablespoons reduced-fat mayonnaise
1 tablespoon fresh lemon juice
1 tablespoon fresh tangerine or orange juice
1/2 teaspoon sugar
1 large, slightly tart apple, such as Braeburn, Gala, or Mutsu, cored, seeded, and cut into 1/2-inch cubes
1 cup halved green seedless grapes
1/3 cup pecan halves, toasted and finely chopped

Talk about retro! This sweet, crunchy salad was created at the turn of the last century at the famed Waldorf-Astoria Hotel in New York City, but remained popular through the ages. Here, we've updated its profile by adding fiber-rich barley.

1 Combine the water, barley, and salt in a medium saucepan; bring to a boil. Reduce the heat, cover, and simmer until tender, about 30 minutes. Drain in a colander, rinsing briefly with cold water to stop the cooking.

2 Stir together the yogurt, onion, mayonnaise, lemon juice, tangerine juice, and sugar in a large bowl. Add the barley, apple, and grapes; toss gently to coat evenly. Sprinkle the top with the pecans.

PER SERVING (generous 3/4 cup): 205 Cal, 6 g Total Fat, 1 g Sat Fat, 1 mg Chol, 85 mg Sod, 35 g Carb, 6 g Fib, 4 g Prot, 37 mg Calc. ***PointsPlus value: 5.***

iceberg salad with blue cheese dressing

SERVES 4

20 Min or Less

¼ cup crumbled blue cheese
3 tablespoons reduced-fat mayonnaise
3 tablespoons plain low-fat Greek yogurt
1 tablespoon cider vinegar
½ teaspoon Worcestershire sauce
⅛ teaspoon ground pepper
½ medium head iceberg lettuce, torn
2 Kirby cucumbers, peeled and sliced
2 plum tomatoes, cut into wedges
1 small red onion, thinly sliced
1 small red bell pepper, thinly sliced

The iceberg–blue cheese combo has been a classic for decades, and a wedge of crisp lettuce with a drizzle of creamy, tangy Roquefort or Danish Blue dressing remains de rigueur on countless steak house menus. Our updated version still features fabulously refreshing iceberg, but we've lightened the dressing considerably, and added a host of brightly colored vegetables. And our version goes great with steak!

1 To prepare the dressing, stir together the blue cheese, mayonnaise, yogurt, vinegar, Worcestershire sauce, and pepper in a small bowl until well mixed. Cover and refrigerate up to 4 days.

2 To prepare the salad, combine the lettuce, cucumbers, tomatoes, onion, and bell pepper in a large bowl. Drizzle with the dressing and toss to coat.

PER SERVING (1¾ cups): 106 Cal, 6 g Total Fat, 2 g Sat Fat, 10 mg Chol, 216 mg Sod, 8 g Carb, 2 g Fib, 4 g Prot, 85 mg Calc.
PointsPlus value: 3.

You can serve this salad on its own, but it also makes a perfect starter for a special occasion meal featuring our Roasted Beef Tenderloin with Mushroom Sauce, page 105.

---

greek salad with oregano dressing

SERVES 4

20 Min or Less

¼ cup reduced-sodium vegetable broth
4 teaspoons olive oil
1 tablespoon white- or red-wine vinegar, or cider vinegar
1½ tablespoons chopped oregano, or 1½ teaspoons dried
1 garlic clove, bruised
¼ teaspoon salt
Freshly ground pepper
1 head romaine, Bibb, iceberg, or green-leaf lettuce, torn into bite-size pieces (6 cups)
1 cucumber, peeled, seeded and chopped
1 green bell pepper, seeded, and cut into ½-inch strips
1 tomato, cut into 8 wedges
¼ cup chopped dill
10 small black olives, pitted and sliced
4 anchovies, rinsed and chopped (optional)
½ cup crumbled feta cheese

Forty years ago, you'd find this salad featured at any corner diner. It's become a classic, so you're just as likely to find it today. This savory version includes all the traditional ingredients but only a fraction of the fat.

1 Combine the broth, oil, vinegar, oregano, garlic, salt, and black pepper in a small bowl. Let stand 5 minutes to allow the flavors to blend, then discard the garlic.

2 Meanwhile, combine the lettuce, cucumber, bell pepper, tomato, dill, and olives in a large salad bowl. Pour the dressing over the salad; toss to coat evenly. Top with the anchovies, if using, and sprinkle with the cheese.

PER SERVING (2½ cups): 128 Cal, 10 g Total Fat, 4 g Sat Fat, 17 mg Chol, 449 mg Sod, 7 g Carb, 3 g Fib, 4 g Prot, 134 mg Calc.
PointsPlus value: 3.

lemon-basil three-bean salad

SERVES 6

20 Min or Less
Vegetarian

1 teaspoon grated lemon zest
1½ tablespoons fresh lemon juice
1 tablespoon extra-virgin olive oil
½ teaspoon salt
Freshly ground pepper
1 (15-ounce) can black beans, rinsed and drained
1 (15-ounce) can small white beans, rinsed and drained
⅔ cup cooked shelled green soybeans (edamame)
⅓ sweet onion, finely diced
⅓ red bell pepper, finely diced
5 large basil leaves, thinly sliced

This popular salad of picnics past takes on a new profile with fresh slivers of basil, tangy lemon juice, and green soybeans (edamame) for their sweet flavor and bright color.

Combine the lemon zest, lemon juice, oil, salt, and ground pepper in a medium bowl. Add the black beans, white beans, soybeans, onion, bell pepper, and basil; toss to coat evenly. Serve at once, or cover and refrigerate for up to 2 days.

PER SERVING (¾ cup): 160 Cal, 3 g Total Fat, 0 g Sat Fat, 0 mg Chol, 427 mg Sod, 26 g Carb, 8 g Fib, 9 g Prot, 94 mg Calc.
PointsPlus value: 4.

Lemon-Basil
Three-Bean Salad

chef's salad with russian dressing

SERVES 4

20 Min or Less

2 tablespoons reduced-fat mayonnaise
¼ cup plain fat-free yogurt
2 tablespoons ketchup
Freshly ground pepper
1 head romaine lettuce, torn into bite-size pieces (6 cups)
1 cucumber, peeled and sliced
1 green bell pepper, sliced into thin rings
1 tomato, cut into 8 wedges
2 ounces reduced-sodium turkey breast, cut into matchstick-size strips
2 ounces reduced-fat Swiss cheese, cut into matchstick-size strips
1 hard-cooked egg, quartered

Weight Watchers members were among the first to be clued in that a typical American chef's salad—loaded with cold cuts and cheese and doused in dressing—was anything but diet food. Here's our take on the classic, packed with more veggies and a leaner but still creamy-rich dressing.

Whisk together the mayonnaise, yogurt, ketchup, and ground pepper in a salad bowl. Add the lettuce and cucumber to the bowl; toss to coat evenly. Arrange the bell pepper, tomato, turkey, cheese, and egg on top of the salad in an attractive pattern and serve at once.

PER SERVING (2½ cups): 139 Cal, 7 g Total Fat, 2 g Sat Fat, 66 mg Chol, 289 mg Sod, 10 g Carb, 2 g Fib, 12 g Prot, 244 mg Calc. ***PointsPlus value: 4.***

spinach-mushroom-bacon salad with warm onion dressing

SERVES 6

1 (10-ounce) bag triple-washed fresh spinach, torn into bite-size pieces, or 8 cups spinach leaves
1 (10-ounce) package sliced mushrooms
2 tablespoons vegetable oil
2 cups reduced-sodium vegetable broth
1 red onion, thinly sliced and separated into rings
1 teaspoon grated orange zest
¼ cup fresh orange juice
2 tablespoons red-wine or cider vinegar
¼ teaspoon salt
1 crisp-cooked bacon slice, crumbled
Freshly ground pepper

The nineties bistro craze made this favorite salad even more popular; who knows how many diners thought their bacon-and-dripping-soaked salads were light eating? Our version cuts the fat dramatically, with a savory, warm dressing that wilts the spinach just enough to make it tender.

1 Place the spinach and mushrooms in a salad bowl; set aside.

2 Heat a large nonstick skillet. Swirl in the oil, then add the broth, onion, orange zest, orange juice, vinegar, and salt. Cook over medium heat, stirring occasionally, until the onions are very tender and the liquid has thickened and reduced to ½ cup, about 15 minutes. Let stand 10 minutes.

3 Pour the warm dressing over the spinach and mushrooms; sprinkle with the bacon pieces and pepper. Serve at once.

PER SERVING (2 cups): 86 Cal, 5 g Total Fat, 1 g Sat Fat, 1 mg Chol, 238 mg Sod, 8 g Carb, 2 g Fib, 3 g Prot, 58 mg Calc.
PointsPlus value: 2.

If you're using bunch spinach, you'll need to wash it carefully. Immerse the leaves in cold standing water and swish gently to free the grit. Lift the spinach out of the water and repeat the rinsing with clean water until the spinach is free of grit, usually three changes of water. Drain and dry in a salad spinner.

Cobb Salad with Green Goddess Dressing

cobb salad with green goddess dressing

SERVES 4

20 Min or Less

- 4 slices turkey bacon
- ½ small iceberg lettuce head, chopped (about 3 cups)
- 1 bunch arugula, chopped (about 1 cup)
- 8 ounces skinless cooked chicken breast, sliced
- 3 large hard-cooked egg whites, chopped
- ½ medium (8-ounce) Hass avocado, peeled and chopped
- 4 plum tomatoes, seeded and chopped
- ½ cup plain fat-free yogurt
- ¼ cup fat-free mayonnaise
- ½ cup chopped parsley
- ¼ cup chopped chives
- 1 scallion, chopped
- 1 teaspoon white-wine vinegar
- ¼ teaspoon salt
- ⅛ teaspoon freshly ground pepper

Like so many of our classic salads, this one comes from 1920s California. Bob Cobb, of the famed Brown Derby restaurant in Hollywood, is said to have created the salad out of leftovers in the refrigerator. The dressing, named to honor the actor George Arliss and a play he starred in, The Green Goddess, *hails from San Francisco's Palace Hotel.*

1 Heat a medium nonstick skillet over medium heat. Add the bacon and cook until crisp. Drain on paper towels until cool enough to handle; coarsely chop.

2 Scatter the lettuce and arugula over a platter. Top with neat rows of the chicken, egg whites, avocado, tomatoes, and bacon.

3 To prepare the dressing, place the yogurt, mayonnaise, parsley, chives, scallion, vinegar, salt, and pepper in a blender; pulse until smooth.

4 Lightly drizzle half of the dressing over the salad and serve at once, passing the remaining dressing separately.

PER SERVING: (1½ cups with ¼ cup dressing): 224 Cal, 8 g Total Fat, 2 g Sat Fat, 56 mg Chol, 580 mg Sod, 12 g Carb, 3 g Fib, 26 g Prot, 110 mg Calc.
PointsPlus value: 5.

We prefer Hass avocados for this recipe. With their distinctive black pebbly skin, Hass avocados contain slightly more fat than the green-skinned Mexican types grown in Florida—but their buttery taste and velvety texture justify every ***PointsPlus*** value.

fruit salad with yogurt-mint dressing

SERVES 4

Vegetarian

1 cup sliced strawberries
2 medium kiwi fruit, pared and sliced
1 banana, sliced
1 (8-ounce) can unsweetened pineapple chunks, drained
3 tablespoons orange juice
¼ cup fat-free vanilla yogurt
2 tablespoons chopped mint
4 small fresh mint sprigs (optional)

In the past, Weight Watchers fruit salads were served in limited quantities—and usually bulked up with vegetables like green peppers and pimientos. And, of course, kiwi fruits were unknown and bananas were forbidden. What a pleasure it is to improve on the past and enjoy this refreshing fruit salad, as perfect for lunch as it is for dessert.

1 Combine the strawberries, kiwi, banana, and pineapple with 1 tablespoon of the orange juice in a large bowl.

2 Puree the yogurt, chopped mint, and the remaining 2 tablespoons orange juice in a food processor. Pour over the fruit mixture; toss to coat evenly. Refrigerate, covered, until thoroughly chilled, at least 1 hour and up to 8 hours. Garnish with the mint sprigs, if using, and serve.

PER SERVING (¾ cup): 104 Cal, 0 g Total Fat, 0 g Sat Fat, 0 mg Chol, 11 mg Sod, 25 g Carb, 3 g Fib, 2 g Prot, 57 mg Calc.
PointsPlus value: 3.

watermelon, tomato, and orange salad

SERVES 4

Vegetarian

1 large navel orange
½ teaspoon ground coriander
½ teaspoon ground cumin
½ teaspoon salt
Pinch cayenne
4 cups 1-inch cubes seedless watermelon
2 cups cherry tomatoes, halved
2 tablespoons chopped fresh mint

Believe it or not, watermelon was once considered forbidden fruit: The first Weight Watchers cookbook omitted it from the list of "legal" fruits. Times have changed, and this refreshing, savory salad combines cubed watermelon with cherry tomatoes, orange segments, mint, and an irresistible combination of warm spices.

1 With a small knife, cut away the peel and white pith from the orange. Working over a large bowl, cut between the membranes to release the segments. Squeeze the juice from the membranes into the bowl. Stir in the coriander, cumin, salt, and cayenne.

2 Add the watermelon, tomatoes, and mint to the bowl; toss to combine.

PER SERVING (1½ cups): 87 Cal, 1 g Total Fat, 0 g Sat Fat, 0 mg Chol, 302 mg Sod, 21 g Carb, 3 g Fib, 2 g Prot, 45 mg Calc.
PointsPlus value: 2.

This is an ideal salad to serve at a casual summer barbecue. Try it with our Soy-Sesame Grilled Tuna, page 166, or our Grilled T-Bone with Steak House Spices, page 108.

california salad sandwiches

SERVES 4

20 Min or Less
Vegetarian

- 1 cup cooked small white beans (such as Great Northern or flageolets), or rinsed drained canned white beans
- 2 tablespoons water
- 1 tablespoon fresh lemon juice
- 2 tablespoons Dijon mustard
- 8 slices multigrain bread
- 8 slices reduced-fat Swiss or cheddar cheese, about 4 ounces
- 1 small avocado, peeled, pitted, and thinly sliced
- 2 cups alfalfa sprouts
- 1 medium tomato, cut into 8 slices

There was a time when this sandwich's alfalfa sprouts, avocado, and whole-grain bread would have pegged it as pure Californian, if not pure hippie. But today, these ingredients are staples in sandwiches everywhere. Instead of slathering the sandwiches with mayonnaise, we use flavorful pureed beans.

1 Combine the beans, water, and lemon juice in a blender; puree until smooth.

2 Spread 1½ teaspoons of the mustard onto each of 4 bread slices, then spread all 8 slices with a layer of the bean puree. Layer each mustard-spread bread slice in the following order: 1 slice of cheese, ¼ of the avocado slices, ½ cup alfalfa sprouts, 2 tomato slices, and another cheese slice. Top each sandwich with the remaining (bean-puree-spread) bread slices.

3 Heat a large nonstick skillet over medium heat. Lightly spray both sides of each sandwich with nonstick spray, then place in the skillet. Cover and cook, turning once, until the cheese melts and the bread toasts slightly, 4 minutes. Serve at once.

PER SERVING (1 sandwich): 339 Cal, 13 g Total Fat, 4 g Sat Fat, 9 mg Chol, 418 mg Sod, 42 g Carb, 10 g Fib, 20 g Prot, 445 mg Calc.
PointsPlus value: 9.

mexican chicken wraps

SERVES 4

- 4 (¼-pound) skinless boneless chicken breast halves
- 1 teaspoon olive oil
- 1 tablespoon Mexican seasoning mix
- ¼ teaspoon salt
- ⅓ cup reduced-fat mayonnaise
- 2 tablespoons chopped cilantro
- 1 tablespoon fresh lime juice
- 2 teaspoons chopped canned chipotles in adobo
- 4 (8-inch) fat-free flour tortillas
- 1 bunch arugula, cleaned
- 1 plum tomato, seeded and chopped
- ½ red onion, chopped

The sandwich wrap was one of the hottest grab-and-go eating trends in the nineties. Wraps can be made with just about any flatbread, from lavash to crêpes, but the most popular is the flour tortilla. Here, we've stuffed tortillas with a mildly spicy warm chicken filling that's tamed with cool, crunchy vegetables.

1 Preheat the broiler or grill; spray the broiler pan or grill rack with nonstick spray. (Or, if you have one, spray a ridged grill pan with nonstick spray and set over medium-high heat until hot.)

2 Combine the chicken and oil in a small bowl. Sprinkle with the Mexican seasoning and salt, tossing to coat. Grill or broil the chicken, turning once, until cooked through, 10–12 minutes. Let cool 5 minutes, then slice ¼ inch thick.

3 Combine the mayonnaise, cilantro, lime juice, and chipotles in a small bowl.

4 To assemble the wraps, place the tortillas on a work surface. Spread each with 1½ tablespoons of the mayonnaise mixture. Top each tortilla with one-fourth of the arugula, then with one-fourth of the chicken. Sprinkle each with one-fourth of the tomato and onion. Fold the bottom flap up over the filling, then fold over the sides to enclose; roll up to form a package. Wrap the bottom of each sandwich in foil, if desired, to prevent them from opening.

PER SERVING (1 wrap): 348 Cal, 12 g Total Fat, 2 g Sat Fat, 69 mg Chol, 700 mg Sod, 30 g Carb, 2 g Fib, 30 g Prot, 126 mg Calc.
PointsPlus value: 9.

Tote one of these portable lunch treats to the office, to school, or to your favorite picnic spot. Add a piece of fresh fruit and you'll feel satisfied all afternoon.

turkey sloppy joes

SERVES 4

1 tablespoon canola oil
1 medium onion, finely chopped
1 green bell pepper, finely chopped
2 garlic cloves, minced
1 teaspoon chili powder
½ teaspoon dried oregano
½ teaspoon dry mustard
1 pound ground skinless turkey breast
1 cup prepared barbecue sauce
4 multigrain hamburger rolls

Nobody knows who Joe was, but these beloved messy sandwiches certainly pack a flavor punch. Bypass the too-salty packaged flavoring mix—our heady mix of seasonings tastes fresher and better!

1 Heat a large nonstick skillet over medium heat. Swirl in the oil, then add the onion, pepper, and garlic. Cook, stirring occasionally, until softened, about 5 minutes. Stir in the chili powder, oregano, and mustard; let cool 1 minute.

2 Add the turkey and cook, stirring to break up the meat, until no longer pink, 3–4 minutes. Stir in the barbecue sauce and cook until slightly thickened, about 2 minutes. Remove from the heat and serve in the hamburger rolls.

PER SERVING (1 roll with ¾ cup meat): 356 Cal, 10 g Total Fat, 2 g Sat Fat, 67 mg Chol, 813 mg Sod, 33 g Carb, 4 g Fib, 32 g Prot, 86 mg Calc.
PointsPlus value: 9.

---

good idea It's important not to overcook the ground turkey breast in this recipe or it may become dry and chewy. Keep it moving in the pan, and add the sauce as soon as it is cooked through—not browned.

Turkey Sloppy Joes and Coleslaw, page 253

portobello burgers

SERVES 4

20 Min or Less
Vegetarian

- 4 large portobello mushroom caps (about 1 pound)
- 4 tablespoons + 2 teaspoons fat-free balsamic vinaigrette dressing
- ¼ teaspoon salt
- ¼ teaspoon freshly ground pepper
- 4 multigrain hamburger rolls
- 1 cup mixed baby greens
- 1 medium tomato, cut into 4 thick slices
- 1 small sweet onion, cut into 4 thick slices
- 2 ounces goat cheese, at room temperature

Portobello mushrooms look like ordinary brown mushrooms on steroids. They became a restaurant staple in the nineties and still dominate menus today. Their earthy flavor and chewy texture make them a great meat alternative. With their large caps, they also look great on a grill. Here, we've copied a standard restaurant technique, serving them up like classic burgers.

1 Prepare the grill for a hot fire; spray a grill rack with nonstick spray. (Or, if you have one, spray a ridged grill pan with nonstick spray and set over medium-high heat until hot.)

2 Brush the portobellos with 2 tablespoons of the balsamic dressing, then sprinkle with the salt and pepper. Grill, turning once, until softened, about 12 minutes.

3 Layer the bottom half of each roll with a portobello cap, ¼ cup of the greens, and a slice each of the tomato and onion. Drizzle each "burger" with 2 teaspoons of the remaining balsamic dressing. Spread one-fourth of the goat cheese on the top half of each roll, place on top of the burgers, and serve at once.

PER SERVING (1 burger): 220 Cal, 6 g Total Fat, 3 g Sat Fat, 13 mg Chol, 664 mg Sod, 36 g Carb, 5 g Fib, 9 g Prot, 142 mg Calc. ***PointsPlus value: 6.***

multigrain loaf with flaxseeds

SERVES 12

Vegetarian

1¼ cups hot (120°F–130°F) water
2 tablespoons honey
4 tablespoons flaxseed
1 cup spelt flour
1 cup whole-wheat flour
1 cup unbleached all-purpose flour
1 (¼-ounce) envelope quick-rise yeast
1 teaspoon salt
½ tablespoon cornmeal
1 egg, lightly beaten

This is a modern take on homemade bread, with some trendy, healthy ingredients: flaxseed, a powerhouse of fiber and heart-healthy omega-3 fatty acids; and spelt, a nutty-tasting cousin of wheat that's high in protein. Both can be found in healthfood stores and some supermarkets.

1 Stir together the water, honey, and 2 tablespoons of the flaxseed in a measuring cup.

2 Combine the spelt flour, whole-wheat flour, all-purpose flour; yeast, and salt in a food processor. With the machine running, pour the water-honey mixture through the feed tube; pulse until the dough forms a smooth ball, about 1 minute.

3 Spray a large bowl with nonstick spray; put the dough in the bowl. Cover lightly with plastic wrap, and let the dough rise in a warm spot until doubled in size, about 30–40 minutes.

4 Punch down the dough. Kneading lightly, form the dough into a loaf. Spray a 5×9-inch loaf pan with nonstick spray; sprinkle the bottom and sides with the cornmeal. Place dough in the pan; cover and let rise in a warm spot until doubled in size, 30 minutes.

5 Preheat the oven to 400°F. Gently brush the top of the loaf with the egg; sprinkle with the remaining 2 tablespoons flaxseed. Bake the bread until deep golden, 18–20 minutes. Cover the top loosely with a sheet of foil; bake 15–17 minutes more, or until an instant-read thermometer inserted into the center registers 210°F. Loosen the sides of the bread with a knife, and unmold the bread onto a rack to cool.

PER SERVING (¾-inch slice): 139 Cal, 2 g Total Fat, 0 g Sat Fat, 9 mg Chol, 199 mg Sod, 27 g Carb, 4 g Fib, 5 g Prot, 19 mg Calc.
PointsPlus value: 4.

bubble bread with herbs and sun-dried tomatoes

SERVES 12

Vegetarian

1 cup warm (105°F–115°F) water
Pinch sugar
1 envelope active dry yeast
¾ cup milk
2 tablespoons unsalted butter, diced
1 tablespoon honey
4¾–5¼ cups unbleached all-purpose flour
1½ teaspoons salt
2 large eggs
1 tablespoon minced fresh herbs (try rosemary and thyme, or dill)
1 tablespoon drained minced oil-packed sun-dried tomatoes

Remember the fun of pulling off bubbles of tasty bread from a knobby bubble ring? While the terminology plants this recipe firmly in the sixties, our version of what is also known as monkey bread, is decidedly and deliciously modern.

1 Combine the water and sugar in a small bowl. Sprinkle in the yeast and let stand until foamy, 5 minutes. Meanwhile, warm the milk, butter, and honey in a large microwavable measuring cup on High, until just warm and butter is nearly melted, 30–40 seconds.

2 Combine 4¾ cups of the flour with the salt in a food processor. With the machine running, scrape the yeast mixture and then milk mixture through feed tube, followed by one egg; pulse about 1 minute, until dough forms a smooth ball, adding only enough of remaining ½ cup flour, if needed, to form a ball.

3 Spray a large bowl with nonstick spray; put dough in bowl and lightly spray top with nonstick spray. Cover with plastic wrap and let dough rise in a warm spot until it doubles in size, about 1 hour.

4 Combine the herbs and sun-dried tomatoes in a small bowl. Punch down the dough. Sprinkle about one-third of the herb mixture on the surface of the dough. Fold the dough in half over the herbs and repeat twice more, folding the dough a few more times to incorporate the herb mixture completely.

5 Spray a 12-cup tube pan with nonstick spray. Pull off a piece of dough about the size of a golf ball and roll into a ball between your palms; drop it into the pan. Repeat, spacing the balls about ½ inch apart and covering the bottom evenly, until the pan is evenly filled with 2 layers of balls. Cover and let the dough rise until doubled in size, 45 minutes.

6 Preheat the oven to 375°F. Bake the bread until lightly golden, 20 minutes. Lightly beat remaining egg in a small bowl, and lightly brush it onto the top of the bread. Continue baking until deep golden, 10–12 minutes more. Carefully remove bread from the pan and cool on a rack. Serve warm or at room temperature.

PER SERVING (1⁄12 of loaf): 220 Cal, 3 g Total Fat, 2 g Sat Fat, 32 mg Chol, 310 mg Sod, 40 g Carb, 2 g Fib, 7 g Prot, 32 mg Calc.
PointsPlus value: 6.

pumpkin rolls

SERVES 12

Vegetarian

3 cups unbleached all-purpose flour
½ cup whole-wheat flour
1 envelope quick-rise yeast
1 tablespoon sugar
¾ teaspoon salt
½ teaspoon ground ginger
½ teaspoon cinnamon
¾ cup milk
½ cup pumpkin puree
2 tablespoons butter, diced
2 large eggs
1 tablespoon poppy seeds

With their crunchy poppy seed topping, these subtly spiced rolls are all-purpose: They give a special flavor boost to breakfast or lunch, and make uniquely elegant dinner rolls.

1 Combine the all-purpose flour, whole-wheat flour, yeast, sugar, salt, ginger, and cinnamon in a food processor.

2 Whisk the milk and pumpkin in a microwavable bowl and stir in the butter. Microwave on High until the butter is melted and the milk registers 120°F–130°F on an instant-read thermometer, 50–70 seconds. With machine running, scrape the milk mixture through the feed tube, followed by one of the eggs; pulse about 1 minute, until dough forms a smooth ball, adding 1–2 tablespoons extra all-purpose flour only if needed to form a ball.

3 Spray a large bowl with nonstick spray; put the dough in the bowl. Cover lightly with plastic wrap and let the dough rise in a warm spot until doubled in size, about 40 minutes.

4 Punch down the dough. Spray a 12-cup muffin pan with nonstick spray. Roll the dough into a cylinder, then cut it into 12 equal pieces. Roll each piece between your palms to form smooth balls, dropping each into a muffin cup. Cover lightly with plastic wrap and let the dough rise in a warm spot until doubled in size, about 20 minutes.

5 Preheat the oven to 350°F. Beat the remaining egg in a small bowl; lightly brush the tops of the rolls with the beaten egg, and sprinkle evenly with the poppy seeds. Bake until golden, 20 minutes. Transfer to a rack to cool.

PER SERVING (1 roll): 176 Cal, 3 g Total Fat, 2 g Sat Fat, 32 mg Chol, 176 mg Sod, 31 g Carb, 2 g Fib, 6 g Prot, 43 mg Calc.
PointsPlus value: 5.

To make the rolls ahead of time, freeze the cooled rolls in zip-close freezer bags for up to a month. The rolls can be defrosted in the microwave, or overnight on the counter. Or place the unwrapped frozen rolls on a baking sheet and heat in a 350°F oven 8 to 10 minutes.

Sausage Focaccia

sausage focaccia

SERVES 12

- 1⅔ cups warm (105°F–115°F) water
- ¼ teaspoon sugar
- 1 envelope quick-rise yeast
- 3 teaspoons olive oil
- 2¼ teaspoons kosher salt
- 1½ links (6 ounces) Italian-style turkey sausage, casing removed
- 1 tablespoon drained oil-packed sun-dried tomatoes, minced
- 1 tablespoon minced fresh rosemary

Like so many formerly "forbidden" ingredients, a little sausage can provide a lot of flavor—and pleasure. Try this chewy, satisfying bread as an accompaniment for soup or as an appetizer.

1 Combine the water and sugar in a small bowl. Sprinkle in the yeast and let stand until just beginning to foam, about 2 minutes. Add 2 teaspoons of the oil.

2 Combine the flour and 2 teaspoons of the salt in a large bowl. Make a well in the center; add the yeast mixture, and begin stirring the flour into the liquid with a wooden spoon until well incorporated and the dough begins wrapping around the spoon. Scrape the sides of the bowl and turn the dough out onto a lightly floured work surface. Knead the dough gradually, adding only enough of the remaining flour to stop it from sticking, until smooth and elastic, 8–9 minutes. (The dough should remain soft and pliable; flour your hands frequently instead of adding flour to the dough, when possible.)

3 Spray a large bowl with nonstick spray; put the dough in the bowl and lightly spray the top with nonstick spray. Cover lightly with plastic wrap, and let the dough rise in a warm spot until it doubles in size, about 40 minutes.

4 Meanwhile, cook the sausage in a nonstick skillet over medium-high heat, breaking up the large pieces with a wooden spoon, until deep brown, 4 minutes. Let cool.

5 Preheat the oven to 450°F. Spray a large (10½ × 15½-inch) jelly-roll pan with nonstick spray. Punch down the dough. Sprinkle one third of the sausage, tomato, and rosemary on the surface of dough, spreading with fingertips. Fold dough in half over the mixture and repeat twice more, folding the dough a few more times to fully incorporate ingredients. Press dough evenly into the pan. Cover and let stand until just slightly puffed, about 10 minutes. Bake until crisp-edged and golden, 20–22 minutes. Immediately brush the top with the remaining 1 teaspoon oil and sprinkle with the remaining ¼ teaspoon salt.

PER SERVING (1⁄12 of loaf): 183 Cal, 3 g Total Fat, 1 g Sat Fat, 10 mg Chol, 455 mg Sod, 30 g Carb, 1 g Fib, 7 g Prot, 11 mg Calc.
PointsPlus value: 5.

zucchini corn bread

SERVES 12

1½ bacon slices
1½ small zucchini, coarsely shredded (1 cup)
1 cup low-fat buttermilk
1 (8-ounce) can creamed corn
½ cup shredded extra-sharp cheddar cheese
2 large eggs, room temperature
2 scallions, minced
3 tablespoons sugar
1 tablespoon butter, melted
1½ teaspoons salt
¼ teaspoon cayenne
1¼ cups yellow cornmeal
1 cup all-purpose flour
1 tablespoon baking powder
¼ teaspoon baking soda

Don't let the long ingredients list stop you; this recipe can be made in one bowl. Adding zucchini to the batter—inspired by the zucchini breads of the seventies—makes it deliciously moist.

1 Cook the bacon in a large cast-iron skillet over medium heat until crisp; remove and finely chop, leaving the drippings in the skillet. Preheat the oven to 375°F.

2 Combine the bacon with the zucchini, buttermilk, creamed corn, cheese, eggs, scallions, sugar, butter, salt, and cayenne in a large bowl, using a wooden spoon. Toss together the cornmeal, flour, baking powder, and baking soda on a sheet of wax paper; stir into the zucchini mixture until just combined.

3 Heat the skillet until very hot, about 2–3 minutes, then remove from the heat. Scrape the batter into the skillet and even the top with a spatula. Bake until lightly browned around the edges and a toothpick inserted into the center comes out clean, about 25 minutes. Use a knife to loosen the bread around the edges of the skillet, and carefully transfer the bread to a rack. Let cool at least 10 minutes. Cut into 12 wedges, and serve warm or at room temperature.

PER SERVING (1 wedge): 183 Cal, 5 g Total Fat, 3 g Sat Fat, 45 mg Chol, 405 mg Sod, 28 g Carb, 2 g Fib, 6 g Prot, 126 mg Calc.
PointsPlus value: 5.

If you plan to use only portions of the bread at a time, wrap wedges of bread in plastic wrap, then place in zip-close freezer bags. Unwrap and defrost in the microwave on Low power or the Defrost setting until just softened and slightly warmed, 30 to 40 seconds.

irish soda bread

SERVES 12

Vegetarian

2 cups all-purpose flour
3 tablespoons sugar
1 teaspoon baking powder
1 teaspoon salt
½ teaspoon baking soda
2 tablespoons cold unsalted butter, cut into small pieces
½ cup dried currants
1 teaspoon caraway seeds
1 cup low-fat buttermilk

A classic quick bread, this golden loaf is perfect for serving with a soup or salad at lunch or with a cup of tea in the afternoon. If you prefer, you can make the bread with raisins instead of currants.

1 Preheat the oven to 350°F. Spray a baking sheet with nonstick spray and lightly dust with flour.

2 Combine the flour, sugar, baking powder, salt, and baking soda in a large bowl. With a pastry blender, cut in the butter until the mixture is crumbly. Stir in the currants and caraway seeds. Add the buttermilk and stir just until the dry ingredients are moistened. Knead the mixture in the bowl just until it forms a dough, 5–6 times. Shape into a 6-inch circle and transfer to the baking sheet.

3 With a sharp knife, cut a ½-inch-deep X over the surface of the loaf. Bake until golden brown and a toothpick inserted in the center comes out clean, 45–50 minutes. Serve warm or cool completely on a rack. Cut into 12 wedges.

PER SERVING (1 wedge): 130 Cal, 2 g Total Fat, 1 g Sat Fat, 6 mg Chol, 301 mg Sod, 25 g Carb, 1 g Fib, 3 g Prot, 41 mg Calc.
PointsPlus value: 3.

classic starters

tasty light bites and dips

deviled eggs

SERVES 6

Vegetarian

8 large eggs
1 small celery stalk, finely chopped (about ¼ cup)
1 small carrot, shredded (about ¼ cup)
2 tablespoons thinly sliced scallion
2 tablespoons fat-free sour cream
1 tablespoon low-fat mayonnaise
2 teaspoons deli-style mustard
1 teaspoon cider vinegar
¼ teaspoon salt
¼ teaspoon ground pepper

In the sixties, deviled eggs were a mainstay at picnics and dinner parties. Our healthy version of this family classic cuts some of the yolks and mayonnaise and adds chopped veggies. The result is more delicious and decidedly healthier.

1 Place the eggs in a saucepan large enough to hold them in a single layer; add enough cold water to cover. Bring to a boil over medium-high heat; reduce the heat and cook at a bare simmer, 12 minutes. Rinse under cold water and, when cool enough to handle, remove the shells.

2 Halve the eggs lengthwise. Place 4 whole yolks in a medium bowl and discard the remaining yolks. Chop 4 of the egg white halves and add to the bowl; mash well with a fork. Add the celery, carrot, scallion, sour cream, mayonnaise, mustard, vinegar, salt, and pepper; blend with a fork.

3 Spoon the filling into the hollows of the remaining 12 halves of whites, mounding to fill. Place on a platter, cover with plastic, and refrigerate at least 1 hour. Serve cold.

PER SERVING (2 stuffed egg halves): 73 Cal, 4 g Total Fat, 1 g Sat Fat, 142 mg Chol, 232 mg Sod, 3 g Carb, 0 g Fib, 7 g Prot, 36 mg Calc.
PointsPlus value: 2.

No matter how casual or formal the get-together, Deviled Eggs are always a favorite. They're great for the cook, too, since you can make them a day ahead and store them tightly covered with plastic wrap in the refrigerator.

cheese ball

SERVES 16

Vegetarian

- ¾ cup shredded low-fat sharp cheddar cheese
- ¾ cup no-salt-added, reduced-fat (2%) cottage cheese
- 1 tablespoon Dijon mustard
- ⅛ teaspoon cayenne
- 1 (8-ounce) package fat-free cream cheese, cut into quarters, at room temperature
- 1 (.9-ounce) package dry vegetable soup/recipe mix
- ½ cup fresh parsley

The seventies cheese ball was pre-dinner staple, dressing up any table. We've cut the fat but added flavor with subtle spices. Whether you shape it into a ball or a log, the mixture is soft and lusciously spreadable.

1 Pulse the cheddar cheese, cottage cheese, mustard, and cayenne in a food processor until very smooth, about 2 minutes. Add the cream cheese and soup mix; process until smooth, scraping down the sides of the bowl as needed. Scrape with a spatula onto a large sheet of plastic wrap.

2 Wrap the plastic around the cheese mixture and shape it into a 4-inch ball or 7-inch-long log with your hands. Refrigerate until firm, at least 3 hours or overnight.

3 Just before serving, sprinkle about half of the chopped parsley in a circle onto a sheet of plastic wrap. Unwrap the cheese ball or log and place on the parsley. Sprinkle the remaining parsley on top and press to help the leaves adhere. Carefully roll any uncoated areas in the loose parsley, and smooth the shape, if needed. Place on a serving plate and surround with cut-up vegetables of your choice.

PER SERVING (2 tablespoons): 42 Cal, 1 g Total Fat, 1 g Sat Fat, 4 mg Chol, 219 mg Sod, 2 g Carb, 0 g Fib, 5 g Prot, 67 mg Calc.
PointsPlus value: 1.

Instead of the parsley, you can press chopped walnuts into the cheese balls (1 cup of walnut pieces, chopped, will increase the per-serving ***PointsPlus*** value by ***1***.)

(clockwise from top left) Cheese Crisps, page 86, Cheese Ball, page 83, Cheese Puffs, and Deviled Eggs, page 82

cheese puffs

SERVES 15

Vegetarian

1 (12-ounce) can evaporated fat-free milk
2 tablespoons unsalted butter
¾ teaspoon dry mustard
¾ teaspoon salt
¼ teaspoon ground pepper
1 cup all-purpose flour
⅓ cup freshly grated Parmesan cheese
2 large eggs
1 teaspoon baking powder
3 egg whites
½ cup shredded reduced-fat cheddar cheese

Looking for an easy crowd pleaser? Look back to this sixties classic cocktail-party staple. Crispy on the outside with creamy centers, they're irresistible morsels. Even better, you can make them in advance, freeze them, and reheat them at the last minute.

1 Bring the milk, butter, mustard, salt, and pepper to a boil in a medium saucepan; reduce the heat to medium. Beat in the flour and Parmesan cheese with a wooden spoon, stirring vigorously, until the mixture leaves the side of the pan. Cool for 10 minutes.

2 Adjust the racks to divide the oven into thirds; preheat the oven to 400°F. Line two baking sheets with foil and lightly coat with nonstick spray.

3 With an electric mixer on medium speed, beat the eggs into the flour mixture until well blended. Sift in the baking powder, then add the egg whites and continue beating until the mixture is glossy and smooth. Beat in the cheddar cheese on low speed until just combined.

4 Spoon the mixture into a pastry bag or a plastic food-storage bag with a corner cut off. Pipe into 1-inch mounds, spacing 1 inch apart. (You can also pipe the mixture into 1½-inch-long "fingers," if you prefer.) You should have about 75 puffs or fingers. Bake until golden brown and firm to the touch, 22 minutes. Serve hot or warm.

PER SERVING (5 puffs): 96 Cal, 4 g Total Fat, 2 g Sat Fat, 37 mg Chol, 255 mg Sod, 9 g Carb, 0 g Fib, 6 g Prot, 147 mg Calc.
PointsPlus value: 3.

To freeze the cooled puffs, place them on a baking sheet in the freezer until firm. Transfer to zip-close freezer bags and freeze for up to two months. To reheat frozen puffs, arrange on baking sheets. Bake in a preheated 375°F oven until hot and crisp, 10 to 15 minutes.

cheese crisps

SERVES 16

Vegetarian

1 cup shredded part-skim mozzarella cheese
2 tablespoons freshly grated Parmesan cheese
1 tablespoon all-purpose flour

In the nineties, frico—little discs of grated cheese, fried to an irresistible chewy crispness—were all the rage at trendy Italian eateries. Who'd have thought that Weight Watchers anticipated the trend as far back as the sixties, when members made Cheese Crisps in their Teflon frying pans? These savory little treats make great cocktail nibbles.

1 Preheat oven to 400°F. Spray 2 baking sheets with nonstick spray.

2 Combine the mozzarella cheese, Parmesan cheese, and flour in a small bowl. Drop the cheese mixture by tablespoons onto the baking sheets, at least 2 inches apart, making 16 crisps. Bake until the cheese is melted and golden, with darker brown edges, 5–7 minutes.

3 Remove from the oven and let the crisps cool for 1 minute. Carefully remove the crisps from the baking sheets with a thin metal spatula and place on paper towels to cool completely. Serve at once, or store in an airtight container for up to 2 days at room temperature.

PER SERVING (1 crisp): 25 Cal, 2 g Total Fat, 1 g Sat Fat, 4 mg Chol, 52 mg Sod, 1 g Carb, 0 g Fib, 2 g Prot, 63 mg Calc.
PointsPlus value: 1.

Not only are these a terrific cocktail nibble, they're also great to serve alongside a bowl of soup or on top of a tossed green salad.

nachos grande

SERVES 8

- 1 teaspoon canola oil
- 1 cup cooked or rinsed drained canned red kidney beans
- ¼ pound lean ground turkey breast
- 1 small onion, chopped
- 1 (14½-ounce) can diced tomatoes with green chiles
- 2 teaspoons Mexican seasoning mix
- ¼ teaspoon salt
- 6 ounces reduced-fat restaurant-style tortilla chips
- ¾ cup shredded reduced-fat cheddar cheese
- 12 pitted small black olives, sliced
- ¼ cup sliced pickled jalapeño peppers, drained
- ½ cup fat-free sour cream

Walk into any popular bar/restaurant, and you'd find this appetizer on the menu—usually being washed down with Mexican beers or festive frozen Margaritas. You can create all that fun in your own kitchen too, minus the booze if you prefer: Serve up this leaner version at your next party, or as a special midweek treat for the kids.

1 Preheat oven to 425°F. Spray a baking sheet with nonstick spray.

2 Heat a large nonstick skillet over medium-high heat. Swirl in the oil, then stir in the beans, turkey, and onion. Cook, stirring to break up the meat, 3 minutes. Add the tomatoes, Mexican seasoning, and salt; cook until thickened, about 5 minutes. Remove from the heat and keep warm.

3 Spread the tortilla chips on the baking sheet. Sprinkle with the cheese, olives, and jalapeño peppers. Bake until the cheese just melts, about 5 minutes. Transfer the nachos to a serving platter. Top with the turkey mixture and sour cream and serve at once.

PER SERVING (1¼ cups): 204 Cal, 4 g Total Fat, 2 g Sat Fat, 17 mg Chol, 483 mg Sod, 29 g Carb, 4 g Fib, 13 g Prot, 141 mg Calc.
PointsPlus value: 5.

swiss fondue

SERVES 10

Vegetarian

1 (19-ounce) can cannellini (white kidney) beans, rinsed and drained
½ cup reduced-fat (2%) milk
½ small garlic clove
¾ cup dry white wine
5 ounces imported Swiss Gruyère cheese (about 1¾ cups)
1 ounce coarsely grated aged Asiago cheese (about ⅓ cup)
2 teaspoons cornstarch, dissolved in 1 tablespoon water
1 tablespoon kirsch (optional)
⅛ teaspoon nutmeg

Fondues, the quintessential sixties gourmet treat, are back in style, and we've found a way to make them a lot more Weight Watchers friendly. It starts with substituting pureed beans for some of the cheese, then adding some shredded aged Asiago cheese for a flavor boost. Serve it with steamed vegetables like broccoli and carrots, and slices of tart apple (like Granny Smith or Braeburn).

1 Place the beans and milk in a food processor; puree, scraping the sides of the work bowl frequently, until absolutely smooth, at least 3 minutes.

2 Rub a medium nonreactive saucepan with the garlic; discard the garlic. Pour the wine into the saucepan and bring to a simmer over medium heat. Add the Gruyère cheese and Asiago cheese, a handful at a time, stirring constantly with a wooden spoon in a zigzag motion, until the cheese is melted, 5–8 minutes (do not boil or the cheese will clump). Stir in the bean mixture, dissolved cornstarch, kirsch (if using), and nutmeg; continue cooking, stirring gently, until smooth and slightly thickened, 5–6 minutes longer. Transfer to a large fondue pot and set over low heat to keep warm. Serve at once.

PER SERVING (about ⅔ cup): 133 Cal, 6 g Total Fat, 4 g Sat Fat, 19 mg Chol, 192 mg Sod, 11 g Carb, 2 g Fib, 9 g Prot, 212 mg Calc.
PointsPlus value: 3.

If you have leftover fondue, it will keep, covered, in the refrigerator for three days. To reheat, place it in a microwavable bowl, cover loosely, and cook on Medium power, stirring every 10 seconds or so, until just melted.

---

creamy onion dip

SERVES 8

- 2 teaspoons olive oil
- 1 large sweet onion, finely chopped
- ¼ cup water
- 1 beef bouillon cube
- 1 cup plain low-fat Greek yogurt
- ⅓ cup light mayonnaise
- 2 teaspoons fresh lemon juice
- ⅛ teaspoon salt
- 4 cups assorted vegetables (such as carrots, celery, and bell peppers), cut-up

In the 1950s, California Dip—a high-fat, high-sodium combo of sour cream and onion soup mix, usually accompanied by a bowl of equally high-fat, high-sodium potato chips—took the nation by storm. The good news is that our from-scratch version served with healthful veggies gives you tons of great onion flavor without sacrificing your eating plan.

1 Heat a large nonstick skillet over medium heat. Swirl in the oil, then add the onion. Cover and cook, stirring occasionally, until softened, 5 minutes. Reduce the heat to medium-low, uncover and cook, stirring frequently, until onion is very soft and golden brown, 20 to 25 minutes. Spoon the onion onto a plate. Add the water to the skillet and crumble in the bouillon cube, stirring until the cube dissolves. Let the onion and the broth stand until cool, 20 minutes.

2 Stir together the onion, broth, yogurt, mayonnaise, lemon juice, and salt in a medium bowl. Cover and refrigerate until chilled, at least 2 hours or up to 3 days. Serve with the vegetables.

PER SERVING (¼ cup dip with ½ cup vegetables): 78 Cal, 4 g Total Fat, 1 g Sat Fat, 5 mg Chol, 304 mg Sod, 7 g Carb, 1 g Fib, 4 g Prot, 56 mg Calc.
PointsPlus value: 2.

white bean–tomato dip with grilled peppers

SERVES 8

Vegetarian

1 tablespoon olive oil
2 garlic cloves, minced
⅛ teaspoon crushed red pepper
2 plum tomatoes, finely chopped
1 (15 ½-ounce) can cannellini (white kidney) beans, rinsed and drained
¼ cup plain fat-free Greek yogurt
1 teaspoon grated lemon zest
1 tablespoon fresh lemon juice
2 teaspoons minced fresh rosemary
½ teaspoon salt
4 large assorted-color bell peppers, cut into 1-inch strips

This super-flavorful hors d'oeuvre relies on many of the healthful ingredients of the Mediterranean diet, including olive oil, beans, yogurt, and fresh vegetables. It's a great beginning to any meal, but it also makes a brilliant light lunch or a side dish to serve with grilled fish.

1 Heat a large nonstick skillet over medium heat. Swirl in the oil, then add the garlic and red pepper and cook, stirring, until the garlic is golden, about 1 minute. Add the tomatoes and cook, stirring occasionally, until softened, 3 minutes. Set aside.

2 Puree the beans in a food processor, scraping the sides of the work bowl frequently, until absolutely smooth, at least 3 minutes. Add the yogurt, lemon zest, lemon juice, rosemary, and salt and pulse until blended. Add the tomato mixture and pulse just until blended. Spoon the dip into a bowl.

3 Spray a ridged cast-iron grill pan with olive oil nonstick spray and set over medium-high heat until hot. Place the bell peppers in the pan, in batches, and grill, turning often, until charred on their edges, 8–10 minutes. Transfer the bell peppers to a serving platter and serve with the dip.

PER SERVING (¼ cup dip with about ½ cup bell peppers): 100 Cal, 2 g Total Fat, 0 g Sat Fat, 0 mg Chol, 263 mg Sod, 16 g Carb, 3 g Fib, 5 g Prot, 56 mg Calc.
PointsPlus value: 2.

best-loved snacks

It's no surprise to anyone who has ever tried to lose weight that snacks can play a key role. Having a few healthy options on hand can offset hunger (both real and imagined) and help you feel more in control when a craving for something a little sweet—or salty, crunchy, or creamy—hits. Here are a baker's dozen of the easiest, most popular snacks that members have vouched for through the years. The best part? All clock in at *4 PointsPlus* value or less. Each recipe makes one serving.

the classics revisited

stuffed celery redux

Spread 2 tablespoons fat-free cream cheese into 4 celery sticks and dot with 1 tablespoon dried cranberries. ***PointsPlus*** value: *2*

swingin' sixties cheese dip

Purée 6 tablespoons fat-free cottage cheese, 1 tablespoon fat-free milk, and ½ clove garlic in a blender until smooth. Season with salt, paprika, and Worcestershire sauce. ***PointsPlus*** value: *1*

nutty apple slices

Spread slices from 1 small apple with 2 teaspoons peanut butter. Sprinkle with cinnamon if you like. ***PointsPlus*** value: *4*

frozen chocolate-banana pop

Insert a popsicle stick in half a banana and freeze on a wax paper-lined plate. Microwave 2 tablespoons bittersweet chocolate chips in small bowl until melted. Coat banana with chocolate and freeze until firm. ***PointsPlus*** value: *4*

frozen grapes:

Break grapes into small clusters, place in a single layer on a plate and freeze. ***PointsPlus*** value: *0*

buttermilk shake

Blend ½ cup fresh or frozen unsweetened strawberries, a few drops vanilla, 1 teaspoon honey, and 1 cup low-fat buttermilk until smooth. ***PointsPlus*** value: *4*

new snack staples

kale chips

Spray 1 cup torn kale leaves lightly with nonstick spray and toss with a pinch each salt and pepper. Bake in 400°F oven until crisp, about 8 minutes. ***PointsPlus*** value: *1*

spicy roast chickpeas

Rinse and pat dry ½ cup canned chickpeas. Bake on small parchment-lined baking sheet in 375°F oven until very crisp, about 45 minutes. Sprinkle with pinch each cumin powder, chipotle chile power, and salt. ***PointsPlus*** value: *3*

crunchy almond cakes

Spread 2 teaspoons almond butter over 2 large rice cakes. ***PointsPlus*** value: *4*

chocolate yogurt pudding

Combine ¾ cup plain fat-free Greek yogurt with 2 teaspoons unsweetened cocoa powder and 1½ teaspoons honey. ***PointsPlus*** value: *3*

banana "ice cream"

Chop a large ripe banana and freeze until solid, at least 2 hours. Pulse in a food processor until light and creamy. ***PointsPlus*** value: *0*

coffee frappé

Freeze ½ cup coffee in an ice cube tray. Blend with ½ cup fat-free milk and a few drops vanilla extract. ***PointsPlus*** value: *1*

chipotle chili popcorn

Sprinkle 3 cups air-popped popcorn with chipotle chili powder. ***PointsPlus*** value: *2*

spanakopita triangles

SERVES 8

Vegetarian

1 (10-ounce) box frozen chopped spinach, thawed and squeezed dry
⅔ cup crumbled reduced-fat feta cheese
3 scallions, chopped
1 large egg white
1½ tablespoons fresh dill, or ¾ teaspoon dried
¼ teaspoon freshly ground pepper
8 (14 × 18-inch) sheets phyllo dough, at room temperature
2 tablespoons olive oil

Serve this classic Greek spinach pie as an appetizer for eight, or as an entrée for four with a salad or soup on the side. The triangles can be baked up to 3 hours in advance, then reheated in a 375°F oven until crisp, about 8 minutes.

1 Place the oven rack in the center of the oven; preheat the oven to 375°F. Spray a baking sheet with nonstick spray.

2 Press the spinach between layers of paper towels to remove any excess moisture. Place the cheese in a medium bowl and mash with a fork. Add the spinach, scallions, egg white, dill, and pepper; stir together until combined.

3 Set the stack of phyllo sheets to one side; keep covered with a sheet of wax paper and a damp towel on top as you work.

4 Lay 1 phyllo sheet lengthwise in front of you and brush the sheet lightly with oil. Top with another sheet and brush lightly with oil. Cut crosswise into 6 even strips. Place a scant tablespoon of the spinach mixture at the end of each strip. Fold one corner up over the filling, then continue folding in a flag fashion, to form a triangle. Place on the baking sheet and repeat with the remaining filling and phyllo sheets to make 24 triangles. Brush the tops of the triangles lightly with any remaining oil.

5 Bake until golden brown, about 25 minutes. Cool for 5 minutes and serve hot or warm.

PER SERVING (3 triangles): 112 Cal, 5 g Total Fat, 2 g Sat Fat, 11 mg Chol, 223 mg Sod, 12 g Carb, 1 g Fib, 4 g Prot, 103 mg Calc.
PointsPlus value: 3.

mushroom "peanuts"

SERVES 8

20 Min or Less
Vegetarian

2 (10-ounce) packages sliced mushrooms, (about 7 cups)
2 tablespoons olive oil
2 teaspoons reduced-sodium soy sauce
1 tablespoon chopped rosemary or thyme, or 1 teaspoon dried
1 large garlic clove, minced
Freshly ground pepper

Once upon a time, Weight Watchers members who craved nuts were encouraged to make "Roast Peanuts" by spreading canned mushrooms on a baking sheet and baking them for hours in a low oven. We broiled our mushrooms instead, flavoring them with garlic and herbs—and the results were addictive! Eat them as a snack, or toss them with pasta. They're also yummy layered in a sandwich or on top of a pizza.

1 Preheat the broiler.

2 Spread the mushrooms in a broiler pan or large roasting pan. Whisk together the oil, soy sauce, rosemary or thyme, and garlic in a small bowl, then drizzle over the mushrooms. Toss well, then let stand for 15 minutes to allow the flavors to blend.

3 Broil 5 inches from the heat until the tops of the mushrooms are crisp, about 2 minutes; turn the pieces with a spatula and broil briefly to crisp the other sides. Sprinkle with the pepper and serve at once.

PER SERVING (¾ cup): 50 Cal, 4 g Total Fat, 1 g Sat Fat, 0 mg Chol, 53 mg Sod, 0 g Carb, 1 g Fib, 2 g Prot, 7 mg Calc.
PointsPlus value: 1.

Although they're best piping hot, you can store the mushrooms in the refrigerator for up to four days. Let them come to room temperature before serving, or reheat them briefly in the microwave until just heated through.

buffalo chicken wings

SERVES 6

3 pounds (12–14) chicken wings, skinned
3 tablespoons cider vinegar
2 tablespoons reduced-sodium chicken broth
2 teaspoons vegetable oil
2 teaspoons hot pepper sauce
¼ cup crumbled blue cheese
¼ cup plain fat-free yogurt
1 tablespoon reduced-fat mayonnaise
6 celery stalks, trimmed

Invented at the Anchor Bar in Buffalo, New York, in the late sixties, the original version of this popular bar snack is a fat-rich nightmare. Our version manages to trim quite a bit of fat by skinning and broiling the wings and marinating them in a wonderfully tangy sauce.

1 Wash and pat the wings dry with paper towels; cut off the tips and reserve for another use. Halve the wings at the joint.

2 Combine the vinegar, broth, oil, and pepper sauce in a large zip-close plastic bag; add the chicken. Squeeze out the air and seal the bag; turn the bag to coat the chicken. Refrigerate, turning the bag occasionally, 30 minutes. Drain and discard any remaining marinade.

3 Spray the broiler rack with nonstick spray; preheat the broiler.

4 Broil the chicken 5 inches from the heat, turning once, until golden and cooked through, about 10 minutes per side.

5 Meanwhile, combine the blue cheese, yogurt, and mayonnaise in a small bowl. Serve with the chicken wings and celery.

PER SERVING (4 wing halves with 1½ tablespoons dip and 1 celery stick): 156 Cal, 8 g Total Fat, 3 g Sat Fat, 47 mg Chol, 182 mg Sod, 3 g Carb, 1 g Fib, 18 g Prot, 76 mg Calc.
PointsPlus value: 4.

The wings can be made ahead and refrigerated for up to two days or frozen for up to three months. They're great to have on hand for an impromptu get-together.

Nachos Grande, page 87,
and Buffalo Chicken Wings

black bean "caviar"

SERVES 8

20 Min or Less
Vegetarian

1 (15-ounce) can black beans, drained and rinsed
1 large garlic clove, minced
1 tablespoon prepared tapenade
1 tablespoon extra-virgin olive oil
⅛ teaspoon freshly ground pepper
24 water crackers

This elegant appetizer would probably have been labeled "mock caviar" in an earlier Weight Watchers era. Deep in color and wonderfully rich, this impostor tops a cracker quite nicely.

Gently toss the beans, garlic, tapenade, oil, and pepper in a medium bowl using a rubber spatula, until just evenly mixed. Transfer to a small serving bowl and serve with the crackers on the side.

PER SERVING (3 crackers, each topped with 1 tablespoon "caviar"): 108 Cal, 3 g Total Fat, 0 g Sat Fat, 0 mg Chol, 134 mg Sod, 17 g Carb, 3 g Fib, 4 g Prot, 38 mg Calc.
PointsPlus value: 3.

Tapenade, a savory paste that hails from France's Provençal region, is made with black olives, capers, lemon, thyme, and other seasonings. A small spoonful packs a big flavor punch. Look for it in the olive section of better supermarkets.

chicken liver crostini

SERVES 8

2 tablespoons unsalted butter or margarine
1 small onion, chopped
1 shallot, chopped
¼ pear, peeled and chopped
½ pound chicken livers, trimmed
1 tablespoon brandy or calvados (optional)
½ teaspoon salt
Freshly ground black pepper
16 (½-ounce) slices Italian or French bread, toasted
1 cup cornichons (small French pickles)

In early Weight Watchers days, cookbooks included plenty of liver recipes; sometimes entire chapters were devoted to liver alone! Today, we've taken a twenty-first-century approach by combining tasty chicken livers with wonderful flavorings to make a divine pâté.

1 Melt the butter or margarine in a large nonstick skillet. Add the onion, shallot, and pear; cook, stirring frequently, until the onion and shallot are translucent and the pear is soft, about 5 minutes. Add the livers and brown them, breaking them apart with a spoon, until they are no longer pink and cooked through, 8–10 minutes. Remove from the heat, and let cool slightly.

2 Combine the liver mixture with its liquid, the brandy or calvados, if using, the salt, and pepper in a food processor. Pulse until very smooth; transfer the mixture to a small bowl or crock. Cover tightly and refrigerate for at least 1 day or up to 5 days. Serve with the toasted bread and the cornichons on the side.

PER SERVING (2 crostini): 141 Cal, 5 g Total Fat, 2 g Sat Fat, 107 mg Chol, 327 mg Sod, 17 g Carb, 1 g Fib, 7 g Prot, 29 mg Calc.
PointsPlus value: 4.

You can also freeze the pâté to have on hand for entertaining; it will last in the freezer for up to three months. Calvados, a dry apple brandy made in the Normandy region of France, lends a subtle apple flavor to meat and poultry dishes. It's well worth investing in a bottle for the kitchen.

Cheesy Pepperoni–
Mushroom Flatbread

cheesy pepperoni-mushroom flatbread

SERVES 24

1 medium onion, halved and thinly sliced
1 red bell pepper, thinly sliced
8 ounces white mushrooms, sliced
1 cup grape tomatoes, halved
1 pound refrigerated or thawed frozen pizza dough, at room temperature
¾ cup fat-free marinara sauce
1½ cups shredded reduced-fat mozzarella cheese
2 tablespoons grated Parmesan cheese
36 slices turkey pepperoni, halved

Cheese, pepperoni, tomato, onion, and mushrooms are frequently cited as the most popular toppings ordered at the nation's pizzerias, and this delicious flatbread features them all. Using reduced-fat cheese, fat-free marinara, and turkey pepperoni lets you enjoy the combination while keeping the fat count in check.

1 Adjust the oven racks to divide the oven in thirds and preheat the oven to 450°F. Spray a 10½ × 15½-inch jelly-roll pan with nonstick spray.

2 Spray a large skillet with nonstick spray and set over medium-high heat. Add the onion, pepper, and mushrooms. Cook, stirring occasionally, until the vegetables are tender and the liquid evaporates, 8–10 minutes. Stir in the tomatoes and cook 1 minute. Set aside.

3 With floured hands, press the dough over the bottom of the prepared pan. If the dough shrinks back, let it rest a few minutes before pressing again. Spread the marinara sauce evenly over the dough. Sprinkle with ½ cup of the mozzarella cheese and 1 tablespoon of the Parmesan cheese. Top evenly with the onion mixture and the pepperoni.

4 Bake on the lowest oven rack until the crust is browned on the bottom, 12–15 minutes. Sprinkle with the remaining 1 cup mozzarella cheese and 1 tablespoon Parmesan cheese. Bake until the cheese melts, 4–5 minutes longer. Cut into 24 squares and serve at once.

PER SERVING (1 square): 95 Cal, 4 g Total Fat, 2 g Sat Fat, 12 mg Chol, 321 mg Sod, 11 g Carb, 1 g Fib, 6 g Prot, 85 mg Calc.
PointsPlus value: 3.

ham-and-swiss mini quiches

SERVES 15

1 ounce lean low-sodium ham, chopped
¼ cup shredded Swiss cheese
1 (1.9-ounce) box frozen mini phyllo pastry shells (15 shells)
2 tablespoons fat-free egg substitute
2 tablespoons fat-free half-and-half
¼ teaspoon Dijon mustard
Pinch salt

The very first Weight Watchers cookbook, published in 1966, advised readers that eggs should not be served at dinner and that they should be limited to 4–7 per week. Today the humble egg is recognized as a nutritious and delicious part of a healthy eating plan, and egg-based dishes are welcome anytime.

1 Preheat the oven to 350°F.

2 Sprinkle the ham and cheese evenly into the pastry shells. Whisk together the egg substitute, half-and-half, mustard, and salt in a small bowl. Spoon the egg mixture evenly into the shells.

3 Place the pastry shells on a baking sheet, and bake until the pastry is lightly crisped and the filling is set, 12–15 minutes. Serve at once.

PER SERVING (1 quiche): 23 Cal, 1 g Total Fat, 0 g Sat Fat, 3 mg Chol, 53 mg Sod, 3 g Carb, 0 g Fib, 1 g Prot, 20 mg Calc.
PointsPlus value: 1.

These mini quiches are best served hot or warm. To speed up the prep for a party, chop the ham, shred the cheese, and whisk together the egg substitute mixture and cover and refrigerate each one separately. Just before your guests arrive, assemble and bake the quiches.

shrimp salsa with tortilla chips

SERVES 12

20 Min or Less

- ½ pound cooked peeled and deveined shrimp, coarsely chopped
- ½ medium jicama, peeled and diced
- 1 jalapeño pepper, seeded and minced
- 2 tablespoons fresh lime juice
- 2 tablespoons chopped fresh cilantro
- 1 scallion, thinly sliced
- ⅛ teaspoon salt
- 48 baked tortilla chips

Once upon a time, anyone hankering for the nutty, earthy flavor of tortilla chips would find fat-laden fried chips their only option. But thanks to a growing interest in healthful snack foods, you'll now find a selection of baked chips at most supermarkets. You can even opt for unsalted chips if you want to lower your sodium intake.

Place the shrimp, jicama, jalapeño, lime juice, cilantro, scallion, and salt in a serving bowl; toss to combine. Serve at once, or cover and refrigerate up to 8 hours. Serve with the chips.

PER SERVING (¼ cup salsa with 4 chips): 78 Cal, 1 g Total Fat, 0 g Sat Fat, 40 mg Chol, 259 mg Sod, 11 g Carb, 2 g Fib, 5 g Prot, 22 mg Calc.
PointsPlus value: 2.

You can turn the salsa into an elegant appetizer by serving it in endive leaves. Or, if it's tomato season, cut plum tomatoes in half lengthwise and scoop out the seeds. Spoon the salsa into the tomato halves.

family entrées

hearty meats, poultry, and seafood

the iconic weight watchers burger

SERVES 4

20 Min or Less

1 pound lean ground beef (7% or less fat)
1 garlic clove, minced
2 teaspoons Worcestershire sauce
¼ teaspoon salt
¼ teaspoon ground pepper
1 teaspoon canola oil
¼ cup plain fat-free Greek yogurt
¼ cup fat-free mayonnaise
¼ cup diced sweet onion
2 tablespoons chopped basil
4 whole wheat hamburger buns, split and warmed
4 slices tomato
1 cucumber, halved crosswise and thinly sliced lengthwise
1 cup baby arugula

Long ago, the classic Weight Watchers hamburger recipe was simply a plain broiled ground beef patty topped wth sautéed mushrooms. Where's the bun? You'll find it here along with creamy basil sauce, crunchy cucumber, and peppery arugula.

1 Combine the beef, garlic, Worcestershire sauce, salt, and pepper in a medium bowl. Form the mixture into 4 (½-inch-thick) patties.

2 Heat a large skillet. Swirl in the oil, then add the patties and cook, turning once, until an instant-read thermometer inserted into the side of each patty registers 160°F, about 8 minutes.

3 Meanwhile, to make the sauce, stir together the yogurt, mayonnaise, onion, and basil in a small bowl.

4 Place the burgers in the buns and top evenly with the tomato slices, cucumber slices, arugula, and sauce.

PER SERVING (1 burger): 338 Cal, 10 g Total Fat, 3 g Sat Fat, 70 mg Chol, 572 mg Sod, 34 g Carb, 6 g Fib, 30 g Prot, 104 mg Calc.
PointsPlus value: 9.

Serve the burgers with a salad made with 1 pound cooked and chilled green beans tossed with segments from 2 medium oranges, 2 teaspoons sesame seeds, and salt and pepper to taste (the per-serving *PointsPlus* value will increase by *2*).

roasted beef tenderloin with mushroom sauce

SERVES 8

beef

½ cup dry red wine or reduced-sodium chicken broth
¼ cup chopped flat-leaf parsley
1 shallot, minced
1 tablespoon balsamic vinegar
1 teaspoon chopped thyme
1 garlic clove, bruised
1 (2-pound) beef tenderloin, trimmed of all visible fat
¼ teaspoon salt
Freshly ground pepper

sauce

2 teaspoons olive oil
1 (10-ounce) package sliced white mushrooms
1 small onion, minced
½ cup chopped flat-leaf parsley
½ cup dry red wine or reduced-sodium chicken broth
½ cup reduced-sodium beef broth
¼ teaspoon red-wine vinegar or fresh lemon juice
¼ teaspoon salt
Freshly ground pepper
Chopped flat-leaf parsley (optional)

The recent revival of steak house cuisine is proof that a good cut of beef is alluring and timeless. And few dishes make the impression that a skillfully prepared beef tenderloin does. It's expensive, but definitely worth the splurge.

1 Place the oven rack on the bottom third of the oven. Preheat the oven to 450°F.

2 To prepare the beef, combine the wine, parsley, shallot, balsamic vinegar, thyme, and garlic in a small bowl. Place the beef on a rack in a large roasting pan. Brush with the wine mixture and sprinkle with the salt and pepper. Roast until an instant-read thermometer inserted in the center registers 145°F for medium-rare, about 45 minutes, or to desired degree of doneness.

3 Meanwhile, to prepare the sauce, heat a large skillet. Swirl in the oil, then add the mushrooms and onion. Sauté until the mushrooms have released some of their liquid and the onion is soft, about 10 minutes. Add the parsley, wine, broth, and wine vinegar or lemon juice. Cook over medium-high heat, watching carefully, until thickened and reduced by one-third; stir in the salt and pepper. Set aside and keep warm.

4 Transfer the beef to a warmed platter; tent with foil and keep warm. Let rest 10 minutes, then cut into ½-inch slices. Serve with the sauce and the additional parsley, if using.

PER SERVING (3 ounces beef with 2 tablespoons sauce): 202 Cal, 8 g Total Fat, 3 g Sat Fat, 71 mg Chol, 215 mg Sod, 4 g Carb, 1 g Fib, 26 g Prot, 23 mg Calc.
PointsPlus value: 5.

individual beef wellingtons

SERVES 4

- 4 (¼-pound) filets mignons, trimmed of all visible fat
- ½ teaspoon salt
- ¼ teaspoon freshly ground pepper
- 1 teaspoon olive oil
- 8 ounces sliced white mushrooms (about 2 cups)
- 1 small onion, chopped
- 1 teaspoon chopped thyme
- 2 garlic cloves, minced
- ¼ cup Madeira
- 4 sheets phyllo dough, thawed, if frozen

In the sixties, few home cooks attempted Beef Wellington. In the classic technique, beef filet is spread with either foie gras (fatty goose or duck liver) or duxelles (sautéed mushroom-shallot-herb paste), then wrapped in puff pastry. Our version is made simpler and lighter by topping filets with sautéed mushrooms and enclosing them in phyllo dough. The results are still deliciously impressive.

1 Preheat the oven to 400°F. Spray a baking sheet with nonstick spray. Sprinkle the filets with the salt and pepper.

2 Heat a large skillet over medium-high heat. Swirl in the oil, then add the filets. Cook until browned on both sides, about 4 minutes. Transfer to a warmed plate.

3 Return the skillet to the heat; add the mushrooms, onion, thyme, and garlic. Cook, stirring occasionally, until the mushrooms are softened, about 6 minutes. Add the Madeira and cook until liquid evaporates, 3 minutes. Remove from heat and let cool 5 minutes.

4 Cover the phyllo sheets with plastic wrap to keep them from drying out as you work. Place one sheet of phyllo on a work surface, with the long side closest to you. Spray with nonstick spray and top with another phyllo sheet. Spray the second sheet with nonstick spray, then cut the stack in half vertically. Place one filet in the center of the lower third of each half. Top each filet with ¼ cup of the mushroom mixture. Fold the short sides of the phyllo over the filets, and roll up the long end, jelly-roll style. Transfer to the baking sheet, and repeat with the remaining phyllo, filets, and mushroom mixture.

5 Spray the Wellingtons with nonstick spray and bake until the crust is golden and the filets are cooked to the desired doneness, 10–12 minutes for medium.

PER SERVING (1 Wellington): 274 Cal, 9 g Total Fat, 3 g Sat Fat, 71 mg Chol, 405 mg Sod, 19 g Carb, 1 g Fib, 28 g Prot, 20 mg Calc.
PointsPlus value: 7.

Individual Beef Wellingtons and Roasted-Garlic Mashed Potatoes, page 271

grilled t-bone with steak house spices

SERVES 4

20 Min or Less

1 teaspoon ground cumin
½ teaspoon salt
½ teaspoon paprika
¼ teaspoon ground pepper
1 (1¼-pound) T-bone steak, trimmed

Grilling has long been a technique favored by Weight Watchers cooks because it produces juicy, flavorful results in lean meats without adding lots of fat. This recipe calls for a grill pan, but an outdoor grill will work as well.

1 Combine the cumin, salt, paprika, and pepper in a small bowl. Rub the mixture on both sides of the steak.

2 Spray a ridged cast-iron grill pan with nonstick spray and set over medium-high heat. Add the steak and grill, turning once, until an instant-read thermometer inserted in the side of the beef registers 145°F, 8–10 minutes, or to desired degree of doneness. Transfer the steak to a cutting board and let stand 5 minutes. Cut into four servings.

PER SERVING (¼ of steak): 165 Cal, 7 g Total Fat, 3 g Sat Fat, 46 mg Chol, 328 mg Sod, 0 g Carb, 0 g Fib, 24 g Prot, 11 mg Calc.
PointsPlus value: 4.

Our deliciously rustic, veggie-packed Tuscan Panzanella, page 55, makes an ideal accompaniment to this classic steak.

soy-lime marinated flank steak

SERVES 4

¼ cup reduced-sodium soy sauce
2 teaspoons grated lime zest
2 tablespoons fresh lime juice
1 tablespoon grated peeled fresh ginger
2 garlic cloves, minced
1 teaspoon honey
½ teaspoon chili-garlic paste
1 (1-pound) flank steak, trimmed
2 teaspoons olive oil

Marinating lean, flavorful flank steak tenderizes it while imparting wonderful flavor. This steak is terrific served over greens—either tossed lettuces or steamed chard, kale, or mustard greens.

1 Combine the soy sauce, lime zest, lime juice, ginger, garlic, honey, and chili-garlic paste in a large zip-close plastic bag; add the steak. Squeeze out the air and seal the bag. Refrigerate, turning the bag occasionally, at least 4 hours or up to 1 day.

2 When ready to serve, preheat the broiler.

3 Remove the steak from the marinade; discard the marinade. Pat the steak dry with paper towels. Rub the oil on both sides of the steak and place on the broiler rack. Broil 5 inches from the heat, turning once, until an instant-read thermometer inserted into side of steak registers 145°F, 8–10 minutes, or to desired degree of doneness. Transfer the steak to a cutting board and let stand 5 minutes. Cut across the grain into 12 slices.

PER SERVING (3 slices): 208 Cal, 7 g Total Fat, 2 g Sat Fat, 83 mg Chol, 176 mg Sod, 1 g Carb, 0 g Fib, 33 g Prot, 6 mg Calc.
PointsPlus value: 5.

In the mood for grilling? This steak will cook up beautifully on a medium-hot grill or in a stovetop grill pan heated over medium-high heat. The cooking time should remain about the same.

Yankee Pot Roast

yankee pot roast

SERVES 8

2 pounds boneless bottom round roast, trimmed
½ teaspoon salt
½ teaspoon black pepper
2 teaspoons olive oil
½ cup reduced-sodium beef broth
1 onion, chopped
3 garlic cloves, chopped
1 tablespoon chopped fresh thyme
1¼ pounds baby potatoes, halved
3 large carrots, cut into 1-inch pieces
2 turnips, peeled and cut into 1-inch pieces

Unlike European pot roasts, Yankee versions of this iconic dish rarely contain wine or garlic. We've taken the liberty of adding a few cloves of garlic to our pot roast, but otherwise it remains true to the original dinner-in-a-pot that Americans have enjoyed for centuries.

1 Preheat the oven to 350°F.

2 Sprinkle the beef with the salt and pepper. Heat a Dutch oven over medium-high heat until hot. Swirl in the oil, then add the beef and cook, turning frequently, until browned on all sides, about 8 minutes. Add the broth, stirring to scrape any browned bits from the bottom of the Dutch oven, then add the onion, garlic, and thyme. Bring to a boil. Cover and bake, turning once, 1½ hours.

3 Add the potatoes, carrots, and turnips to the Dutch oven. Bake, covered, until the beef and vegetables are fork-tender, 45 minutes longer.

4 Transfer the beef to a cutting board and slice across the grain into 16 slices. Serve with the vegetables.

PER SERVING (2 slices beef with generous ½ cup vegetables): 277 Cal, 6 g Total Fat, 2 g Sat Fat, 84 mg Chol, 261 mg Sod, 19 g Carb, 3 g Fib, 36 g Prot, 45 mg Calc.
PointsPlus value: 7.

hearty stovetop beef stew

SERVES 6

1 pound beef top round steak, trimmed and cut into ¾-inch chunks
¾ teaspoon salt
¼ teaspoon ground pepper
1 tablespoon all-purpose flour
2 teaspoons olive oil
4 carrots, cut into 1½-inch pieces
2 celery stalks, cut into 1½-inch pieces
1 medium onion, cut into thin wedges
3 garlic cloves, finely chopped
1 (12-ounce) bottle dark beer
1 cup strong brewed coffee
2 tablespoons ketchup
1 tablespoon dark molasses
1 pound red potatoes, cut into ¾-inch chunks
½ pound green beans, trimmed and halved

Talk about flavor! This easy stew gets deep richness from a combination of beer, coffee, and a touch of molasses. Legend has it that thrifty chuck-wagon cooks often tossed the morning's leftover coffee into the stewpot. We think it's a tradition worth following, judging by the crowd-pleasing response to this hearty meal.

1 Sprinkle the beef with the salt and ⅛ teaspoon of the pepper. Put the beef and flour in a large zip-close plastic bag. Shake the bag until the beef is evenly coated with the flour.

2 Heat a Dutch oven over medium-high heat until hot. Swirl in the oil, then add half of the beef and cook until browned on all sides, about 5 minutes. Transfer to a plate. Repeat with the remaining beef.

3 Add the carrots, celery, onion, and garlic to the Dutch oven. Cook, stirring frequently to scrape up the browned bits from the bottom of the Dutch oven, until the onions are golden, about 3 minutes. Stir in the beef, beer, coffee, ketchup, molasses, and the remaining ⅛ teaspoon pepper. Bring to a boil; reduce the heat and simmer, covered, 1 hour. Add the potatoes and green beans. Simmer, covered, until the beef and potatoes are fork-tender, about 20 minutes longer.

PER SERVING (about 1⅔ cups): 234 Cal, 4 g Total Fat, 1 g Sat Fat, 41 mg Chol, 421 mg Sod, 29 g Carb, 5 g Fib, 19 g Prot, 67 mg Calc.
PointsPlus value: 6.

beef fajitas

SERVES 4

3 tablespoons fresh lime juice
3 garlic cloves, minced
1½ teaspoons ground cumin
12 ounces flank steak, trimmed of all visible fat, thinly sliced on the diagonal
1 small onion, thinly sliced
1 red bell pepper, sliced into thin strips
1 green bell pepper, sliced into thin strips
1 jalapeño pepper, seeded and finely chopped
1½ tablespoons reduced-sodium soy sauce
1 tablespoon Worcestershire sauce
1 teaspoon chili powder
4 (8-inch) fat-free flour tortillas
½ cup fat-free sour cream
½ cup salsa

Eighties eaters were passionate about all things Tex-Mex—especially sizzling fajitas. True to the primordial Texas recipe, we've made ours with flank steak. Though it needs a little time to marinate, it's loaded with beefy flavor and has a good chew. If you can't find flank steak at your market, look for skirt steak, bottom round, or rump steak, and trim it well.

1 Combine the lime juice, garlic, and cumin in a zip-close plastic bag; add the steak. Squeeze out the air and seal the bag; turn to coat the steak. Refrigerate, turning the bag occasionally, 20 minutes. Drain and discard the marinade.

2 Spray a large skillet with nonstick spray and set over medium-high heat. Add the onion, red and green bell peppers, and the jalapeño pepper; cook, stirring occasionally, until softened, 5 minutes. Add the steak and cook until lightly browned but still barely red in the center, 3–4 minutes. Add the soy sauce, Worcestershire sauce, and chili powder; cook 1 minute longer.

3 Warm the tortillas according to package directions. Place a tortilla on a work surface and place one-fourth of the beef mixture in a strip down the center, leaving a 1½-inch border at either end. Fold the bottom flap up over the filling, then fold over the sides to enclose; roll up to form a package. Repeat with the remaining tortillas and filling, and serve the fajitas at once with the sour cream and salsa.

PER SERVING (1 tortilla with 1 cup filling and 2 tablespoons each sour cream and salsa): 307 Cal, 7 g Total Fat, 2 g Sat Fat, 49 mg Chol, 632 mg Sod, 35 g Carb, 3 g Fib, 26 g Prot, 159 mg Calc.
PointsPlus value: 8.

beef, bean, and zucchini chili

SERVES 6

1 pound extra lean ground beef (5% fat or less)
1 onion, chopped
2 garlic cloves, minced
2 (14½-ounce) cans diced tomatoes
1 (15½-ounce) can kidney beans, rinsed and drained
1 (15-ounce) can tomato sauce
1 cup reduced-sodium beef broth
1 red bell pepper, diced
2 tablespoons chili powder
1 teaspoon ground cumin
¼ teaspoon cayenne
1 medium zucchini, halved lengthwise and sliced
24 baked tortilla chips

The word "chili" is Mexican for chile pepper, but the dish loved by game day fans everywhere is definitely all-American. It was even declared the state food of Texas back in 1977, and Texans have an affinity for a big bowl of red. Our version mixes lean ground beef with kidney beans, plenty of spice, and a shot of veggies.

1 Combine the beef, onion, and garlic in a large saucepan and cook over medium-high heat, stirring to break up the beef, until the beef is browned, 5 minutes.

2 Add the tomatoes, beans, tomato sauce, broth, bell pepper, chili powder, cumin, and cayenne. Bring to a boil; reduce the heat and simmer, partially covered, until thickened slightly, 30 minutes, adding zucchini during last 5 minutes of cooking. Serve with tortilla chips.

PER SERVING (1 generous cup with 4 tortilla chips): 257 Cal, 6 g Total Fat, 2 g Sat Fat, 40 mg Chol, 789 mg Sod, 30 g Carb, 7 g Fib, 23 g Prot, 78 mg Calc.
PointsPlus value: 6.

The terms "chili powder" and "chile powder" are often used interchangeably, but they don't mean the same thing. Chili powder is a blend of ground dried chile pods and other seasonings, like cumin, garlic, oregano, and salt. Chile powder refers to pure ground chile pods with few or no additives.

Beef, Bean, and Zucchini Chili

salisbury steaks with mushroom gravy

SERVES 4

1 pound extra lean ground beef (5% fat or less)
1 onion, finely chopped
2 slices thin-sliced whole wheat bread, cut into cubes
½ teaspoon salt
⅛ teaspoon ground pepper
2 teaspoons olive oil
¼ pound white mushrooms, sliced
¼ teaspoon dried thyme
1 tablespoon all-purpose flour
1 cup reduced-sodium beef broth

This dish of chopped meat, shaped to resemble a steak, is named after its inventor, the American physician Dr. J. H. Salisbury (1823–1905). The good doctor believed that a diet of lean beef was the road to health, and advised his readers to eat it three times a day. While his advice is a little extreme, we do appreciate the deliciousness of his eponymous dish!

1 Stir together the beef, onion, bread, salt, and pepper in a large bowl until well mixed. Shape into four oval patties.

2 Spray a large nonstick skillet with nonstick spray and set over medium heat. Place the patties in the skillet and cook until well browned, 2–3 minutes on each side. Transfer to a plate.

3 Return the skillet to the heat. Swirl in the oil, then add the mushrooms and thyme. Cook, stirring occasionally, until the mushrooms are tender, about 8 minutes. Sprinkle the mushrooms with the flour, stirring to coat. Add the broth and bring to a boil, stirring until the sauce bubbles and thickens. Return the patties to the skillet; reduce the heat and simmer, uncovered, until cooked through, 3 to 4 minutes.

PER SERVING (1 patty with ¼ cup gravy): 219 Cal, 8 g Total Fat, 3 g Sat Fat, 60 mg Chol, 509 mg Sod, 10 g Carb, 2 g Fib, 26 g Prot, 31 mg Calc.
PointsPlus value: 5.

Give this recipe a flavor update by substituting shiitake, oyster, or mixed wild mushrooms instead of white mushrooms.

pork loin roast with gingersnap sauce

SERVES 8

2 teaspoons olive oil
1 teaspoon dried thyme
¾ teaspoon salt
¼ teaspoon ground pepper
1 (2-pound) boneless center-cut pork loin roast, trimmed
1 shallot, finely chopped
1 garlic clove, minced
¾ cup reduced-sodium beef broth
4 reduced-fat gingersnap cookies, crushed
1 teaspoon packed brown sugar
1 teaspoon unsalted butter

Pork loin is one of the leanest cuts available, so be sure not to overcook it, or you may end up with a tough, dry roast. For best results, the center of the pork should be just lightly pink. This is a great recipe to try anytime of the year, but it's a superb way to get leftover holiday cookies out of your pantry.

1 Preheat the oven to 375°F. Spray a shallow roasting pan with nonstick spray.

2 Combine 1 teaspoon of the oil, the thyme, ½ teaspoon of the salt, and the pepper in a small bowl. Rub the spice mixture all over the pork. Put the pork in the pan and roast until an instant-read thermometer inserted in the center registers 145°F, about 45 minutes. Transfer the pork to a cutting board, cover loosely with foil, and let stand 10 minutes.

3 Meanwhile, to prepare the sauce, heat a small saucepan over medium heat until hot. Swirl in the remaining 1 teaspoon oil, then add the shallot and garlic; cook, stirring constantly, until fragrant, 1 minute. Add the broth, gingersnaps, sugar, and the remaining ¼ teaspoon salt. Bring to a boil; boil 1 minute. Remove the pan from the heat and swirl in the butter. Cut the pork into 16 slices and serve with the sauce.

PER SERVING (2 slices pork with about 2 tablespoons sauce): 224 Cal, 11 g Total Fat, 4 g Sat Fat, 73 mg Chol, 303 mg Sod, 4 g Carb, 0 g Fib, 26 g Prot, 14 mg Calc.
PointsPlus value: 6.

the new pork and beans

SERVES 8

baked beans

1 pound dried navy beans, soaked according to package directions
1 (14-ounce) can reduced-sodium chicken broth
1 cup water
1 medium onion, chopped
⅓ cup light molasses
5 teaspoons grainy mustard
4–5 teaspoons Asian-style hot chile sauce
2 bacon slices, chopped

pork medallions

1 large garlic clove
¾ teaspoon salt
1½ pounds pork tenderloin, well trimmed and cut into 16 (¾-inch-thick) rounds
1 teaspoon paprika
¼ teaspoon Chesapeake Bay seasoning
1 teaspoon olive or vegetable oil

In the early days of Weight Watchers, many types of beans were virtually verboten, but frankfurters weren't—resulting in such memorable recipes as Franks and Green Beans in the first Weight Watchers Cookbook. Today's version uses richly flavored, slowly baked beans, with savory spiced pork medallions taking the place of the franks.

1 Combine the soaked beans, broth, and water in an ovenproof bean pot or Dutch oven; bring to a boil. Reduce the heat and simmer until just tender, 30–40 minutes.

2 Arrange the oven racks to divide the oven into thirds. Preheat the oven to 300°F. Stir the onion, molasses, mustard, chile sauce, and bacon into the beans, and return to a boil. There should be just enough broth to reach the level of the beans; if necessary, add a little water. Bake, uncovered, on the lower rack, 2 hours. Increase the oven temperature to 400°F. Continue baking until the beans are tender but not mushy, and the liquid is thickened, about 1 hour and 15 minutes more.

3 About 20 minutes before the beans are finished, prepare the pork: Finely chop the garlic on a cutting board, and sprinkle on the salt; mash to a paste with the side of a large knife. Rub paste all over the pork. Combine the paprika and Bay seasoning in a small bowl or cup; sprinkle evenly onto all sides of pork rounds.

4 Heat the oil in a large ovenproof skillet over medium-high heat, add the pork rounds, and cook until browned, 1–2 minutes per side. Bake on the upper rack of the oven, until just cooked through, 6–8 minutes. To serve, top the beans with the pork.

PER SERVING (generous ¾ cup of beans with 2 pork rounds): 379 Cal, 8 g Total Fat, 2 g Sat Fat, 54 mg Chol, 525 mg Sod, 46 g Carb, 10 g Fib, 32 g Prot, 134 mg Calc.
PointsPlus value: 9.

Chesapeake Bay seasoning is a special blend of spices containing celery salt, paprika, allspice, cayenne, and other herbs and spices. Look for it in your supermarket. Our favorite brand is Old Bay.

pork marsala

SERVES 4

4 (¼-pound) boneless loin pork chops, trimmed of visible fat
½ teaspoon salt
Freshly ground pepper
3 teaspoons olive oil
1 medium onion, chopped
1 tablespoon all-purpose flour
2 garlic cloves, minced
8 ounces shiitake mushrooms, stemmed and sliced
½ cup dry Marsala
½ cup reduced-sodium beef broth
2 plum tomatoes, seeded and chopped
2 tablespoons chopped basil

An elegantly simple dish that never goes out of style, this is just as delicious made with chicken or turkey breast pounded to scaloppine-like thinness.

1 Sprinkle the pork with ¼ teaspoon of the salt and a grinding of the pepper.

2 Heat a large skillet over medium-high heat. Swirl in 2 teaspoons of the oil, then add the pork. Cook turning once until just cooked through, 8–10 minutes. Transfer to a plate and keep warm.

3 Return the skillet to the heat and swirl in the remaining 1 teaspoon oil. Add the onion, flour, and garlic; cook, stirring, 30 seconds. Add the mushrooms, the remaining ¼ teaspoon salt, and another grinding of the pepper. Cook until softened, about 3 minutes. Pour in the Marsala and broth; bring to a boil and continue cooking, stirring occasionally, until slightly thickened, 2 minutes. Add the pork and tomatoes; cook 1 minute, turning the pork once, until heated through, 1 minute. Remove from the heat and stir in the basil; serve at once.

PER SERVING (1 cutlet with 2–3 tablespoons sauce): 276 Cal, 12 g Total Fat, 4 g Sat Fat, 70 mg Chol, 402 mg Sod, 13 g Carb, 2 g Fib, 27 g Prot, 25 mg Calc.
PointsPlus value: 7.

Marsala is Italy's most famous fortified wine, and to make this dish without it seems unthinkable. However, dry sherry or Madiera makes a pretty good substitute. For an alcohol-free version, substitute ¼ cup each of reduced-sodium chicken broth and tart apple cider for the Marsala.

Stuffed Pork Chops and Braised Cabbage with Apples, Onions, and Raisins, page 252

stuffed pork chops

SERVES 4

4 (¼-pound) boneless loin pork chops, trimmed of all visible fat
3 tablespoons plain dried bread crumbs
½ celery stalk, finely chopped
½ small onion, finely chopped
2 tablespoons fat-free egg substitute
1 tablespoon chopped flat-leaf parsley
1 tablespoon chopped sage
Freshly ground black pepper

Today's leaner pork isn't the juicy, fat-marbled meat it once was—good news for Weight Watchers, bad news for those who like their pork chops tender. We've solved the problem by starting our chops on the stove and finishing them in the oven, which prevents them from drying out.

1 Cut a large, deep pocket in the side of each chop with a very sharp knife.

2 Combine the bread crumbs, celery, onion, egg substitute, parsley, sage, and pepper in a medium bowl. Fill the pocket of each chop with the mixture; skewer the edges with toothpicks to hold them together, if necessary.

3 Preheat the oven to 400°F. Spray a 1-quart shallow baking pan with nonstick spray.

4 Spray a large nonstick skillet with nonstick spray and set over medium heat. Add the stuffed chops and cook, turning once, until golden brown on each side. Transfer to the baking pan; cover with foil, and bake until the meat is no longer pink and the vegetables in the stuffing are tender, about 10 minutes. Remove the foil and continue baking until the stuffing is golden and slightly crispy, 10 minutes more.

PER SERVING (1 chop with 2 tablespoons stuffing): 208 Cal, 9 g Total Fat, 3 g Sat Fat, 70 mg Chol, 101 mg Sod, 5 g Carb, 1 g Fib, 26 g Prot, 28 mg Calc.
PointsPlus value: 5.

skillet pork chops with onion gravy

SERVES 6

- 4 (6-ounce) bone-in pork loin chops, trimmed
- ½ teaspoon salt
- ¼ teaspoon ground pepper
- 1 teaspoon olive oil
- 2 sweet onions, thinly sliced
- 1¼ cups reduced-sodium chicken broth
- 2 garlic cloves, minced
- 2 teaspoons all-purpose flour
- 1 teaspoon whole-grain Dijon mustard
- 1 tablespoon chopped fresh thyme

Pork chops in onion sauce is a Southern classic, but often it is swimming in too much fat. We gave the dish a healthy makeover that retains all the great flavor but with a mere 1 teaspoon oil. Think of it as comfort food that you can really feel comfortable with!

1 Sprinkle the chops with the salt and pepper. Heat a large nonstick skillet over medium heat. Swirl in the oil, add the chops and cook, turning occasionally, until browned, about 5 minutes. Transfer to a plate.

2 Add the onions, ¼ cup of the broth, and the garlic to the skillet. Bring to a boil. Reduce the heat and simmer, covered, stirring occasionally, until the onions are very tender, 12–15 minutes.

3 Sprinkle the onions with the flour; cook, stirring constantly, 1 minute. Add the remaining 1 cup broth, mustard, and thyme. Bring to a boil, stirring until the sauce bubbles and thickens. Return the chops and any accumulated juices to the skillet. Reduce the heat and simmer, uncovered, until the chops are heated through, 2–3 minutes.

PER SERVING (1 chop with ¼ cup sauce): 253 Cal, 11 g Total Fat, 4 g Sat Fat, 76 mg Chol, 420 mg Sod, 9 g Carb, 2 g Fib, 29 g Prot, 30 mg Calc.
PointsPlus value: 6.

Steamed kale or collards sprinkled with a touch of cider vinegar and red pepper flakes makes a fresh and flavorful side for this dish.

Skillet Pork Chops with Onion Gravy

lamb chops with rosemary and red wine

SERVES 4

20 Min or Less

3 tablespoons all-purpose flour
4 (5-ounce) boneless loin lamb chops, trimmed of all visible fat
4 teaspoons olive oil
½ cup dry red wine or reduced-sodium beef broth
1 tablespoons chopped rosemary
¼ teaspoon salt
Freshly ground pepper
Rosemary sprigs (optional)

Flavorful, elegant, and easy to prepare, quick-cooking lamb chops are the perfect dish to serve for last-minute company.

1 Place the flour on a sheet of wax paper. Dip the lamb into the flour, coating on both sides and shaking off the excess. (Discard any leftover flour.)

2 Heat a large skillet over medium-high heat. Swirl in the oil, then add the lamb chops. Cook, turning once, about 8 minutes for medium or to desired degree of doneness. Transfer the chops to a warmed serving platter; keep warm.

3 Add the wine or broth, rosemary, salt, and pepper to the skillet; bring to a boil and cook, scraping up the browned bits from the bottom of the pan, until the liquid has reduced to ¼ cup. Pour the wine mixture over the chops; garnish with the rosemary sprigs, if using, and serve at once.

PER SERVING (1 chop with 1 tablespoon sauce): 271 Cal, 14 g Total Fat, 4 g Sat Fat, 93 mg Chol, 220 mg Sod, 4 g Carb, 0 g Fib, 29 g Prot, 13 mg Calc.
PointsPlus value: 7.

lamb chops with mint pesto

SERVES 4

- 4 (1/4-pound) loin lamb chops, 1-inch thick, trimmed of all visible fat
- 1½ cups packed flat-leaf parsley
- ½ cup packed mint leaves
- ¼ cup reduced-sodium chicken broth
- 3 tablespoons chopped walnuts
- 2 tablespoons freshly grated Parmesan cheese
- 4 teaspoons olive oil
- 1 garlic clove, chopped
- ¼ teaspoon salt
- Freshly ground pepper
- 1 lemon, cut into 4 wedges
- Mint sprigs (for garnish)

Lamb and mint are longtime flavor partners: the sweet freshness of the herb complements the intense flavor of the meat. Only fresh mint will do, though, so if it's unavailable, save this recipe for another time.

1 Spray the broiler rack with nonstick spray; preheat the broiler.

2 Pulse the parsley, mint, broth, walnuts, cheese, oil, garlic, salt, and pepper in a mini food processor, scraping the sides often, until the mixture forms a coarse paste.

3 Squeeze 1 lemon wedge over each lamb chop; place on the broiler rack. Broil the chops 4 inches from the heat, turning once, about 7 minutes on each side for medium or to desired degree of doneness. Serve each chop with a dollop of the mint pesto, and garnish all with the mint sprigs.

PER SERVING (1 chop with 2 tablespoons pesto): 269 Cal, 17 g Total Fat, 4 g Sat Fat, 77 mg Chol, 306 mg Sod, 4 g Carb, 1 g Fib, 26 g Prot, 98 mg Calc.
PointsPlus value: 7.

We love the combo of savory lamb chops and silky mashed potatoes. Try our Roasted-Garlic Mashed Potatoes, page 271, for a terrifically flavorful version.

---

lamb kebabs

SERVES 4

1 onion, chopped
¼ cup dry red wine or reduced-sodium chicken broth
Grated zest of 1 lemon
3 tablespoons fresh lemon juice
4 teaspoons olive oil
1 tablespoon chopped rosemary
1 tablespoon chopped thyme
1 tablespoon chopped oregano
1 tablespoon chopped mint
1 garlic clove, minced
⅛ teaspoon crushed red pepper
15 ounces boneless beef tenderloin or boneless leg of lamb, well trimmed and cut into 1-inch cubes
1 medium onion, cut into 8 wedges (remove the thick inner pieces and reserve for another use)
1 medium green bell pepper, seeded and cut into 8 (1-inch) squares
8 medium mushroom caps
8 cherry tomatoes
½ teaspoon salt

In this simple recipe, a variety of vegetables make this meal-on-a-stick great do-ahead company fare. You'll need at least 12-inch skewers, and if you're using wooden or bamboo ones, be sure to soak them in hot water for 30 minutes first so they don't catch fire under the broiler.

1 Puree the chopped onion, wine or broth, lemon zest, lemon juice, oil, rosemary, thyme, oregano, mint, garlic, and red pepper in a food processor. Place the mixture in a large zip-close plastic bag; add the meat. Squeeze out the air and seal the bag; turn to coat the meat. Refrigerate, turning the bag occasionally, 1 hour. Remove the meat from the marinade; discard the marinade.

2 Spray the broiler rack with nonstick spray; preheat the broiler.

3 Thread the onion wedges, bell pepper, mushroom caps, tomatoes, and meat onto 4 long skewers, beginning and ending with the onions. Set the skewers on the rack. Broil, turning once, until the meat is browned on the outside and vegetables are charred on their edges, about 5 minutes per side. Sprinkle with the salt and serve at once.

PER SERVING (1 kebab): 199 Cal, 8 g Total Fat, 3 g Sat Fat, 67 mg Chol, 331 mg Sod, 8 g Carb, 2 g Fib, 25 g Prot, 25 mg Calc.
PointsPlus value: 5.

irish lamb stew

SERVES 4

1 pound boneless lamb shoulder, trimmed and cut into 1-inch cubes
½ teaspoon salt
¼ teaspoon ground pepper
1 teaspoon olive oil
1 onion, chopped
2 tablespoons all-purpose flour
3 cups reduced-sodium beef broth
1 (14½-ounce) can diced tomatoes
5 red potatoes, cut into 1-inch cubes
2 carrots, cut into 1-inch cubes
1 cup frozen peas

Here's a perfect dish for St. Paddy's day, or anytime you're craving a little Celtic flavor. Lamb shoulder is flavorful and an excellent choice for stew, though it can be quite fatty. As with all Weight Watchers recipes, it's important to well trim all meats before cooking.

1 Sprinkle the lamb with the salt and pepper. Heat a Dutch oven over medium-high heat until hot. Swirl in the oil, then add the lamb and cook, turning occasionally, until browned, about 6 minutes. Transfer to a plate. Add the onion to the Dutch oven and cook, stirring occasionally, until tender, about 5 minutes. Stir in the flour; cook 1 minute.

2 Add the broth, tomatoes, and lamb. Bring to a boil; reduce the heat and simmer, covered, until the meat is almost tender, about 30 minutes. Add the potatoes and carrots. Bring to a boil. Reduce the heat and simmer, covered, until the vegetables are tender, about 25 minutes. Stir in the peas and cook until heated through, 2 minutes.

PER SERVING (1½ cups): 473 Cal, 10 g Total Fat, 3 g Sat Fat, 81 mg Chol, 895 mg Sod, 62 g Carb, 10 g Fib, 35 g Prot, 128 mg Calc.
PointsPlus value: 12.

roast chicken with lemon and herbs

SERVES 8

1 (4½-pound) roasting chicken
½ teaspoon salt
½ teaspoon ground pepper
1 lemon, halved
6 garlic cloves, peeled
3 thyme sprigs, or 1 teaspoon dried thyme
3 sage sprigs, or 1 teaspoon dried sage
Thyme sprigs (optional)
Sage sprigs (optional)

Classic comfort food, our roasted chicken gets a flavor boost from herbs, lemon, and garlic. Wrap and refrigerate any leftovers for the week's lunches.

1 Preheat the oven to 350°F. Rub the chicken inside and out with the salt and pepper. Squeeze the lemon halves over the outside of the chicken. Place the squeezed lemon halves, the garlic, thyme, and sage into the large cavity of the chicken; truss.

2 Place the chicken, breast-side up, on a rack in a roasting pan; roast until the juices run clear when pierced with a fork, or until an instant-read thermometer inserted in the thigh registers 165°F, about 2 hours. Remove from the oven; let stand 10 minutes before carving.

3 Remove the lemons, garlic, and herbs from the cavity and discard. Carve the chicken. Garnish with the additional thyme and sage, if using. Remove the skin before eating.

PER SERVING (⅛ chicken, without skin): 161 Cal, 6 g Total Fat, 2 g Sat Fat, 74 mg Chol, 216 mg Sod, 0 g Carb, 0 g Fib, 26 g Prot, 19 mg Calc.
PointsPlus value: 4.

good idea

Keep the skin on whole chicken when you roast it to hold in moisture and prevent the meat from becoming too dry. But, remember to remove the skin before serving.

spice-rubbed beer can chicken

SERVES 6

2 garlic cloves, minced
1 tablespoon chili powder
1 teaspoon ground cumin
¾ teaspoon salt
⅛ teaspoon cayenne
1 (3½-pound) whole chicken, giblets discarded
1 (12-ounce) can beer

Cooking a whole chicken with an open can of beer in the cavity—an only-in-America recipe! We can't deny that the steam from the beer adds a subtle flavor while keeping the chicken wonderfully moist as it cooks.

1 Preheat the oven to 375°F. Spray a medium roasting pan with nonstick spray.

2 Stir together the garlic, chili powder, cumin, salt, and cayenne in a small bowl. Loosen the skin from the breasts and legs of the chicken, then rub the seasoning mixture under and over the skin.

3 Pour off one-fourth of the beer. Hold the chicken upright with the opening of the cavity pointing down. Slide the cavity of the chicken over the can. Set the chicken, standing upright, with the can bottom in the prepared roasting pan.

4 Roast the chicken until an instant-read thermometer inserted in a thigh registers 165°F, 1 to 1¼ hours. Remove the chicken from the oven and transfer to a carving board. Let stand 10 minutes. Carefully remove and discard the beer can before carving. Discard the chicken skin before eating.

PER SERVING (⅙ of chicken): 183 Cal, 7 g Total Fat, 2 g Sat Fat, 83 mg Chol, 397 mg Sod, 1 g Carb, 1 g Fib, 27 g Prot, 23 mg Calc.
PointsPlus value: 4.

saucy oven-baked bbq chicken

SERVES 6

1 tablespoon paprika
1 tablespoon + 1 teaspoon chili powder
2 teaspoons ground cumin
2 teaspoons packed dark brown sugar
¾ teaspoon salt
1 (3½-pound) chicken, skin and wings discarded, cut into 6 pieces
⅓ cup ketchup
2 tablespoons white-wine vinegar
½ teaspoon Worcestershire sauce

Cooking chicken first with a dry rub, and then finishing it with a flavorful "wet mop" is the preferred technique of many a BBQ pit master. We've adapted this method for easy oven cooking so that you can enjoy moist, flavorful, barbecue-style chicken at home any night of the week.

1 Preheat the oven to 425°F. Line a roasting pan with foil and spray with nonstick spray.

2 Stir together the paprika, 1 tablespoon of the chili powder, the cumin, 1 teaspoon of the sugar, and the salt in a small bowl. Rub the mixture all over the chicken to coat. Stir together the remaining 1 teaspoon chili powder, 1 teaspoon sugar, the ketchup, vinegar, and Worcestershire sauce in a small bowl. Set aside.

3 Place the chicken in the prepared roasting pan and bake 35 minutes. Remove from the oven, drizzle with the ketchup mixture, and turn to coat. Bake until the chicken is cooked through, 15 minutes longer.

PER SERVING (⅙ of chicken): 194 Cal, 7 g Total Fat, 2 g Sat Fat, 77 mg Chol, 554 mg Sod, 7 g Carb, 1 g Fib, 26 g Prot, 32 mg Calc.
PointsPlus value: 5.

Nothing beats a piece of hot barbecued chicken than serving it with a side of cooling potato salad. Try our Potato Salad with Tarragon-Chive Dressing, page 273, for an herb-packed version that features flavorful Yukon Gold potatoes.

---

skillet-braised chicken with roasted vegetables

SERVES 6

4 plum tomatoes, cut into wedges
1 large onion, sliced
1 red bell pepper, sliced
1 large fennel bulb, sliced
3 teaspoons olive oil
¾ teaspoon salt
½ teaspoon ground pepper
1 (3½-pound) chicken, skin and wings discarded, cut into 6 pieces
4 garlic cloves, sliced
1 (14-ounce) can reduced-sodium chicken broth
1 teaspoon dried oregano

This savory chicken with rich sauce braises on the stovetop while a batch of roasted vegetables cook in the oven. Serve it all with mashed potatoes for a robust meal (½ cup of mashed potatoes will increase the per-serving ***PointsPlus*** *value by* ***3****).*

1 Preheat the oven to 400°F. Spray a large rimmed baking sheet with nonstick spray.

2 Combine the tomatoes, onion, bell pepper, fennel, 2 teaspoons of the oil, ¼ teaspoon of the salt, and ¼ teaspoon of the pepper in a large bowl; toss to coat. Arrange the vegetables on the baking sheet in a single layer and roast, tossing occasionally, until the onion begins to brown, about 30 minutes. Set aside.

3 Meanwhile, sprinkle the chicken with the remaining ½ teaspoon salt and ¼ teaspoon pepper and add to the skillet. Heat a 12-inch nonstick skillet over medium heat. Swirl in the remaining 1 teaspoon oil. Cook the chicken until browned, about 4 minutes on each side. Add the garlic and cook until fragrant, about 30 seconds. Add the broth and oregano. Bring to a boil; reduce the heat and simmer, covered, turning the chicken occasionally, until cooked through, about 25 minutes.

4 Transfer the chicken to a platter and keep warm. Increase the heat to high and bring the broth to a boil; cook until very slightly thickened, about 5 minutes. Stir in the roasted vegetables and serve with the chicken.

PER SERVING (1 piece chicken with ½ cup vegetable mixture): 228 Cal, 9 g Total Fat, 2 g Sat Fat, 77 mg Chol, 549 mg Sod, 9 g Carb, 3 g Fib, 27 g Prot, 57 mg Calc.
PointsPlus value: 6.

chicken cordon bleu

SERVES 4

4 (¼-pound) skinless boneless chicken breast halves, pounded to ¼-inch thickness
4 thin slices lean ham (about 2 ounces)
4 thin slices reduced-fat Swiss cheese (about 2 ounces)
4 tablespoons all-purpose flour
½ teaspoon salt
Freshly ground pepper
1 large egg, lightly beaten
½ cup cornflake crumbs
½ cup reduced-fat (2%) milk
½ cup reduced-sodium chicken broth
1 tablespoon Madeira
⅛ teaspoon nutmeg
2 tablespoons freshly grated Parmesan cheese

Chicken cordon bleu is a glamorous dish that graced many a dinner-party table in the sixties. The method is simple: A layer of fine ham and cheese is sandwiched between thin medallions of chicken or veal, then sautéed. Here, we've simplified and lightened the recipe to use a single layer of chicken rolled around the filling to make an elegant presentation.

1 Preheat the oven to 400°F. Spray a baking sheet with nonstick spray.

2 Working one at a time, place a chicken breast half on a work surface. Top with one slice of the ham, then one slice of the Swiss cheese. Roll up, jelly-roll style, and secure with a toothpick. Repeat with the remaining chicken, ham and cheese.

3 Combine 2 tablespoons of the flour, ¼ teaspoon of the salt, and a grinding of the pepper on a sheet of wax paper. Place the egg in a shallow bowl, and the cornflake crumbs in another shallow bowl.

4 Working one at a time, lightly coat the chicken rolls first with the flour mixture, shaking off the excess, then dip into the egg to coat. Lightly coat with the cornflake crumbs, and place on the baking sheet (discard any leftover flour mixture, egg, and crumbs). Lightly spray the chicken rolls with nonstick spray. Bake until a thermometer inserted into the thickest part of each roll reaches 165°F, about 30 minutes.

5 Meanwhile, to prepare the sauce, combine the milk, broth, the remaining 2 tablespoons flour, the Madeira, nutmeg, the remaining ¼ teaspoon salt, and another grinding of the pepper in a medium saucepan. Whisk until smooth; cook over medium heat, whisking constantly, until thickened, about 6 minutes. Remove from the heat and stir in the Parmesan cheese; cover and keep warm.

6 When the chicken rolls are ready, drizzle with the sauce and serve them at once.

PER SERVING (1 breast with ¼ cup sauce): 291 Cal, 8 g Total Fat, 4 g Sat Fat, 121 mg Chol, 835 mg Sod, 13 g Carb, 0 g Fib, 36 g Prot, 287 mg Calc.
PointsPlus value: 7.

Chicken Cordon Bleu

chicken cacciatore

SERVES 6

- 1 (3½-pound) chicken, skin and wings discarded, cut into 6 pieces
- ½ teaspoon salt
- ¼ teaspoon freshly ground pepper
- 3 teaspoons olive oil
- 2 red bell peppers, seeded and chopped
- 1 onion, chopped
- ¼ pound mushrooms, sliced
- 1 stalk celery, chopped
- 3 garlic cloves, minced
- ½ teaspoon dried oregano
- 1 (14½-ounce) can diced tomatoes
- ½ cup reduced-sodium chicken broth
- 2 tablespoons chopped fresh basil

Also known as hunter's chicken, cacciatore is one of the world's favorite chicken dishes. A recipe for it, using only breast meat, appeared in the very first Weight Watchers cookbook in 1966. This veggie-packed version features both light and dark meat braised in a deliciously aromatic sauce.

1 Sprinkle the chicken with the salt and pepper. Heat a large skillet over medium-heat until hot. Swirl in 2 teaspoons of the oil, then add the chicken and cook until browned, 3–4 minutes on each side. Transfer the chicken to a plate and set aside.

2 Return the skillet to the heat. Swirl in the remaining 1 teaspoon of oil, then add the bell peppers, onion, mushrooms, celery, garlic, and oregano. Cook, stirring occasionally, until the vegetables are softened, 5–6 minutes. Return the chicken to the skillet; add the tomatoes and chicken broth. Bring to a boil. Reduce the heat and simmer, covered, until the chicken is cooked through and the vegetables are tender, about 20 minutes. Stir in the basil.

PER SERVING (1 piece chicken with ⅔ cup vegetables and sauce): 249 Cal, 10 g Total Fat, 2 g Sat Fat, 89 mg Chol, 436 mg Sod, 8 g Carb, 2 g Fib, 31 g Prot, 54 mg Calc.
PointsPlus value: 6.

Serving this chicken dish over pasta is a good way to make the most of its abundant sauce. A ½ cup of cooked whole wheat linguine per serving will increase the ***PointsPlus*** value by ***2***.

---

chicken satay with peanut sauce

SERVES 8

2½ tablespoons Thai fish sauce
1 tablespoon minced peeled fresh ginger
2 garlic cloves, minced
1 tablespoon + 2 teaspoons fresh lime juice
1½ pounds skinless boneless chicken breast halves, cut into thin 2-inch strips
6 tablespoons light coconut milk
3 tablespoons reduced-fat chunky peanut butter
2 tablespoons chopped cilantro
4 teaspoons honey
1 teaspoon grated lime zest
⅛ teaspoon crushed red pepper

A Southeast Asian treat that became ubiquitous in the Asian food–obsessed nineties, satays make great party fare. We've lightened the traditional peanut dipping sauce considerably by using unsweetened light or "lite" coconut milk, available in most supermarkets. It has the flavor of regular coconut milk with about half the fat and calories.

1 Combine 1½ tablespoons of the fish sauce, the ginger, garlic, and 2 teaspoons of the lime juice in a zip-close plastic bag; add the chicken. Squeeze out the air and seal the bag; turn to coat the chicken. Refrigerate, turning the bag occasionally, 1 hour.

2 Meanwhile, soak 40 long wooden skewers in enough cold water to cover for at least 30 minutes (this prevents them from burning); drain and set aside.

3 To prepare the peanut sauce, combine the coconut milk, peanut butter, cilantro, honey, the remaining 1 tablespoon each fish sauce and lime juice, the lime zest, and red pepper in a medium bowl; whisk until smooth.

4 Preheat the broiler or prepare the grill for a hot fire; spray the broiler pan or grill rack with nonstick spray. Thread the chicken strips onto the skewers, then broil or grill the skewers 4 inches from the heat, turning once, until they are cooked through, 3–4 minutes per side. Serve at once with the peanut sauce.

PER SERVING (5 skewers with about 2 tablespoons peanut sauce): 162 Cal, 6 g Total Fat, 2 g Sat Fat, 47 mg Chol, 200 mg Sod, 7 g Carb, 0 g Fib, 21 g Prot, 18 mg Calc.
PointsPlus value: 4.

Freeze any leftover coconut milk in an airtight container for future recipes; it will stay fresh for up to two months.

chicken salad véronique

SERVES 4

½ cup plain fat-free yogurt
2 tablespoons reduced-fat mayonnaise
1 tablespoon honey
1 teaspoon cider vinegar
½ teaspoon Dijon mustard
¼ teaspoon celery seeds
¼ teaspoon salt
Freshly ground pepper
¾ pound cooked skinless boneless chicken breast, coarsely chopped
1 cup seedless green grapes
1 celery stalk, finely chopped
¼ cup chopped walnuts
4 small grape bunches (optional)

In the French culinary canon, any dish labeled "Véronique" includes grapes—and it is a tasty pleasure to add these sweet, juicy (and formerly forbidden) morsels to a chicken salad. Serve it with multigrain bread or rolls.

Combine the yogurt, mayonnaise, honey, vinegar, mustard, celery seeds, salt, and pepper in a large bowl. Add the chicken, grapes, celery, and walnuts; toss to coat evenly. Cover and refrigerate at least 1 hour or up to 8 hours. Garnish with the small grape bunches, if using, and serve.

PER SERVING (¾ cup): 277 Cal, 11 g Total Fat, 2 g Sat Fat, 66 mg Chol, 303 mg Sod, 16 g Carb, 1 g Fib, 29 g Prot, 95 mg Calc.
PointsPlus value: 7.

chicken parmigiana

SERVES 4

1 large egg
1 tablespoon water
⅓ cup plain dried bread crumbs
¼ cup chopped flat-leaf parsley
3 tablespoons freshly grated Parmesan cheese
Freshly ground pepper
4 (¼-pound) skinless boneless chicken breasts, pounded thin
2 teaspoons olive oil
2 cups fat-free marinara sauce
4 tablespoons shredded reduced-fat mozzarella cheese

One of those beloved Italian-American dishes that never goes out of style. You can substitute turkey cutlets for the chicken.

1 Preheat the oven to 400°F. Spray a 1-quart shallow baking dish with nonstick spray.

2 Beat the egg with the water in a shallow bowl. Combine the bread crumbs, parsley, Parmesan, and pepper on a sheet of wax paper.

3 Dip the chicken breasts first in the egg mixture, then coat lightly on both sides with the bread crumb mixture, shaking off the excess.

4 Heat a large nonstick skillet; swirl in the oil, then add the chicken. Cook, turning once, until the chicken is browned and cooked through, about 8 minutes.

5 Add the marinara sauce to the prepared baking dish. Top with the chicken. Sprinkle evenly with the mozzarella. Bake until mozzarella is melted, 10–15 minutes.

PER SERVING (1 breast): 310 Cal, 9 g Total Fat, 3 g Sat Fat, 121 mg Chol, 738 mg Sod, 18 g Carb, 3 g Fib, 34 g Prot, 129 mg Calc. ***PointsPlus value: 7.***

The chicken breasts need to be uniformly thin to cook evenly. To pound your own, lay the breasts between two sheets of plastic wrap, or put them in a partially sealed zip-close plastic bag (don't seal the bag, or it will pop). Use a rubber mallet or heavy skillet to pound the breasts to uniform thinness.

poached chicken breasts with green sauce

SERVES 4

chicken

2 teaspoons olive oil
1 onion, chopped
1 green bell pepper. seeded and chopped
1 carrot, peeled and chopped
1 celery stalk, chopped
4 (¼-pound) skinless boneless chicken breasts
3 cups reduced-sodium chicken broth
½ cup dry white wine
2 tablespoons chopped flat-leaf parsley
1 tablespoon chopped thyme
1 garlic clove
1 bay leaf
Freshly ground white pepper

sauce

1 cup packed flat-leaf parsley leaves
5 small green olives, pitted and chopped
1 tablespoon fresh lemon juice
½ tablespoon plain dried bread crumbs
1 teaspoon capers, drained
1 teaspoon olive oil
1 garlic clove
Freshly ground white pepper

Poaching is one of the all-time-great low-fat cooking techniques, and Weight Watchers members have relied upon it for years. The technique of gently cooking foods in not-quite-simmering liquid is well suited for delicate and mild-flavored foods. In this case, chicken breasts soak up the subtle flavors of vegetables, chicken broth, and white wine. The green sauce makes for a tangy contrast.

1 To prepare the chicken: Heat a large nonstick skillet; swirl in the oil, then add the onion, green pepper, carrot, and celery. Sauté until the vegetables are wilted, about 5 minutes.

2 Add the chicken, broth, wine, parsley, thyme, garlic, bay leaf, and white pepper. Bring to a boil; reduce the heat and simmer, covered, until the chicken is cooked through, 12–15 minutes.

3 Meanwhile, prepare the sauce: Pulse the parsley, olives, lemon juice, bread crumbs, capers, oil, garlic, and pepper in a food processor until the mixture forms a coarse pesto-like sauce.

4 Transfer the chicken and vegetables with a slotted spoon to a warmed platter. Discard the bay leaf; reserve the liquid remaining in the pan for another use. Arrange the chicken and vegetables on a platter, and top each chicken breast with a dollop of the sauce.

PER SERVING (1 breast with ¼ cup vegetables and 2 tablespoons sauce): 218 Cal, 8 g Total Fat, 2 g Sat Fat, 70 mg Chol, 277 mg Sod, 8 g Carb, 2 g Fib, 28 g Prot, 62 mg Calc.
PointsPlus value: 5.

grilled chicken with corn–cherry tomato relish

SERVES 4

3 ears of corn, husks and silk removed
2 cups cherry tomatoes, halved
2 scallions, thinly sliced
1 jalapeño pepper, seeded and minced
2 tablespoons fresh lime juice
1 tablespoon chopped fresh cilantro
½ teaspoon salt
4 (¼-pound) boneless skinless chicken breast halves
1 tablespoon olive oil
1 teaspoon ground cumin

Here's a simple recipe for grilled chicken that makes the most of summer flavors. Grilling is one of the most popular ways to cook sweet corn, and with good reason: It's quick, it doesn't require heating up a big pot of water on a hot summer day, and the end result is sweet, roasted kernels with a delightfully firm texture.

1 Prepare the grill for a medium fire; spray the grill rack with nonstick spray.

2 Place the corn on the grill rack. Grill, turning often, until tender and well marked, about 6 minutes. Transfer the corn to a cutting board and let cool 5 minutes. With a sharp knife, cut the kernels from the cobs; transfer the kernels to a large bowl. Stir in the tomatoes, scallions, jalapeño, lime juice, cilantro, and ¼ teaspoon of the salt. Set aside.

3 Rub the chicken with the oil, then sprinkle with the cumin and the remaining ¼ teaspoon salt. Place on the grill rack and grill, turning once, until chicken is cooked through, 8–10 minutes. Serve the chicken with the relish.

PER SERVING (1 chicken breast with 1 cup salsa): 273 Cal, 9 g Total Fat, 2 g Sat Fat, 70 mg Chol, 367 mg Sod, 22 g Carb, 3 g Fib, 29 g Prot, 41 mg Calc.
PointsPlus value: 7.

Got leftovers? Wrap each serving of chicken and salsa in a tortilla and tote it to the office for a delicious lunch. A medium (7-inch) whole wheat tortilla has a ***PointsPlus*** value of *2*.

Orange Chicken

orange chicken

SERVES 6

1 medium orange
1 teaspoon olive oil
1 teaspoon paprika
1 teaspoon dried rosemary, crumbled
½ teaspoon garlic salt
¼ teaspoon ground pepper
6 (¼-pound) skinless, boneless chicken thighs, trimmed of visible fat

Anyone who joined Weight Watchers in the seventies will remember this beloved recipe, which we've updated with a fresh citrus and rosemary flavor. Juicy chicken thighs are a tasty alternative to the usual breasts, (and a lot more forgiving when it comes to cooking). Just be sure to trim them well, as they tend to have lots of fatty pockets.

1 Preheat the oven to 350°F. Peel off the zest (the colorful outer layer of the orange rind) with a zester or vegetable peeler, making sure to avoid the bitter white pith underneath; mince the zest. Trim off the remaining orange rind with a knife, then cut the orange into 8 wedges.

2 Stir the orange zest, oil, paprika, rosemary, garlic salt, and pepper in a small bowl. Rub the orange mixture all over the chicken. Transfer to a roasting pan and scatter the orange wedges around the chicken pieces.

3 Roast until the juices run clear and an instant-read thermometer inserted into the chicken reads 165°F, about 35 minutes.

PER SERVING (1 thigh): 189 Cal, 8 g Total Fat, 2 g Sat Fat, 77 mg Chol, 155 mg Sod, 3 g Carb, 1 g Fib, 25 g Prot, 33 mg Calc.
PointsPlus value: 5.

If you have one, use a razor-sharp rasp grater to remove the zest from the orange—it will produce tissue-thin shreds.

chicken with lemon-caper sauce

SERVES 4

20 Min or Less

- 2 tablespoons all-purpose flour
- 4 (¼-pound) skinless boneless chicken breast halves
- ½ teaspoon salt
- ¼ teaspoon ground pepper
- 1 tablespoon olive oil
- ½ cup dry white wine or reduced-sodium chicken broth
- ¼ cup fresh lemon juice
- 1 tablespoon drained capers
- 1 tablespoon chopped flat-leaf parsley

Briny capers with tangy lemon is a classic combination in French, Italian, and Greek cooking, and with good reason: The duo imparts big flavor without a lot of fat. We suggest garnishing this dish with chopped fresh parsley, but you could also use a tablespoon of chopped dill for a Greek accent or a teaspoon of chopped tarragon for a French touch.

1 Place the flour on a sheet of wax paper. Sprinkle the cutlets with ¼ teaspoon of the salt and ⅛ teaspoon of the pepper, then coat with the flour. Discard any remaining flour.

2 Heat a large nonstick skillet over medium heat. Swirl in the oil, then add the cutlets and cook until lightly browned, about 2 minutes on each side. Add the wine, lemon juice, and capers. Bring to a boil; reduce the heat and simmer, turning the chicken once to coat with the sauce, until cooked through, about 2 minutes.

3 Remove the skillet from the heat and stir in the parsley, the remaining ¼ teaspoon salt, and the remaining ⅛ teaspoon pepper. Transfer the chicken and sauce to a platter.

PER SERVING (1 cutlet with generous 1 tablespoon sauce): 198 Cal, 7 g Total Fat, 2 g Sat Fat, 70 mg Chol, 424 mg Sod, 4 g Carb, 0 g Fib, 26 g Prot, 20 mg Calc.
PointsPlus value: 5.

chicken with 40 cloves of garlic

SERVES 8

- 1 tablespoon extra-virgin olive oil
- 4 skin-on bone-in chicken breast halves (about 2 pounds)
- 4 skin-on bone-in chicken thighs (about 2 pounds)
- ½ cup dry white wine
- ½ cup reduced-sodium chicken broth
- 2 tablespoons tomato paste
- 40 garlic cloves, unpeeled
- 1 rosemary sprig, or ½ teaspoon dried
- 1 thyme sprig, or ½ teaspoon dried
- 1 bay leaf
- ¾ teaspoon salt
- ¼ teaspoon freshly ground pepper

Why 40 garlic cloves and not 35? Who knows where the number of cloves for this eighties classic came from, but fear not: The long cooking time mellows the garlic. Serve the unpeeled garlic alongside the chicken and let everyone have fun squeezing the creamy fat-free paste onto the chicken. Have extra napkins on hand!

1 Preheat the oven to 375°F.

2 Heat a large heavy-bottomed roasting pan or flameproof casserole large enough to hold the chicken in a single layer over medium heat. Swirl in the oil, then add the chicken breast and thigh pieces, skin-side down. Cook until browned on all sides, about 5 minutes, and transfer the chicken pieces to a plate.

3 Pour off and discard any fat remaining in the pan. Stir in the wine, broth, and tomato paste, scraping up any browned bits from the bottom of the pan. Remove from the heat and add the garlic, rosemary, thyme, bay leaf, salt and pepper. Return the chicken to the pan and toss to coat with the sauce. Cover tightly with foil and bake until the chicken is cooked through and the garlic is softened, 1¼–1½ hours. Discard the bay leaf. Remove the skin before eating.

PER SERVING (1 chicken piece with 5 garlic cloves and 2–3 tablespoons sauce): 247 Cal, 9 g Total Fat, 3 g Sat Fat, 87 mg Chol, 369 mg Sod, 6 g Carb, 1 g Fib, 32 g Prot, 55 mg Calc.
PointsPlus value: 6.

For an alcohol-free version of this dish [as well as the Poached Chicken Breasts with Green Sauce on page 138] substitute ½ cup nonalcoholic dry white wine and a tablespoon of white vinegar for the white wine—or omit the wine, and increase the chicken broth by ½ cup.

---

southern-style chicken and dumplings

SERVES 4

- 2 teaspoons olive oil
- 3 celery stalks, chopped
- 2 carrots, chopped
- 1 onion, chopped
- 1 garlic clove, minced
- ¼ teaspoon dried thyme
- 4 cups reduced-sodium chicken broth
- 1½ cups chopped skinless cooked chicken breast
- ¼ pound green beans, trimmed and cut into ½-inch lengths
- ¼ cup chopped fresh parsley
- 1 cup all-purpose flour
- ½ teaspoon baking powder
- ¼ teaspoon salt
- ⅛ teaspoon ground pepper
- 1 cup water

This comfort classic will bring the alluring aromas of chicken stew and steaming dumplings to your kitchen in record time. It's a terrific recipe for using up leftover roast chicken, or you can purchase precooked roast chicken breast from either the prepared foods case or the refrigerated meat section at supermarkets.

1 Heat a large saucepan over medium heat until hot. Swirl in the oil, then add the celery, carrots, onion, garlic, and thyme. Cook, stirring occasionally, until the vegetables are softened, 5 to 6 minutes. Add the broth and chicken. Bring to a boil; reduce the heat, cover, and simmer 10 minutes. Add the green beans and simmer until the vegetables are tender, 10–15 minutes. Stir in the parsley.

2 Meanwhile, combine the flour, baking powder, salt, and pepper in a medium bowl. Stir the water into the flour mixture just until moistened. Drop the dough, by rounded teaspoonfuls, onto the simmering stew, making 12 dumplings. Cover and simmer until the dumplings have doubled in size and are cooked through, 15–20 minutes.

PER SERVING (1½ cups chicken mixture with 3 dumplings): 277 Cal, 5 g Total Fat, 1 g Sat Fat, 43 mg Chol, 939 mg Sod, 34 g Carb, 4 g Fib, 24 g Prot, 113 mg Calc.
PointsPlus value: 7.

Southern-Style Chicken and Dumplings

shake-in-the-bag chicken

SERVES 4

2/3 cup cornflake crumbs
1 tablespoon all-purpose flour
2 teaspoons paprika
1 teaspoon dark brown sugar
3/4 teaspoon garlic powder
3/4 teaspoon onion powder
3/4 teaspoon salt
1/2 teaspoon ground cumin
4 bone-in chicken breast halves, skinned (about 2 pounds)

Remember those commercials for oven-fried-chicken coating mix, so common in the seventies? Little did we know how easy it was to make our own version—with much less sodium and fresher flavorings. Best of all, our mix makes simple skinless chicken breasts positively delicious. Enjoy the chicken hot or cold.

1 Preheat oven to 400°F. Spray a baking sheet with nonstick spray.

2 Combine the cornflake crumbs, flour, paprika, sugar, garlic powder, onion powder, salt, and cumin in a large zip-close plastic bag. Spray the chicken pieces lightly with nonstick spray, then place one piece in the bag. Shake the bag to evenly coat the chicken, then transfer chicken to the baking sheet. Repeat with the remaining chicken pieces; discard any remaining coating mix.

3 Bake until a thermometer inserted into the thickest part of each breast registers 165°F, 35–40 minutes.

PER SERVING (1 breast half): 244 Cal, 5 g Total Fat, 1 g Sat Fat, 89 mg Chol, 597 mg Sod, 11 g Carb, 1 g Fib, 36 g Prot, 28 mg Calc.
PointsPlus value: 6.

marinated mediterranean chicken

SERVES 8

8 skinless bone-in chicken thighs (about 2 pounds)
1 (14-ounce) can quartered artichoke hearts, drained
¾ cup chopped pitted dates
¼ cup golden raisins
12 pimiento-stuffed Manzanilla olives, halved
2 tablespoons balsamic vinegar
3 garlic cloves, minced
1 tablespoon dried basil
1 tablespoon drained capers
1 tablespoon extra-virgin olive oil
2 teaspoons dried oregano
1 teaspoon packed light brown sugar
½ teaspoon salt
¼ teaspoon freshly ground pepper
½ cup reduced-sodium chicken broth

Almost every eighties dinner party served up a version of this chicken dish, and no wonder: It's easy to make, great hot or at room temperature, delicious as leftovers, and perfect for toting in a covered dish.

1 Combine the chicken, artichoke hearts, dates, raisins, olives, vinegar, garlic, basil, capers, oil, oregano, sugar, salt, and pepper in a large zip-close plastic bag. Squeeze out the air and seal the bag; turn to coat the chicken. Refrigerate, turning the bag occasionally, at least 8 hours or overnight.

2 Preheat the oven to 350°F. Remove the chicken pieces from the marinade and arrange them in a single layer in a large roasting pan. Pour the marinade over the chicken, then pour in the broth. Bake until a thermometer inserted into the thickest part of the chicken registers 165°F, 30–35 minutes.

PER SERVING (1 thigh with about ½ cup sauce): 224 Cal, 9 g Total Fat, 2 g Sat Fat, 45 mg Chol, 446 mg Sod, 21 g Carb, 5 g Fib, 17 g Prot, 51 mg Calc.
PointsPlus value: 6.

Pair this sweet-and savory-chicken with a crisp green salad of chopped romaine, arugula, and scallions tossed with balsamic vinegar and a sprinkle of salt and pepper.

biscuit-topped chicken potpie

SERVES 5

- 1½ cups reduced-sodium chicken broth
- ½ cup low-fat (1%) milk
- 2 tablespoons all-purpose flour
- ¼ teaspoon ground pepper
- 1 tablespoon unsalted butter
- 2 stalks celery, chopped
- 1 medium onion, chopped
- 2 garlic cloves, minced
- 2 cups frozen mixed vegetables (corn, carrots, peas, and green beans)
- 1½ cups chopped skinless cooked chicken breast
- 2 tablespoons minced fresh parsley
- 1 (6-ounce) package refrigerated buttermilk biscuits

What could be better than a luscious potpie baked under a crust of tender, golden biscuits? One that allows you to stick to your eating plan, of course! Our recipe calls for healthy ingredients like low-fat milk, lean chicken breast, and plenty of vegetables, so you can have all the flavor of an old-fashioned potpie without the excess fat.

1 Preheat the oven to 425°F. Spray a 3-quart shallow baking dish with nonstick spray.

2 Whisk together the broth, milk, flour, and pepper in a medium bowl until blended. Set aside.

3 Melt the butter in a large skillet over medium-high heat. Add the celery, onion, and garlic, and cook, stirring occasionally, until softened, 6 minutes. Stir in the mixed vegetables and chicken, and cook until heated through, 3 minutes. Add the broth mixture and cook, stirring constantly, until the mixture comes to a boil and thickens, 2–3 minutes. Stir in the parsley. Pour into the prepared baking dish. Arrange the biscuits on top of the chicken mixture.

4 Bake until the filling is bubbling and the biscuits are golden brown, 10–12 minutes.

PER SERVING (generous 1 cup chicken and vegetables with biscuit): 292 Cal, 9 g Total Fat, 3 g Sat Fat, 42 mg Chol, 666 mg Sod, 32 g Carb, 4 g Fib, 20 g Prot, 95 mg Calc.
PointsPlus value: 7.

tandoori-marinated turkey breast

SERVES 8

- 3/4 cup plain fat-free yogurt
- 1 small onion, finely chopped
- 2 tablespoons grated peeled fresh ginger
- 2 tablespoons red-wine vinegar
- 1 tablespoon Dijon mustard
- 1 teaspoon ground cumin
- 1 garlic clove, minced
- 1/2 teaspoon cinnamon
- 1/4 teaspoon crushed red pepper
- 8 (1/4-pound) skinless turkey cutlets

It's hard to believe that until the seventies, yogurt was only found in ethnic or health-food stores. In Indian cookery, plain yogurt is often used as a marinade; its acid is a great tenderizer, and its tangy flavors are a great match for spices and herbs. Here, it turns ordinary turkey breast into something juicy and special.

1 Combine the yogurt, onion, ginger, vinegar, mustard, cumin, garlic, cinnamon, and red pepper in a large zip-close plastic bag; add the turkey. Squeeze out the air and seal the bag; turn to coat the turkey. Refrigerate, turning the bag occasionally, at least 2 hours or overnight. Drain and discard the marinade.

2 Spray the broiler rack with nonstick spray; preheat the broiler. Broil the turkey 5 inches from the heat, turning once, until cooked through, about 4 minutes per side.

PER SERVING (1 cutlet): 156 Cal, 3 g Total Fat, 1 g Sat Fat, 67 mg Chol, 83 mg Sod, 2 g Carb, 0 g Fib, 27 g Prot, 43 mg Calc.
PointsPlus value: 3.

Diner-Style Meatloaf and
Creamed Spinach, page 264

diner-style meatloaf

SERVES 8

1 medium onion, finely chopped
1 red bell pepper, finely chopped
1 pound lean ground turkey
1 pound lean ground turkey breast
1 cup ketchup
½ cup seasoned dried bread crumbs
1 large egg white
2 tablespoons prepared mustard
1 teaspoon Worcestershire sauce
1 teaspoon garlic powder
¼ teaspoon salt
¼ teaspoon freshly ground pepper

Diner food was all the rage in the fifties, making a comeback in the eighties. Our slimmed-down version of meatloaf substitutes a mix of ground turkey and turkey breast for the fattier beef-pork-veal combination served up at the corner diner.

1 Preheat the oven to 400°F. Place the oven rack in the center of the oven. Spray a baking sheet with nonstick spray.

2 Spray a large nonstick skillet with nonstick spray and set over medium heat. Add the onion and bell pepper; cook, stirring occasionally, until softened, about 5 minutes. Remove from the heat and let cool 10 minutes.

3 Blend together the ground turkey and turkey breast, the onion mixture, ½ cup of the ketchup, the bread crumbs, egg white, mustard, Worcestershire sauce, garlic powder, salt, and pepper in a large bowl. Transfer the mixture to the baking sheet and shape into a 5 × 10-inch loaf, about 2½ inches thick. Spread the remaining ½ cup ketchup over the top of the meat loaf. Bake until a thermometer inserted into the center of the meatloaf registers 165°F, about 45 minutes. Remove from the oven and let stand 10 minutes before slicing.

PER SERVING (⅛ of loaf): 245 Cal, 8 g Total Fat, 2 g Sat Fat, 72 mg Chol, 615 mg Sod, 16 g Carb, 1 g Fib, 27 g Prot, 47 mg Calc.
PointsPlus value: 6.

turkey tetrazzini casserole

SERVES 8

8 ounces spaghetti
3 cups cooked cubed skinless turkey breast (about 1 pound)
2 (10¾-ounce) cans reduced-fat condensed cream of mushroom soup
1 cup low-fat (1%) milk
⅓ cup grated Romano cheese
½ teaspoon garlic powder
½ teaspoon ground cumin
¼ teaspoon freshly ground pepper
¼ cup plain dried bread crumbs
2 tablespoons unsalted light butter, melted

This comfort-food specialty—originally made with chicken—is said to have been created in honor of the Italian opera singer Luisa Tetrazzini. But for decades, Americans have used the recipe as a creative way to recycle leftover Thanksgiving turkey. Either way, it's irresistible, especially with our creative seasonings.

1 Preheat the oven to 375°F. Spray a 7 × 11-inch baking dish with nonstick spray. Cook the spaghetti according to package directions. Drain and keep warm.

2 Combine the turkey, soup, milk, cheese, garlic powder, cumin, and pepper in a large bowl; add the spaghetti and toss well. Transfer to the baking dish.

3 Combine the bread crumbs and butter in a small bowl. Sprinkle over the spaghetti mixture and bake until the top is golden, 20–25 minutes.

PER SERVING (1 cup): 296 Cal, 9 g Total Fat, 4 g Sat Fat, 58 mg Chol, 403 mg Sod, 30 g Carb, 1 g Fib, 23 g Prot, 105 mg Calc.
PointsPlus value: 8.

Romano is a hard salty cheese made from sheep's milk. You can substitute Parmesan for it in this recipe.

turkey meatballs

SERVES 4

¾ pound ground skinless turkey breast
3 tablespoons plain dried bread crumbs
1 large egg white, lightly beaten
2 tablespoons chopped flat-leaf parsley
2 tablespoons chopped dill
1 tablespoon Dijon mustard
1 teaspoon grated lemon zest
4 teaspoons olive oil
1 medium (8-ounce) zucchini, chopped
1 onion, finely chopped
1 green bell pepper, finely chopped
1 (28-ounce) can whole plum tomatoes, chopped, with their juice
1 (10-ounce) package frozen cut green beans, thawed
¼ teaspoon salt
Freshly ground pepper

These are not your traditional serve-with-pasta meatballs. Our herb-laced orbs are cooked in a chock-full-of-veggies tomato sauce and are great with rice, mashed potatoes, noodles, and spaghetti! Perfect for a covered-dish supper or buffet, too.

1 Combine the turkey, bread crumbs, egg white, parsley, dill, mustard, and lemon zest in a large bowl. Shape into 20 meatballs.

2 Heat a large nonstick skillet over medium heat. Swirl in the oil, then add the meatballs. Cook, turning frequently, until browned on all sides, about 6 minutes. Transfer to a heatproof plate with a slotted spoon; keep warm.

3 Return the skillet to the heat and add the zucchini, onion, and green bell pepper; sauté until wilted, about 5 minutes. Stir in the tomatoes, beans, salt, and black pepper; bring to a simmer. Add the meatballs to the sauce; simmer, partially covered, frequently spooning the sauce over the meatballs, until the meatballs are cooked through and tender, 10 minutes.

PER SERVING (5 meatballs with ½ cup sauce): 257 Cal, 8 g Total Fat, 2 g Sat Fat, 50 mg Chol, 631 mg Sod, 22 g Carb, 6 g Fib, 26 g Prot, 129 mg Calc.
PointsPlus value: 6.

At many fresh-produce markets and farm stands, you can find herbs with their roots still attached. In that form, they will keep fresh for days. Just place them in a glass with enough water to cover their roots, cover their leaves loosely with an upturned plastic bag, and refrigerate.

grilled duck breasts with orange-balsamic glaze

SERVES 8

- 1¼ cups orange juice
- ½ cup balsamic vinegar
- 1 whole (1¾-pound) boneless duck breast, trimmed of all skin and visible fat, and separated into 4 equal pieces
- 2 small shallots, minced
- ½ cup dry red wine or reduced-sodium chicken broth
- 1 tablespoon grated orange zest
- ¼ teaspoon salt
- Freshly ground white pepper
- 1 bunch arugula, torn into bite-size pieces (optional)

Remember Duck à l'Orange? The dish that was the height of elegance in the sixties soon became a culinary cliché. This thoroughly modern version brings it back in all its glory, using sophisticated flavorings and easy-to-cook duck breasts. Try it for a special-occasion meal.

1 Combine 1 cup of the orange juice and ¼ cup of the vinegar in a large zip-close plastic bag; add the duck. Squeeze out the air and seal the bag; turn to coat the duck. Refrigerate, turning the bag occasionally, at least 2 hours or overnight. Drain and discard the marinade.

2 Spray the grill rack with nonstick spray; prepare the grill.

3 Meanwhile, to prepare the glaze, combine the shallots, wine or broth, the remaining ¼ cup each orange juice and vinegar, the orange zest, salt, and pepper in a medium saucepan; bring to a boil. Reduce the heat and simmer, watching carefully and stirring occasionally, until the mixture is reduced by half, about 15 minutes. Remove from the heat.

4 Grill the duck, turning once and basting with the glaze, until the juices run clear when pierced with a fork, about 8 minutes per side.

5 Transfer the duck to a carving board, let cool slightly. Thinly slice lengthwise. Arrange the slices on serving plates and drizzle with any leftover glaze. Serve each portion with ⅓ cup of the arugula, if using.

PER SERVING (3 ounces): 121 Cal, 1 g Total Fat, 0 g Sat Fat, 58 mg Chol, 115 mg Sod, 5 g Carb, 0 g Fib, 21 g Prot, 19 mg Calc.
PointsPlus value: 3.

Duck breasts are now available at many supermarkets, however, they are very likely to be frozen. Be sure they are solidly frozen and haven't begun to thaw. If you're lucky enough to find them fresh, store them in the refrigerator in their original packaging and cook them within two days.

---

duck stir-fry with sugar snap peas

SERVES 4

2/3 cup reduced-sodium chicken broth
1/4 cup hoisin sauce
2 tablespoons reduced-sodium soy sauce
3 teaspoons cornstarch
4 teaspoons Asian (dark) sesame oil
1 pound skinless boneless duck breast halves, cut into thin strips
1 small red onion, thinly sliced
1 tablespoon grated peeled fresh ginger
1/2 pound sugar snap peas, trimmed
1 small yellow bell pepper, thinly sliced
1 cup cherry tomatoes, halved
1/4 cup thinly sliced fresh basil

Stir-frying's reputation as a healthy cooking technique is well deserved: Using high heat while constantly keeping ingredients in motion requires little added fat, and it also helps vegetables retain their nutrients. A wok, of course, is the classic vessel for stir-frying, but a large heavy skillet will do fine, as well.

1 Whisk together the broth, hoisin sauce, soy sauce, and cornstarch in a small bowl until smooth; set aside.

2 Heat a large skillet or wok over medium-high heat until hot. Swirl in 2 teaspoons of the oil, then add the duck and stir-fry until browned and cooked through, about 4 minutes. Transfer the duck to a plate and set aside.

3 Return the skillet to the heat. Swirl in the remaining 2 teaspoons oil, then add the onion and ginger and stir-fry until fragrant, about 30 seconds. Add the sugar snap peas and pepper; stir-fry until crisp-tender, about 3 minutes. Add the tomatoes and stir-fry 1 minute. Return the duck along with the broth mixture to the skillet. Cook, stirring constantly, until the mixture bubbles and thickens, about 1 minute longer. Remove from the heat and stir in the basil.

PER SERVING (1 cup): 245 Cal, 6 g Total Fat, 1 g Sat Fat, 67 mg Chol, 667 mg Sod, 19 g Carb, 3 g Fib, 27 g Prot, 60 mg Calc.
PointsPlus value: 6.

baked halibut with lemon and capers

SERVES 4

4 (¼-pound) halibut fillets
¼ cup fresh lemon juice
4 teaspoons olive oil
2 tablespoons plain dried bread crumbs
2 tablespoons capers, drained
¼ teaspoon salt
Freshly ground pepper
½ cup minced flat-leaf parsley
4 lemon wedges

Recreate the pleasures of a time-honored way to cook fish: baking it with a crust of flavorful bread crumbs. Try our caper and savory herbed bread crumb topping. Use the freshest fish you can find; if halibut isn't available, flounder, sole, catfish, and cod are also good choices.

1 Preheat the oven to 350°F. Spray a 9 × 13-inch baking dish with nonstick spray.

2 Place the fillets skin-side down in the baking dish; sprinkle them with the lemon juice. Brush each fillet with the oil, then sprinkle with the bread crumbs, capers, salt, and pepper.

3 Bake until the fish flakes easily when tested with a fork, 15– 20 minutes, depending on the thickness of the fish. Spoon any pan juices over the fish and sprinkle with the parsley. Serve at once, with the lemon wedges.

PER SERVING (1 fillet): 168 Cal, 6 g Total Fat, 1 g Sat Fat, 60 mg Chol, 388 mg Sod, 5 g Carb, 1 g Fib, 22 g Prot, 40 mg Calc.
PointsPlus value: 4.

Wondering how to tell if fish fillets are fresh? Look first for a slight sheen on the flesh that indicates that it is moist and has been properly stored. If skin is attached, it should look flexible and moist, not dried out. Finally, give the fish a sniff; it should have a pleasant, ocean-like aroma.

---

moroccan swordfish with couscous

SERVES 4

- 4 teaspoons olive oil
- 1 onion, chopped
- 1 green bell pepper, chopped
- 4 (5-ounce) swordfish steaks
- 1 (14-ounce) can diced tomatoes
- 1 cup fish broth or bottled clam juice
- Juice of 1 lemon
- ½ cup chopped flat-leaf parsley
- 1 teaspoon ground cumin
- 1 garlic clove, chopped
- ½ teaspoon turmeric
- ¼ teaspoon salt
- Freshly ground black pepper
- 1 cup couscous
- ¼ cup dry white wine or reduced-sodium chicken broth

Swordfish is a very firm-fleshed white fish with a mild flavor. Its partner in this dish, couscous, is a staple of North African and Middle Eastern cuisines. A pasta rather than a grain, it's made of tiny balls of semolina dough, which are steamed and then dried. It can be found in most supermarkets and cooks in just a few minutes.

1 Heat a large nonstick skillet. Swirl in 2 teaspoons of the oil, then add the onion and green pepper. Sauté until wilted, about 5 minutes. Transfer to a heatproof plate and keep warm.

2 Return the skillet to the heat; swirl in the remaining 2 teaspoons oil, then add the swordfish. Cook, turning once, until lightly browned on each side. Place the onion-pepper mixture on top of the fish in the skillet; add the tomatoes, broth, lemon juice, parsley, cumin, garlic, turmeric, salt, and pepper. Stir gently, then cover and cook, stirring the vegetables and turning the fish occasionally, until the fish flakes when tested with a fork, about 12 minutes. Transfer the fish and vegetables to a warmed platter; keep warm.

3 Meanwhile, cook the couscous according to package directions.

4 Add the wine or broth to the remaining liquid in the skillet; cook over high heat, stirring, until thickened and reduced by half. Spoon over the fish and serve with the couscous.

PER SERVING (1 steak with 1 cup couscous and ½ cup sauce): 420 Cal, 12 g Total Fat, 3 g Sat Fat, 76 mg Chol, 840 mg Sod, 45 g Carb, 5 g Fib, 32 g Prot, 95 mg Calc.
PointsPlus value: 11.

cajun catfish

SERVES 4

¼ cup all-purpose flour
¼ cup chopped flat-leaf parsley
2 teaspoons ground cumin
1 teaspoon dried oregano
1 teaspoon dried thyme
½ teaspoon cayenne
¼ teaspoon salt
¼ cup fat-free egg substitute
4 (6-ounce) catfish fillets
4 teaspoons vegetable oil
Chopped flat-leaf
parsley (optional)

No wonder we all fell in love with Cajun cuisine in the eighties. This hybrid of French and Southern culinary influences makes great use of crawfish, chicken, pork, and seasonal game. It also often includes filé powder (the powdered leaves of the sassafras tree), parsley, bay leaves, cayenne, black pepper, and a variety of hot peppers. This recipe evokes those flavors.

1 Combine the flour, parsley, cumin, oregano, thyme, cayenne, and salt on a sheet of wax paper. Place the egg substitute in a shallow dish.

2 Dip the fish first in the egg substitute, then coat lightly with the flour mixture and transfer to a plate. (Discard any leftover egg or flour mixture.) Cover the fish and refrigerate for 30 minutes.

3 Heat a large nonstick skillet over medium heat. Swirl in the oil, then add the fish. Cook, turning once, until it is golden brown and flakes easily when tested with a fork, about 10 minutes. Sprinkle with the additional chopped parsley, if using, and serve at once.

PER SERVING (1 fillet): 261 Cal, 7 g Total Fat, 1 g Sat Fat, 104 mg Chol, 330 mg Sod, 7 g Carb, 1 g Fib, 39 g Prot, 55 mg Calc.
PointsPlus value: 6.

How long will the fish take to cook? Here's a good rule of thumb: Lay the fish flat and measure it at its thickest point. Count on approximately 10 minutes of cooking time for each inch of thickness.

Cajun Catfish and Sweet Potato Fritters, page 274

blackened tilapia with remoulade

SERVES 4

6 tablespoons reduced-fat mayonnaise
½ small onion, finely chopped
2 tablespoons chopped parsley
1 tablespoon fresh lemon juice
2 teaspoons drained capers, chopped
1 teaspoon Dijon mustard
½ teaspoon sugar
1 tablespoon Cajun seasoning mix
2 teaspoons paprika
2 teaspoons canola oil
4 (6-ounce) tilapia fillets

The eighties saw the arrival of Cajun cuisine on a national level. Paul Prudhomme, one of New Orleans's most famous chefs, brought the notion of blackening into our homes with his frequent television appearances.

1 To prepare the remoulade (a French cousin of tartar sauce), combine the mayonnaise, onion, parsley, lemon juice, capers, mustard, and sugar in a medium bowl; blend well and set aside.

2 Combine the Cajun seasoning and paprika on a piece of wax paper. Heat a large skillet over medium-high heat until hot; swirl in the oil. Dip one side of each fillet into the seasoning mixture, then immediately place seasoned-side down into the hot skillet. Repeat with the remaining seasoning mixture and fillets. Cook, turning once, until the skin is blackened and the fish flakes easily with a fork, about 4 minutes. Serve immediately with the remoulade.

PER SERVING (1 fillet with 2 tablespoons remoulade): 199 Cal, 11 g Total Fat, 2 g Sat Fat, 81 mg Chol, 815 mg Sod, 4 g Carb, 1 g Fib, 21 g Prot, 43 mg Calc.
PointsPlus value: 5.

If tilapia isn't available in your fish market, any small, firm-fleshed, mild fish, such as catfish or striped bass, will do. The versatile blackening mix is also delicious and cooks beautifully on boneless skinless chicken breast halves, pork chops, or shrimp.

salmon en papillote

SERVES 4

4 carrots, peeled and cut into matchstick-size pieces
1 fennel bulb, cleaned and very thinly sliced
1 leek, cleaned and thinly sliced
2 medium (5-ounce) potatoes, peeled and cut into matchstick-size pieces
4 (¼-pound) salmon fillets
½ cup hot reduced-sodium vegetable broth
4 tablespoons dry white wine
4 teaspoons olive oil
2 tablespoons chopped dill
1 tablespoon grated peeled fresh ginger
½ teaspoon salt
Freshly ground pepper
4 lemon slices
Dill sprigs (optional)

The classic French term for baking a dish in parchment or foil is en papillote. Here we use salmon, a rich source of heart-healthy omega-3 fatty acids. Serve this dinner-in-an-envelope with Asparagus en Papillote [page 248], and you've got yourself a virtually pot-and-pan-free dinner.

1 Preheat the oven to 425°F.

2 Combine the carrots, fennel, leek, and potatoes in a steamer basket; set in a saucepan over 1 inch of boiling water. Cover tightly and steam until slightly wilted but still crunchy, 2 minutes.

3 Tear off 4 (12-inch) squares of foil. Divide the vegetable mixture in half, then evenly divide one-half among the foil squares, placing the vegetables in the center of each square. Top with the salmon, then with another layer of the remaining vegetables. Spoon 2 tablespoons of the hot broth over each salmon-vegetable stack, then drizzle each with a tablespoon of wine and a teaspoon of oil. Sprinkle with the dill, ginger, salt, and pepper, then top with a lemon slice.

4 Fold the foil into packets, making a tight seal. Place the packets on a baking sheet and bake until the salmon is just opaque in the center, about 15 minutes (watch for escaping steam as you open the foil to check). Place each packet on a serving plate. Standing back to avoid the steam, cut each packet open slightly in the center. Garnish with the dill sprigs, if using, and serve at once.

PER SERVING (1 fillet with 1 cup vegetables): 343 Cal, 11 g Total Fat, 3 g Sat Fat, 75 mg Chol, 499 mg Sod, 32 g Carb, 6 g Fib, 27 g Prot, 87 mg Calc.
PointsPlus value: 9.

oven-fried fish and chips

SERVES 4

- 2 large (8 ounce) russet potatoes, scrubbed
- 1 teaspoon salt
- ¼ + ⅛ teaspoon ground pepper
- ⅓ cup panko
- ¼ cup cornmeal
- 2 large egg whites
- 1 tablespoon Dijon mustard
- 2 (8-ounce) tilapia or catfish fillets, each cut into 4 pieces

There's nothing more British than a piping hot fish fillet surrounded by crisp fries. We've done away with the deep-frying to make the dish healthier and easier to recreate at home. Our version uses panko and cornmeal in the crust for superb oven browning.

1 Preheat the oven to 475°F.

2 Cut each potato lengthwise into eight wedges. Place on a medium rimmed baking sheet; spray lightly with nonstick spray. Sprinkle with ½ teaspoon of the salt and ¼ teaspoon of the pepper, and toss to coat. Arrange the potatoes in a single flat layer and bake, without turning, until the bottoms are deep golden and crisp, about 15 minutes. Turn the potatoes to the opposite cut side and bake until crisp, 10–15 minutes longer.

3 Meanwhile, to prepare the fish, spray another medium rimmed baking sheet with nonstick spray.

4 Combine the panko and cornmeal in a food processor and pulse until finely ground. Spread the mixture on a piece of wax paper. Whisk together the egg whites and mustard in a shallow bowl.

5 Sprinkle the fish with the remaining ½ teaspoon salt and the remaining ⅛ teaspoon pepper. Dip each piece into the egg white mixture, then into the panko mixture, pressing to adhere. (Discard any leftover panko or egg mixture.) Place the fish on the baking sheet and bake until the fish is golden brown and flakes easily when tested with a fork, 6–8 minutes.

PER SERVING (2 pieces fish with 4 potato wedges): 235 Cal, 4 g Total Fat, 2 g Sat Fat, 50 mg Chol, 847 mg Sod, 31 g Carb, 3 g Fib, 19 g Prot, 50 mg Calc.
PointsPlus value: 6.

The Japanese-style bread crumbs known as panko have become so popular in the last few years that you'll now find them on the shelves of most supermarkets. Panko features large, airy flakes that cook up light and crisp, making them perfect for dishes like this.

Oven-Fried Fish and Chips

Fish Tacos with Chipotle Cream

fish tacos with chipotle cream

SERVES 4

½ cup light sour cream
1 teaspoon minced chipotles en adobo
½ teaspoon chili powder
½ teaspoon salt
½ teaspoon black pepper
1 pound firm-fleshed skinless cod or halibut fillets, cut into 1-inch pieces
8 (6-inch) corn tortillas, warmed
½ cup thinly sliced green or red cabbage or a combination

They may sound Mexican, but almost everyone agrees that the fish taco has its origins in the surf towns of Southern California. Traditionally, the fish was battered and fried, but today beachside stands and restaurants are just as likely to grill it. Our recipe calls for broiling the fish so that the dish comes together quickly and easily year-round.

1 Spray a broiler rack with nonstick spray; preheat the broiler.

2 Stir together the sour cream and chipotles in a small bowl. Set aside.

3 Sprinkle the fish with the chili powder, salt, and pepper. Spray lightly with olive oil nonstick spray and place on the broiler rack. Broil 5 inches from the heat until the fish flakes easily when tested with a fork, 3–5 minutes. Divide the fish among the tortillas, and top with the sour cream mixture and cabbage.

PER SERVING (2 tacos): 231 Cal, 8 g Total Fat, 3 g Sat Fat, 61 mg Chol, 441 mg Sod, 24 g Carb, 3 g Fib, 17 g Prot, 100 mg Calc.
PointsPlus value: 6.

You'll find small cans of smoky chipotle en adobo in the Mexican section of most grocery stores. To store what you'll have leftover, remove it from the can and transfer it to an airtight container. It will keep for several weeks refrigerated or up to a year frozen.

soy-sesame grilled tuna

SERVES 4

- 2 tablespoons reduced-sodium soy sauce
- 2 tablespoons fresh lemon juice
- 2 tablespoons dry white wine or reduced-sodium vegetable broth
- 2 teaspoons sesame oil
- 2 garlic cloves, minced
- Freshly ground pepper
- 4 (6-ounce) tuna steaks, 1½ inches thick

In the Asian food–obsessed nineties, this flavorful dish would have been right at home on any elegant restaurant menu. It's simple—and impressive—to make at home too. If you prefer your tuna medium or rare, just reduce the grilling time accordingly.

1 Combine the soy sauce, lemon juice, wine or broth, oil, garlic, and 2 grindings of the pepper in a large zip-close plastic bag; add the tuna. Squeeze out the air and seal the bag; turn to coat the tuna. Refrigerate, turning the bag once or twice, 30 minutes. Remove the tuna from the marinade; discard the marinade.

2 Spray the grill rack with nonstick spray; prepare the grill.

3 Grill the tuna 5 inches from the heat, turning once, until the outside is golden and the center is barely pink, about 13 minutes.

PER SERVING (1 steak): 225 Cal, 9 g Total Fat, 3 g Sat Fat, 101 mg Chol, 157 mg Sod, 0 g Carb, 0 g Fib, 33 g Prot, 19 mg Calc.
PointsPlus value: 5.

Add some extra flavor by tossing a handful of soaked fruitwoods, mesquite, or whole herb sprigs on the fire just before grilling the fish.

crab with homemade cocktail sauce

SERVES 4

20 Min or Less

- ½ cup ketchup-based chili sauce
- 4 teaspoons prepared horseradish, drained
- 5 teaspoons fresh lemon juice
- 12 ounces jumbo-lump crabmeat, picked over
- 1 celery stalk, finely chopped
- ½ small red onion, finely chopped
- 1 tablespoon chopped fresh parsley

For those who believe that shrimp cocktail is the highlight of retro cuisine, we present an equally heavenly version, made with sweet crabmeat. For the best appearance, lump or jumbo-lump crabmeat is preferable to pasteurized canned or frozen crabmeat; look for it in fish markets or better supermarkets. Serve the dish plain or with water crackers.

1 To prepare the cocktail sauce, combine the chili sauce, horseradish, and 3 teaspoons of the lemon juice in a small bowl.

2 Combine the crabmeat, celery, onion, the remaining 2 teaspoons lemon juice, and the parsley in a medium bowl; mix gently. Serve chilled with the cocktail sauce.

PER SERVING (½ cup with 2 tablespoons sauce): 126 Cal, 2 g Total Fat, 0 g Sat Fat, 85 mg Chol, 609 mg Sod, 10 g Carb, 1 g Fib, 18 g Prot, 105 mg Calc.
PointsPlus value: 3.

For an elegant presentation, spoon each serving of the crabmeat into a Boston or Bibb lettuce leaf or into the bottom of a small martini glass.

crab cakes with tartar sauce

SERVES 4

½ cup + ⅓ cup reduced-fat mayonnaise
2 tablespoons chopped parsley
1½ tablespoons pickle relish
2 teaspoons drained capers
1 large egg, lightly beaten
2 teaspoons Dijon mustard
1 teaspoon Chesapeake Bay seasoning
½ teaspoon Worcestershire sauce
1 pound fresh, canned, or thawed frozen lump crabmeat, picked over

These wonderful cakes are all about crab. We've made them without any bread-crumb filler so each bite is pure seafood delight. Tartar sauce a taboo, you say? Not today, we say. Enjoy!

1 Preheat oven to 400°F. Spray a baking sheet with nonstick spray.

2 To prepare the tartar sauce, combine ½ cup of the mayonnaise, the parsley, relish, and capers in a small bowl. Cover and refrigerate until ready to use.

3 Combine the remaining ⅓ cup mayonnaise, the egg, mustard, Chesapeake Bay seasoning, and Worcestershire sauce in a large bowl; mix well. Gently fold in the crabmeat until well combined. Cover and refrigerate 30 minutes.

4 Divide the crab mixture into 8 portions, and shape each into a ½-inch-thick patty. Spray a large nonstick skillet with nonstick spray and set over medium heat. Add 4 of the crab cakes and cook, turning once, until light golden, 4 minutes. Transfer to the baking sheet and repeat with the remaining crab cakes. Bake until the crab cakes are heated through, about 5 minutes. Serve with the tartar sauce.

PER SERVING (2 cakes with 3 tablespoons sauce): 294 Cal, 19 g Total Fat, 3 g Sat Fat, 177 mg Chol, 995 mg Sod, 7 g Carb, 0 g Fib, 22 g Prot, 117 mg Calc.
PointsPlus value: 8.

mussels in white wine with garlic

SERVES 4

- 4 pounds mussels
- 2 teaspoons olive oil
- 1 medium shallot, chopped
- 3 large garlic cloves, minced
- ¼ cup dry white wine or reduced-sodium vegetable broth
- 2 tablespoons chopped thyme
- 4 (1-ounce) slices French or Italian bread, toasted

This is one of those timeless dishes that always seems special (even though mussels remain one of the best bargains in the fish market). In our version, we've doubled the satisfaction: After you've polished off your last mussel, there's still a delicious piece of toasted bread soaked with all that wonderful broth in the bottom of your dish to enjoy.

1 Scrub the mussels well with a vegetable brush under cold running water. Pull off the hairy beards that may be attached to some of the mussel shells; if it's difficult, use a small knife. Place the mussels in a large pot of cold water; let them soak a few minutes to release any residual grit, then drain. Repeat for several changes of water, until no sand falls to the bottom of the pot.

2 Heat a large nonstick saucepan. Swirl in the oil, then add the shallot. Sauté until golden, 3 minutes. Add the garlic and sauté until just fragrant. Add the mussels, wine or broth, and thyme; cook, covered, shaking the pan occasionally, until the mussels open, about 5 minutes. Discard any that don't open.

3 Place a slice of the bread into each of 4 large soup bowls. Ladle the mussels with their shells and broth into the bowls and serve at once.

PER SERVING (about 30 mussels with 1 slice bread and ¼ cup broth): 265 Cal, 5 g Total Fat, 1 g Sat Fat, 51 mg Chol, 263 mg Sod, 25 g Carb, 1 g Fib, 29 g Prot, 112 mg Calc.
PointsPlus value: 7.

If they're available at your fish market, farm-raised mussels are a more convenient choice for this dish. They tend to be cleaner and rarely have any beards, so they save you lots of prep time.

---

tabbouleh niçoise

SERVES 4

3 cups boiling water
1 cup bulgur
1 pound tuna steaks
1 teaspoon salt
½ teaspoon coarsely ground pepper
½ red onion, thinly sliced
2 tablespoons red-wine vinegar
1 tablespoon extra-virgin olive oil
¼ teaspoon sugar
1 cup thinly sliced romaine lettuce
1 cup halved grape or cherry tomatoes
⅓ cup slivered basil leaves
8 pitted kalamata olives, halved

It's an old Weight Watchers trick to find substitutes for potatoes, which were once a limited treat on the program. Here, we've used bulgur—steamed and dried cracked wheat—as a substitute for the boiled potatoes traditionally served in a Niçoise salad. The result? Chewier texture, nuttier flavor, and a lot more fiber and magnesium, to boot.

1 Pour the boiling water over the bulgur in a large heatproof bowl; cover and let stand 30 minutes. Drain well.

2 Meanwhile, sprinkle both sides of the tuna with ½ teaspoon of the salt and the pepper. Spray a skillet with nonstick spray and heat over high heat. Add the tuna and sear 1 minute per side for a red center, 2 minutes per side for medium. Cool and thinly slice.

3 Combine the onion, vinegar, oil, the remaining ½ teaspoon of the salt, and the sugar in a large bowl. Add the drained bulgur, the lettuce, tomatoes, basil, and olives; toss to coat evenly. Arrange the salad on a platter and top with the tuna slices, fanned out into an attractive pattern.

PER SERVING (1¼ cups salad with about 3 ounces tuna):
343 Cal, 10 g Total Fat, 2 g Sat Fat, 43 mg Chol, 708 mg Sod, 32 g Carb, 8 g Fib, 32 g Prot, 46 mg Calc.
PointsPlus value: 8.

Tabbouleh Niçoise

paella valenciana

SERVES 6

16 littleneck clams
1 tablespoon extra-virgin olive oil
8 ounces skinless boneless chicken thighs, trimmed of visible fat and cut into 1-inch chunks
2 medium red bell peppers, chopped
1 medium yellow onion, chopped
4 ounces turkey kielbasa, sliced ¼ inch thick
4 garlic cloves, chopped
½ teaspoon saffron threads, crushed
1 cup reduced-sodium chicken broth
¾ cup long-grain white rice
½ cup frozen peas
½ pound large shrimp, peeled and deveined
1 (15-ounce) can quartered artichoke hearts, drained

Paella is arguably Spain's most beloved dish—and in the sixties it was the ultimate dinner-party entrée. Today, it's easier to find its ingredients, but the dish hasn't lost any of its glamour. Our streamlined version is still perfect for serving to company or for a Sunday family dinner.

1 Scrub the clams well with a vegetable brush under cold running water. Place them in a large pot of cold water; let them soak a few minutes to release any residual grit, then drain. Repeat for several changes of water until no sand falls to the bottom of the pot.

2 Heat a large skillet over medium-high heat. Swirl in the oil, then add the chicken, peppers, onion, kielbasa, garlic, and saffron. Cook, stirring occasionally, until the vegetables begin to soften, 2–3 minutes. Add the broth, rice, and peas; bring to a boil. Reduce the heat to medium-low, cover, and simmer 15 minutes.

3 Add the clams, shrimp, and artichoke hearts to the skillet; cover and cook until the clams open and the shrimp are pink and opaque, about 10 minutes longer. Discard any clams that do not open. Serve at once.

PER SERVING (1½ cups): 286 Cal, 6 g Total Fat, 1 g Sat Fat, 80 mg Chol, 491 mg Sod, 33 g Carb, 5 g Fib, 25 g Prot, 76 mg Calc.
PointsPlus value: 7.

Saffron, the key flavoring and coloring element of this dish, is the world's most expensive spice. Luckily, a little goes a long way in imparting its distinctive flavor to the dish. Look for saffron threads (not the inferior powdered form) in gourmet stores and better supermarkets.

spicy grilled shrimp and scallops

SERVES 4

20 Min or Less

4 teaspoons olive oil
2 teaspoons fresh lemon juice
2 garlic cloves, minced
½ teaspoon paprika
½ teaspoon kosher salt
¼ teaspoon cayenne
½ pound medium shrimp, peeled and deveined
½ pound bay scallops, rinsed and patted dry with paper towels
4 lemon wedges

Served hot or at room temperature, as an hors d'oeuvre, appetizer, or entrée, this fare from the deep blue is a real crowd pleaser. Adjust the cayenne and paprika up or down ¼ teaspoon, depending on how hot or mild you like your food.

1 Spray the broiler rack with nonstick spray; preheat the broiler.

2 Combine the oil, lemon juice, garlic, paprika, salt, and cayenne in a medium bowl. Toss with the shrimp and scallops, then place them on the broiler rack. Broil until golden brown on both sides, turning once, 6–8 minutes. Serve at once with the lemon wedges.

PER SERVING (4 ounces): 116 Cal, 5 g Total Fat, 1 g Sat Fat, 65 mg Chol, 349 mg Sod, 3 g Carb, 1 g Fib, 14 g Prot, 59 mg Calc.
PointsPlus value: 3.

Bay scallops are small (about ½- to ¾-inch diameter) and have a wonderfully sweet flavor. They're pricey but worth the splurge. The larger, somewhat less tender sea scallops can be used if you prefer, but cut them in half. Pass up tiny calico scallops, which can become rubbery during cooking.

Prosciutto-Wrapped Scallops and
Asparagus en Papillote, page 248

prosciutto-wrapped scallops

SERVES 4

1 cup orange juice
¼ cup balsamic vinegar
1 teaspoon sugar
1 teaspoon grated orange zest
5 paper-thin proscuitto slices (about 2½ ounces)
1 pound jumbo sea scallops (about 20)

Prosciutto is ham that has been salt-cured and air-dried rather than smoked, producing an incomparably sweet-tasting meat. Pairing it with sweet scallops is a match made in heaven. You don't have to buy the priciest, best prosciutto (which hails from Parma, Italy) for this recipe; domestic prosciutto is fine, as long as it is sliced paper-thin.

1 Preheat oven to 450°F. Spray a baking sheet with nonstick spray.

2 Combine the juice, vinegar, and sugar in a medium saucepan. Bring to a boil over high heat; continue boiling until syrupy, about 8 minutes. Remove from the heat and stir in the zest.

3 Place one slice of proscuitto on a cutting board; slice into 4 (¾ × 5-inch) strips. Repeat with the remaining proscuitto. Wrap each scallop in a proscuitto strip and place it, seam-side down, on the baking sheet. Bake the scallops 5 minutes; brush them with the orange-balsamic syrup and roast until cooked through, 2–3 minutes more. Brush the scallops with any remaining syrup just before serving.

PER SERVING (5 scallops): 148 Cal, 2 g Total Fat, 1 g Sat Fat, 33 mg Chol, 425 mg Sod, 11 g Carb, 0 g Fib, 21 g Prot, 94 mg Calc.
PointsPlus value: 4.

the modern pantry

A well-stocked pantry can be one of your strongest allies in losing weight. Here's a list of the best staples available in supermarkets everywhere that will go a long way in helping you get healthful meals on the table quickly and easily. And remember: Be sure to keep plenty of your favorite fresh fruits and vegetables on hand to round out your meals and snacks.

on your shelves

Canned seafood (tuna, salmon, clams)
No-salt-added canned beans (assorted varieties)
Quick-cooking and regular brown rice, white rice, Arborio rice, Wehani rice
Assorted whole grains (quinoa, quick-cooking barley, bulgur, and grits)
Dried pastas (assorted varieties)
Whole wheat couscous
Old-fashioned and quick-cooking oats
Whole wheat panko bread crumbs
Canned reduced-sodium chicken, beef, and vegetable broths; reduced-fat cream of mushroom soup
Canned whole tomatoes, diced tomatoes, tomato paste, and tomato sauce
Canola oil, olive oil, sesame oil, and nonstick spray
Red-wine, white-wine, cider, and balsamic vinegars
Brine-cured olives and capers
Bottled roasted red bell peppers (not packed in oil)
Fat-free and reduced-calorie salad dressings
Fat-free salsa and hot pepper sauce
Dijon mustard
Prepared horseradish
Ketchup
Fat-free mayonnaise
Soy, hoisin, and fish sauces
Light (reduced-fat) coconut milk
No-sugar-added fruit preserves
Onions, garlic, and shallots
Peanut butter
Low-fat baked tortilla chips
Salt, black pepper, and all common dried herbs (such as basil, oregano, and thyme) and spices (such as cinnamon, nutmeg, and cumin)

in your freezer

Lean ground beef (7% fat or less)
Lean beef, pork, and lamb (assorted cuts)
Chicken (assorted cuts)
Skinless turkey breast (cuts and ground)
Sausage (turkey and chicken)
Canadian bacon
Fish and shellfish (assorted varieties)
Reduced-calorie sandwich bread
Whole wheat pitas
Tortillas and wraps (assorted varieties)
Reduced-calorie hot dog and hamburger buns
Frozen vegetables (assorted varieties)
Frozen unsweetened berries (assorted varieties)

in your refrigerator

Lean, low-sodium sandwich meats
Fat-free and low-fat cheeses (assorted varieties, hard and soft)
Goat cheese
Parmesan cheese
Tofu and tempeh
Fresh fruits and vegetables (assorted varieties)
Fresh herbs (assorted varieties)
Large eggs
Fat-free egg substitute
Fat-free milk
Unsalted butter
Fat-free half-and-half
Fat-free sour cream
Plain fat-free yogurt (Greek and regular)
Fresh ginger

baking essentials

All-purpose flour
Whole wheat flour
Cornmeal
Granulated, brown, and confectioners' sugars
Honey, maple syrup, and molasses
Unsweetened cocoa powder
Baking soda and baking powder
Dried fruits and nuts (assorted varieties)
Vanilla extract

cornmeal-crusted shrimp with grits and greens

SERVES 4

⅓ cup cornmeal
½ teaspoon paprika
¼ teaspoon salt
½ teaspoon black pepper
2 large egg whites, lightly beaten
1 pound large shrimp, peeled and deveined
1 cup reduced-sodium chicken broth
1 cup fat-free milk
½ cup quick-cooking grits
1 medium sweet onion, thinly sliced
1 pound kale or collard greens, thinly sliced
½ teaspoon hot sauce, optional

Shrimp and creamy hominy grits is a traditional breakfast of Southern fishermen during the shrimping season. Today the dish has gone upscale and appears as breakfast, lunch, or dinner in regional cookbooks and on restaurant menus across the country. We've added wilted greens to this recipe for extra Southern charm.

1 Preheat the oven to 475°F. Line a baking sheet with foil and spray the foil with nonstick spray.

2 Combine the cornmeal, paprika, ⅛ teaspoon of the salt, and ¼ teaspoon of the pepper on a piece of wax paper. Place the egg whites in a shallow bowl. Dip the shrimp into the egg whites, then into the cornmeal mixture. Arrange in a single layer on the baking sheet and spray lightly with nonstick spray. Bake until the shrimp are just opaque in the center, 8–10 minutes.

3 Meanwhile, bring the broth and milk to a boil in a medium saucepan over medium-high heat. Gradually stir in the grits and cook, stirring frequently, until the grits are thick and smooth, about 5 minutes.

4 Spray a large nonstick skillet with olive oil nonstick spray and set over medium heat. Add the onion and cook, stirring frequently, until softened, 5 minutes. Stir in the kale and the remaining ⅛ teaspoon salt, the remaining ¼ teaspoon pepper, and hot sauce, if using. Cook, stirring occasionally, until the greens are crisp-tender, 5 minutes. Serve with the shrimp and grits.

PER SERVING (5 shrimp, ½ cup kale, and ⅓ cup grits): 288 Cal, 2 g Total Fat, 0 g Sat Fat, 117 mg Chol, 903 mg Sod, 44 g Carb, 4 g Fib, 24 g Prot, 293 mg Calc.
PointsPlus value: 7.

shrimp scampi with fresh linguine

SERVES 4

1 (9-ounce) package refrigerated fresh linguine
4 teaspoons butter
1¼ pounds medium shrimp, peeled and deveined
¼ teaspoon black pepper
6 garlic cloves, minced
½ cup reduced-sodium chicken broth
½ cup dry white wine
¼ cup fresh lemon juice
¼ cup finely chopped fresh parsley

A recipe for this iconic shrimp dish appeared in the very first Weight Watchers cookbook in 1966. Not surprisingly, that recipe contained no butter or wine. Our recipe is closer (in ingredients) to the original dish, but uses only a fraction of the fat.

1 Cook the linguine according to package directions.

2 Meanwhile, melt 2 teaspoons of the butter in a large skillet over medium-high heat. Sprinkle the shrimp with ⅛ teaspoon of the pepper. Add the shrimp to the skillet and cook until just opaque in the center, about 3 minutes. Add the garlic and cook, stirring, until fragrant, 30 seconds. With a slotted spoon, transfer the shrimp to a platter and keep warm.

3 Add the broth, wine, and lemon juice to the skillet. Bring to a boil; boil until the sauce is reduced by half, about 5 minutes. Return the shrimp to the skillet, and stir in the parsley, the remaining 2 teaspoons butter, and the remaining ⅛ teaspoon pepper. Serve the shrimp mixture over the pasta.

PER SERVING (scant 1 cup pasta, about 8 shrimp, and 3 tablespoons sauce): 353 Cal, 6 g Total Fat, 3 g Sat Fat, 154 mg Chol, 943 mg Sod, 46 g Carb, 3 g Fib, 24 g Prot, 93 mg Calc.
PointsPlus value: 9.

Fresh pasta cooks up with a soft, luscious texture that is noticeably different from that of dried pasta, but if you'd prefer to use dried linguine in this recipe you can. Just remember to measure the pasta after cooking and use only a scant 1 cup for each serving.

salmon cakes with red pepper sauce

SERVES 4

salmon cakes

1 (14½-ounce) can red sockeye salmon, drained, skin and larger bones discarded
½ cup plain dried bread crumbs
2 scallions, thinly sliced
¼ cup plain fat-free Greek yogurt
1 large egg, lightly beaten
2 tablespoons chopped fresh flat-leaf parsley
1 teaspoon grated lemon zest
¼ teaspoon black pepper
2 teaspoons olive oil

sauce

3 tablespoons plain fat-free Greek yogurt
1 (5-ounce) jar roasted red bell peppers
2 teaspoons fresh lemon juice
⅛ teaspoon salt
Pinch black pepper

Keeping canned fish such as salmon and tuna on hand makes it easy and economical to work heart-healthy seafood meals into your eating, something that the Weight Watchers plan has championed since its founding.

1 To prepare the salmon cakes, combine the salmon, bread crumbs, scallions, yogurt, egg, parsley, lemon zest, and pepper in a medium bowl. Stir, breaking up any large chunks of salmon, until just combined. Form the mixture into 4 cakes.

2 Heat a large nonstick skillet over medium heat. Swirl in the oil, then add the cakes and cook until browned and heated through, 3–4 minutes on each side.

3 To prepare the sauce, combine all the sauce ingredients in a blender; puree. Serve with the salmon cakes.

PER SERVING (1 cake with 2 tablespoons sauce): 259 Cal, 9 g Total Fat, 2 g Sat Fat, 131 mg Chol, 685 mg Sod, 14 g Carb, 1 g Fib, 30 g Prot, 359 mg Calc.
PointsPlus value: 6.

If you'd like, serve these salmon cakes burger-style for a heartier meal. You can place each cooked patty in a 1½-ounce light hamburger bun and increase the per-serving ***PointsPlus*** value by ***2***.

---

tuna noodle casserole

SERVES 6

6 cups extra-wide egg noodles
1 (10 ¾-ounce) can reduced-fat condensed cream of mushroom soup
1 cup low-fat (1%) milk
2 tablespoons unsalted light butter
2 garlic cloves, minced
2 cups sliced white mushrooms (8 ounces)
4 scallions, chopped
1 cup frozen peas
2 teaspoons chopped thyme
2 teaspoons chopped rosemary
2 (5-ounce) cans solid white tuna in water, rinsed, drained, and flaked
¼ cup chopped parsley
1 ounce reduced-fat baked potato chips, lightly crushed (about 1 cup)

One reason this sixties classic is so timeless is its convenience. Designed to use canned and frozen ingredients and pantry staples, it's one of those dishes you can assemble in no time. We've given it a fresher spin, adding fresh herbs and sautéed mushrooms, but kept the beloved potato-chip topping.

1 Preheat the oven to 350°F. Spray a 2-quart baking dish with nonstick spray. Cook the noodles according to package directions; drain and keep warm.

2 Combine the soup and milk in a large bowl; set aside.

3 Melt the butter in a large nonstick skillet over medium-high heat. Add the garlic and sauté until fragrant, 30 seconds. Stir in the mushrooms, scallions, peas, thyme, and rosemary; cook, stirring occasionally, until the mushrooms are softened, about 5 minutes. Stir into the soup mixture. Add the noodles, tuna, and parsley; toss well. Transfer to the baking dish and sprinkle with the potato chips. Bake until bubbly and the top is golden, 30–35 minutes.

PER SERVING (generous 1 cup): 311 Cal, 6 g Total Fat, 2 g Sat Fat, 52 mg Chol, 465 mg Sod, 43 g Carb, 4 g Fib, 21 g Prot, 132 mg Calc.
PointsPlus value: 8.

Steamed baby carrots sprinkled with lemon juice make a colorful, healthful side dish for this all-American casserole.

Tuna Noodle Casserole

california rolls

SERVES 8

2 cups water
1½ cups short-grain rice
3 tablespoons rice vinegar
1 tablespoon sugar
¼ teaspoon salt
8 sheets nori
1 teaspoon prepared wasabi paste
1 Hass avocado, peeled, pitted, and cut into 16 long, thin strips
10 ounces surimi (imitation crabmeat), cut into long, thin strips
2 teaspoons toasted sesame seeds

Most Americans became acquainted with sushi through a Japanese-American creation known as the California roll. With cooked crabmeat (or its cousin, surimi) rather than raw fish in its center, it was a good gateway dish for those timid about raw fish. But even sushi aficionados love these beautiful, flavorful easy-to-make rolls.

1 Combine the water and rice in a medium saucepan. Bring to a boil, reduce the heat to medium-low, and simmer, covered, until the water evaporates, about 20 minutes. Remove from the heat and let stand 10 minutes. Meanwhile, combine the vinegar, sugar, and salt in a small bowl. Stir into the rice, tossing gently with a spatula to combine, and let cool 15 minutes.

2 Place a bamboo sushi mat on a work surface so that the slats run horizontally. Put a nori sheet, with a long side facing you, on top of the mat. With moistened hands, spread ½ cup of the vinegar rice onto it, leaving a 1-inch border along the top edge. Spread ⅛ teaspoon of the wasabi paste horizontally across the center of the rice. Arrange 2 avocado slices end to end in a horizontal line over the wasabi, and top with one-eighth of the surimi. Sprinkle with ¼ teaspoon of the sesame seeds. Grasp the edges of the nori and the mat closest to you. Roll the nori evenly and tightly away from you, pressing down slightly with each quarter turn. Seal the roll with a few drops of water on the far edge of the nori, being sure to press the seam closed. Repeat with the remaining rice, wasabi, avocado, surimi, and sesame seeds to make 8 rolls. If not serving immediately, cover the rolls with plastic wrap and refrigerate up to 6 hours.

3 Just before serving, place the rolls on a cutting board. With a serrated knife dipped in hot water, cut each roll crosswise into 6 pieces.

PER SERVING (6 pieces): 212 Cal, 4 g Total Fat, 1 g Sat Fat, 11 mg Chol, 399 mg Sod, 35 g Carb, 3 g Fib, 9 g Prot, 26 mg Calc.
PointsPlus value: 5.

meatless mainstays

satisfying vegetarian entrées

tofu-lentil burgers

SERVES 4

Vegetarian

3 cups water
1 cup brown lentils, picked over, rinsed, and drained
6 ounces extra-firm tofu, cubed
2 scallions, sliced
¼ cup chopped fresh parsley
1 large egg white
1 garlic clove, minced
1 teaspoon grated lemon zest
1 tablespoon fresh lemon juice
¾ teaspoon salt
½ teaspoon dried oregano
¼ teaspoon black pepper
2 whole wheat English muffins, split and toasted
4 tomato slices
4 leaf lettuce leaves

America's love affair with the burger is long-standing, and seems to be on the upswing again, thanks, in part, to a proliferation of new lower-fat varieties: chicken, turkey, bison, salmon, veggie, and more. This unique open-face burger mixes two vegetarian staples—tofu and lentils—in a recipe that's easy and delicious enough to become a household standby.

1 Bring the water and lentils to a boil in a medium saucepan. Reduce the heat and simmer gently until the lentils are tender but still retain their shape, about 25 minutes. Drain.

2 Combine the lentils, tofu, scallions, parsley, egg white, garlic, lemon zest, lemon juice, salt, oregano, and pepper in a food processor; pulse until a thick chunky mixture forms. Shape into 4 patties.

3 Spray a large nonstick skillet with nonstick spray and set over medium heat. Add the patties and cook until browned and firm, about 3 minutes per side. Serve the burgers on the English muffins with the tomato slices and lettuce leaves.

PER SERVING (1 open-face burger): 286 Cal, 5 g Total Fat, 1 g Sat Fat, 0 mg Chol, 589 mg Sod, 43 g Carb, 11 g Fib, 22 g Prot, 231 mg Calc.
PointsPlus value: 7.

When you know you'll need a dinner you can get on the table in just a few minutes, make the patties a day ahead. Place them in a single layer on a tray, cover, and refrigerate. To complete the meal, serve the burgers with Coleslaw, page 253, which you can also make a day ahead.

tempeh-vegetable stir-fry with peanut sauce

SERVES 6

Vegetarian

1 cup reduced-sodium vegetable broth
¼ cup creamy peanut butter
2 tablespoons reduced-sodium soy sauce
1 tablespoon grated peeled fresh ginger
¼ teaspoon crushed red pepper
4 teaspoons canola oil
1 (8-ounce) package tempeh, cut into ¼-inch slices
½ pound green beans, trimmed
1 red bell pepper, cut into thin strips
6 scallions, cut into 2-inch lengths
1 zucchini, halved lengthwise and sliced
¼ cup chopped fresh cilantro
2 tablespoons unsalted dry-roasted peanuts, chopped

Dense, nutty tempeh is made from pressed fermented soybeans, and has a meaty texture as well as a high protein content. You can find it in the refrigerator section in some supermarkets and in natural foods stores.

1 Whisk together the broth, peanut butter, soy sauce, ginger, and crushed red pepper in a small bowl until smooth.

2 Heat a wok or large skillet over medium-high heat until hot. Swirl in 2 teaspoons of the oil, then add the tempeh and stir-fry until lightly browned, about 5 minutes. Transfer to a plate. Return the wok to the heat. Swirl in the remaining 2 teaspoons oil, then add the green beans and bell pepper. Stir-fry until the vegetables are crisp-tender, about 5 minutes.

3 Add the peanut-butter mixture, scallions, and zucchini to the wok; stir-fry until the scallions are softened, about 2 minutes. Return the tempeh to the wok and stir-fry just until heated through, 2 minutes. Remove from the heat and stir in the cilantro. Sprinkle with the peanuts.

PER SERVING (1½ cups): 216 Cal, 14 g Total Fat, 2 g Sat Fat, 0 mg Chol, 311 mg Sod, 14 g Carb, 4 g Fib, 12 g Prot, 81 mg Calc.
PointsPlus value: 6.

vegetarian stuffed cabbage rolls

SERVES 4

Vegetarian

8 large green cabbage leaves
2 teaspoons olive oil
2 celery stalks, chopped
1 onion, chopped
1 carrot, chopped
3 garlic cloves, minced
¾ teaspoon dried thyme
¼ teaspoon black pepper
8 ounces frozen soy crumbles, thawed
1 cup cooked brown rice
1 (14½-ounce) can diced tomatoes
1 (8-ounce) can no-salt-added tomato puree

Cabbage is nutrient-dense and wonderfully versatile. This recipe calls for using only the largest outer leaves as wrappers, so you'll have plenty of cabbage left to include in salads, and slaws, and as a topping for sandwiches. Or you can cook it in sautés, soups, and stews as well as boil wedges with corned beef or other meats.

1 Preheat the oven to 400°F. Spray a 9-inch square baking dish with nonstick spray.

2 Bring a large pot of water to a boil. Add the cabbage leaves and return to a boil. Cook until the cabbage is pliable, about 8 minutes. Drain, then rinse the cabbage under cold running water. Transfer to a cutting board. Trim away the thick ribs at the base of the leaves.

3 Meanwhile, to make the filling, heat a medium nonstick skillet over medium heat. Swirl in the oil, then add the celery, onion, and carrot. Cook, stirring, until the vegetables are softened, about 5 minutes. Add the garlic, ½ teaspoon of the thyme, and ⅛ teaspoon of the pepper; cook, stirring, until fragrant, about 30 seconds. Transfer the vegetables to a large bowl. Stir in the soy crumbles and rice.

4 Place about ¼ cup of the filling in the center of each cabbage leaf. Fold the sides of the cabbage leaves over the filling, then roll up to enclose the filling. Place the cabbage rolls, seam side down, in the prepared baking dish.

5 Stir together the diced tomatoes, tomato puree, the remaining ¼ teaspoon thyme, and the remaining ⅛ teaspoon pepper in a small bowl; pour over the cabbage rolls. Cover the baking dish with foil; bake until cabbage is tender, about 1 hour 15 minutes.

PER SERVING (2 cabbage rolls with about ½ cup sauce): 237 Cal, 4 g Total Fat, 1 g Sat Fat, 0 mg Chol, 212 mg Sod, 31 g Carb, 7 g Fib, 23 g Prot, 133 mg Calc.
PointsPlus value: 6.

black bean and soy chili

SERVES 6

Vegetarian

2 teaspoons olive oil
1 large onion, chopped
1 red bell pepper, chopped
1 jalapeño pepper, seeded and minced
3 garlic cloves, minced
1 tablespoon chili powder
2 teaspoons ground cumin
2 teaspoons dried oregano
¼ teaspoon salt
2 (14½-ounce) cans diced tomatoes
1 (12-ounce) package frozen soy crumbles
1 small eggplant, unpeeled, chopped
½ cup water
2 (15½-ounce) cans black beans, rinsed and drained
¼ cup chopped fresh cilantro
6 tablespoons plain fat-free Greek yogurt

Meatless chilis became popular in the sixties and seventies with an increasing interest in vegetarianism. Almost all recipes contained beans, as well as a vegetable-based protein like tempeh, tofu, or TVP (textured vegetable protein). This version calls for beeflike soy crumbles, black beans, and an unusual chili vegetable, eggplant.

1 Heat a large saucepan over medium-high heat until hot. Swirl in the oil, then add the onion, bell pepper, and jalapeño. Cook, stirring, until the vegetables are softened, about 5 minutes. Add the garlic, chili powder, cumin, oregano, and salt; cook, stirring, until fragrant, 30 seconds.

2 Add the tomatoes, soy crumbles, eggplant, and water. Bring to a boil. Reduce the heat and simmer, covered, stirring occasionally, until the vegetables are tender, about 20 minutes. Add the beans and simmer, partially covered, 10 minutes longer. Remove from the heat and stir in the cilantro. Top each serving with a tablespoon of the yogurt.

PER SERVING (1⅓ cups chili with 1 tablespoon yogurt): 311 Cal, 4 g Total Fat, 1 g Sat Fat, 0 mg Chol, 707 mg Sod, 42 g Carb, 16 g Fib, 31 g Prot, 195 mg Calc.
PointsPlus value: 7.

Make a double batch of this chili and freeze it in single-serving containers to pack for lunch. Just zap it in the office microwave for a healthy, filling meal.

Curried Vegetable Stew

curried vegetable stew

SERVES 8

Vegetarian

4 teaspoons vegetable oil
2 teaspoons curry powder
2 onions, chopped
1 tablespoon minced peeled fresh ginger
2 garlic cloves, minced
1 (14-ounce) can diced tomatoes, with juice
1 cup reduced-sodium vegetable broth
1 medium (1¼-pound) eggplant, peeled and chopped
1 medium (8-ounce) zucchini, chopped
1 (10-ounce) box frozen cut green beans
4 carrots, sliced ¼-inch thick
1 (5-ounce) potato, chopped
1 cup hot water
1 (10-ounce) box frozen cauliflower florets
1 (15-ounce) can chickpeas, rinsed and drained
½ teaspoon salt
Freshly ground pepper
¼ cup chopped cilantro

Like some of the most beloved Weight Watchers recipes, this one is a delicious way to enjoy lots of vegetables. Don't be put off by the long list of ingredients; the stew is one of those throw-everything-together-in-a-pot dishes that makes a great family meal, company dish, or addition to a potluck supper. Don't be afraid to add or substitute your favorite veggies.

1 Heat a large nonstick saucepan. Swirl in the oil, then add the curry powder. Cook, stirring constantly, until fragrant, about 30 seconds. Add the onions, ginger, and garlic; sauté until the onions are wilted and the garlic is fragrant, about 2 minutes.

2 Add the tomatoes and broth; simmer over low heat until heated through. Add the eggplant, zucchini, green beans, carrots, potato, and water. Cover and simmer, stirring occasionally, until the vegetables are tender, about 20 minutes. Add the cauliflower, chickpeas, salt, and pepper; simmer, covered, until heated through, about 15 minutes. Sprinkle with the cilantro and serve.

PER SERVING (1¼ cups): 168 Cal, 4 g Total Fat, 1 g Sat Fat, 0 mg Chol, 367 mg Sod, 30 g Carb, 8 g Fib, 6 g Prot, 82 mg Calc.
PointsPlus value: 4.

soyful scalloped potatoes

SERVES 6

Vegetarian

½ pound firm tofu, cut into ½-inch slices
3 teaspoons unsalted butter
1 large sweet onion, sliced into very thin wedges
1 teaspoon minced fresh rosemary, or ½ teaspoon dried
½ teaspoon salt
¼ teaspoon freshly ground pepper
1¾ pounds Yukon Gold potatoes, peeled and cut into ¼-inch slices
½ cup coarsely shredded Gruyère cheese
1¼ cups reduced-sodium vegetable broth

Heart-healthy soy is de rigueur *these days, and here, in the form of tofu, it lends creamy richness to a classic potato dish. Thanks to the sweet, caramelized onions and buttery cheese, even those who say they dislike tofu will never know it's there. Be sure to use imported Swiss Gruyère; its rich flavor goes a long way.*

1 To press some of the moisture out of the tofu, line a baking sheet with a double layer of paper towels. Arrange the tofu in a single layer and then top with another double layer of towels. Cover with another baking sheet and weight with 2 large cans. Let stand 15 minutes, then pat tofu dry with more paper towels.

2 Meanwhile, preheat the oven to 400°F. Spray a 2-quart shallow baking dish with nonstick spray.

3 Melt 2 teaspoons of the butter in a large nonstick skillet over medium heat. Add the onion and cook, stirring occasionally, until tender, 20 minutes. Add the rosemary, salt, and pepper and toss.

4 Arrange half the potatoes in the baking dish, overlapping them slightly. Crumble the pressed tofu on top, then scatter over half of the onions and ¼ cup of the cheese. Repeat to make a second layer of potatoes, onion, and cheese on top of that. Pour in the broth and dot with the remaining 1 teaspoon butter. Cover and bake 45 minutes. Uncover and continue baking until the potatoes are tender and the cheese is melted and slightly golden, about 15 minutes more.

PER SERVING (about ¾ cup): 228 Cal, 8 g Total Fat, 3 g Sat Fat, 13 mg Chol, 330 mg Sod, 28 g Carb, 4 g Fib, 12 g Prot, 183 mg Calc.
PointsPlus value: 6.

Serve a green vegetable alongside the potatoes for a satisfying vegetarian meal. Try Green Beans with Tomato and Oregano, page 259, or Asparagus en Papillote, page 248.

memorable mushroom recipes

Mushrooms were an "unlimited" ingredient in the early days of Weight Watchers. They were utilized in dozens of recipes to add their meaty flavor to members' favorite dishes. These timeless mushroom recipes are just as good today as they were when they were first introduced.

mushroom sandwich spread circa 1970

SERVES 2
***PointsPlus* value: 4 per serving (1 open-face sandwich)**

1 cup cooked sliced mushrooms
¾ cup finely diced green pepper
¼ cup diced pimiento
2 tablespoons light mayonnaise
1 teaspoon chopped fresh chives
Salt and black pepper to taste
2 slices reduced-calorie whole wheat bread, toasted

Combine all the ingredients except the bread in a small bowl; stir to mix well. Top each bread slice evenly with the mushroom mixture.

vegetarian mushroom patties circa 1990

SERVES 6
***PointsPlus* value: 8 per serving (1 patty)**

2½ cups chopped fresh mushrooms
1 cup plus 2 tablespoons seasoned dried bread crumbs
⅔ cup low-fat (1%) cottage cheese
½ cup chopped onion
2 large eggs, lightly beaten
2 ounces shredded mozzarella cheese
2 ounces chopped walnuts or almonds
1 teaspoon reduced-sodium soy sauce
¼ teaspoon garlic powder
Dash salt
Dash black pepper
2 teaspoons vegetable oil

Spray a large baking pan with nonstick spray.

Combine all the ingredients except the oil in a large bowl; stir to mix well. Shape the mixture into 6 patties.

Heat a large nonstick skillet over medium heat. Swirl in the oil. Add the patties and cook, turning once, until lightly browned, 6 minutes. Transfer to the baking pan and bake until firm, about 15 minutes.

mushroom-cheese pâté circa 1980

SERVES 2
***PointsPlus* value: 6 per serving (1 pâté)**

4 cups sliced fresh mushrooms
2 tablespoons sliced scallions
2 teaspoons dry red wine
1 (1-ounce) envelope dry onion soup mix
⅔ cup cottage cheese
3 tablespoons plain dried bread crumbs

Spray 2 (6-ounce) custard cups with nonstick spray. Set aside.

Spray a medium nonstick skillet with nonstick spray and set over medium heat. Add the mushrooms, scallions, wine, and soup mix and cook, stirring often, until the mushrooms are tender and the liquid has evaporated, about 8 minutes. Transfer to a blender and puree.

Add the cottage cheese and bread crumbs to the blender; pulse until combined. Spoon the mixture evenly into the custard cups. Cover and refrigerate at least 2 hours or up to 3 days. To serve, run a knife around the edge of the custard cups and invert the pâté onto plates.

Note: All ***PointsPlus*** values were calculated using the Weight Watchers online recipe builder.

chickpea croquettes with roasted tomato sauce

SERVES 4

Vegetarian

10 medium very ripe plum tomatoes, halved
2 large garlic cloves
½ teaspoon salt
¼ teaspoon freshly ground pepper
3 teaspoons olive oil
1 medium onion, chopped
1 tablespoon sesame seeds
1 teaspoon cumin seeds
1 (15-ounce) can chickpeas, drained and rinsed
½ small jalapeño pepper, seeded and chopped
1 large egg, separated (room temperature)
¼ teaspoon baking powder
1 egg white (room temperature)
3 tablespoons all-purpose flour

Chickpeas are deliciously nutty tasting, high-fiber, and virtually fat-free. Here, we've pureed them into a tasty croquette reminiscent of the Spanish tapas treat known as croquetas.

1 To prepare the sauce, preheat the oven to 450°F. Spray a broiler pan with nonstick spray. Arrange the tomatoes, cut-side up, spray the tops with nonstick spray, and roast until charred on the bottoms, 15 minutes. Puree the tomatoes (with their charred skins), garlic, ¼ teaspoon of the salt, and the pepper in the food processor until smooth.

2 Heat a large nonstick skillet over medium heat. Swirl in 1 teaspoon of the oil, then add the onion. Sauté until lightly browned, about 8 minutes, adding the sesame and cumin seeds in the last minute of cooking time. Transfer to a food processor.

3 Add the chickpeas, jalapeño pepper, the egg yolk, baking powder, and remaining ¼ teaspoon of the salt to the processor. Pulse until a chunky paste forms and transfer to a medium bowl.

4 With an electric mixer on high speed, whip the 2 egg whites in a medium bowl until soft peaks form. Fold half of the whipped whites into the chickpea mixture; sprinkle the flour over the top and fold it in lightly, then add the remaining whipped whites and fold in until just combined.

5 Return the skillet to medium heat; swirl in ½ teaspoon of the oil. Drop 10 tablespoonfuls of the batter into the pan, flattening them slightly to form croquettes. Cook until golden, about 1½ minutes, then turn. Add another ½ teaspoon oil to the pan, swirling pan gently to distribute. Cook until croquettes are golden, 1–1½ minutes more. Transfer to a platter; keep warm; repeat to make 10 more croquettes. Serve immediately, with the sauce.

PER SERVING (5 croquettes with a scant ⅓ cup sauce): 243 Cal, 8 g Total Fat, 1 g Sat Fat, 53 mg Chol, 532 mg Sod, 34 g Carb, 6 g Fib, 11 g Prot, 82 mg Calc.
PointsPlus value: 6.

red bean, spinach, and tomato burritos

SERVES 4

20 Min or Less
Vegetarian

- 2 teaspoons olive oil
- 1 onion, chopped
- 1 jalapeño, seeded and minced
- 2 garlic cloves, minced
- 1 tablespoon chili powder
- 2 teaspoons ground cumin
- 6 cups lightly packed baby spinach, chopped
- 2 plum tomatoes, chopped
- 1 (15½-ounce) can red kidney beans, rinsed and drained
- 4 (8-inch) whole wheat flour tortillas
- ½ cup shredded reduced-fat Monterey Jack cheese

We've published dozens of recipes for burritos over the years, and with good reason: Not only are they a delicious way to combine a number of healthy favorites, including tortillas, protein-packed beans, great vegetables, and low-fat cheese, they're also quick and easy to put together.

1 Heat a large nonstick skillet over medium heat. Swirl in the oil, then add the onion and jalapeño; cook, stirring occasionally, until softened, about 5 minutes. Add the garlic, chili powder, and cumin, and cook, stirring, until fragrant, about 30 seconds. Add the spinach, tomatoes, and beans. Cook, covered, until the spinach is wilted, about 4 minutes. Uncover and cook until the liquid has evaporated, about 2 minutes longer.

2 Place one-fourth of the spinach mixture down the center of each tortilla; sprinkle each with 2 tablespoons of the cheese. Fold the two opposite sides of each tortilla over to enclose the filling.

PER SERVING (1 burrito): 285 Cal, 8 g Total Fat, 3 g Sat Fat, 9 mg Chol, 512 mg Sod, 42 g Carb, 10 g Fib, 16 g Prot, 207 mg Calc.
PointsPlus value: 7.

Serve the burritos with brown rice tossed with thinly sliced scallions and chopped fresh cilantro (⅔ cup cooked brown rice will increase the ***PointsPlus*** value by *3*).

vegetable quesadillas

SERVES 4

Vegetarian

8 (6-inch) flour tortillas
½ teaspoon olive oil
1 medium red onion, thinly sliced
1 large red bell pepper, thinly sliced
1 cup frozen corn kernels
1 teaspoon ground cumin
¾ teaspoon dried oregano
¼ cup chopped cilantro
1 tablespoon fresh lime juice
1½ cups shredded reduced-fat Monterey Jack or cheddar cheese
1⅓ cups salsa
¼ cup reduced-fat sour cream

Once Americans discovered quesadillas in the eighties, there was no turning back. Our version is baked in the oven, making it an extra-easy choice for a weeknight supper. If you'd rather not heat up the oven, prepare the quesadillas one at a time in a nonstick skillet sprayed with nonstick spray.

1 Adjust the oven racks to divide the oven into thirds; preheat the oven to 375°F. Arrange 4 of the tortillas on a baking sheet.

2 Heat a nonstick skillet over medium heat. Swirl in the oil, then add the onion and pepper. Sauté until softened, 6 minutes. Stir in the corn, cumin, and oregano; cook until the vegetables are tender-crisp, 4 minutes more. Remove from the heat; stir in the cilantro and lime juice.

3 Sprinkle half of the cheese evenly over the tortillas on the baking sheet, leaving a ½-inch border. Spoon the vegetable mixture on top, dividing evenly among the tortillas and spreading level. Sprinkle on the remaining cheese and top with the 4 remaining tortillas, pressing lightly on top.

4 Bake until golden brown and the cheese is melted, 10 minutes, rotating the baking sheet halfway through. Cut each quesadilla into 8 wedges and serve with the salsa and sour cream.

PER SERVING (1 quesadilla with ⅓ cup salsa and 1 tablespoon sour cream): 368 Cal, 14 g Total Fat, 6 g Sat Fat, 29 mg Chol, 685 mg Sod, 45 g Carb, 5 g Fib, 19 g Prot, 442 mg Calc.
PointsPlus value: 10.

Vegetable Quesadillas

italian bean and vegetable stuffed mushrooms

SERVES 4

Vegetarian

- 12 (4-inch) portobello mushrooms
- 2 teaspoons olive oil
- 1 small red bell pepper, chopped
- 1 fennel bulb, chopped
- 1 onion, chopped
- 3 garlic cloves, minced
- 2 (15½-ounce) cans garbanzo beans, rinsed and drained
- ¼ cup chopped fresh basil
- ½ teaspoon salt
- ¼ teaspoon crushed red pepper
- ½ cup shredded reduced-fat mozzarella cheese

Meaty, oversized portobello mushrooms make a satisfying vegetarian dish. This recipe stuffs them with a satisfying mixture of veggies and garbanzo beans, then gilds them with a rich layer of mozzarella for a dish that's hearty enough for a main course.

1 Preheat the oven to 400°F.

2 Remove the stems from the mushrooms and coarsely chop; set aside. Using a small spoon, scrape out and discard the dark gills from the underside of the mushroom caps. Place the mushroom caps, stemmed side up, in a jelly-roll pan.

3 To prepare the filling, heat a large nonstick skillet over medium heat. Swirl in the oil, then add the bell pepper, fennel bulb, onion, and chopped mushroom stems. Cook, stirring frequently, until the vegetables are softened, about 5 minutes. Add the garlic and cook, stirring, until fragrant, about 30 seconds. Transfer the vegetable mixture to a large bowl. Stir in the beans, basil, salt, and red pepper.

4 Spoon the vegetable mixture evenly into the mushroom caps, mounding in the center. Cover loosely with foil and bake 15 minutes. Uncover and sprinkle evenly with the mozzarella; bake until the mushrooms are browned and the cheese is melted, about 5 minutes longer.

PER SERVING (3 stuffed mushrooms): 402 Cal, 10 g Total Fat, 2 g Sat Fat, 8 mg Chol, 643 mg Sod, 60 g Carb, 15 g Fib, 24 g Prot, 229 mg Calc.
PointsPlus value: 10.

warm lentils with escarole

SERVES 4

Vegetarian

3 cups water
1 cup brown lentils, picked over, rinsed, and drained
1 small carrot, diced (⅓ cup)
½ bunch escarole, coarsely chopped (about ½ pound)
1 teaspoon olive oil
2 large garlic cloves, minced
½ medium red onion, diced
¼ cup reduced-sodium vegetable broth
2 tablespoons sherry vinegar
½ teaspoon salt
¼ teaspoon freshly ground pepper

All good seventies cookbooks included a recipe for lentil soup, but it wasn't until the nineties that these wonderful legumes got their sophisticated due. Here, the earthy-tasting beans are paired with slightly bitter escarole, a classic Italian combination. Cook the lentils in gently boiling water until they are just tender and holding their shape.

1 Bring the water and lentils to a boil in a medium saucepan; reduce the heat and simmer gently until the lentils are tender but still retain their shape, about 25 minutes. Just before the lentils are finished, add the carrot and cook 30 seconds. Drain in a colander, rinsing briefly with cold water to stop cooking. Transfer to a medium bowl.

2 Meanwhile, heat a large nonstick skillet over medium heat. Add the escarole, with water still clinging to the leaves; cover and cook until wilted, 3–4 minutes. Drain, if necessary, and add to the lentils; wipe out the skillet and return it to the stove over medium heat.

3 Swirl the oil in the center of the skillet; drop in the garlic and heat until it begins to sizzle. Add the onion and sauté 1 minute. Add the broth, vinegar, salt, and pepper; let the mixture bubble about 5 seconds. Pour over the lentil mixture and toss gently.

PER SERVING (about ¾ cup): 196 Cal, 2 g Total Fat, 0 g Sat Fat, 0 mg Chol, 341 mg Sod, 33 g Carb, 13 g Fib, 14 g Prot, 66 mg Calc. ***PointsPlus value: 4.***

For an additional ***3 PointsPlus*** value per serving, complete this rustic Italian meal with a 1-ounce slice of crusty Italian bread drizzled with 1 teaspoon of olive oil.

pasta primavera

SERVES 6

Vegetarian

2 cups boiling water
10 sun-dried tomato halves (not oil-packed)
3¼ cups farfalle (bow-tie pasta)
2 tablespoons extra-virgin olive oil
4 garlic cloves, sliced
1 medium fennel bulb, chopped (about 1 cup)
½ pound asparagus, trimmed and cut into 1-inch pieces
1 medium onion, chopped
1 cup thawed frozen peas
½ cup dry white wine
½ teaspoon salt
¼ teaspoon freshly ground pepper
½ cup freshly grated Parmesan cheese (preferably Parmigiano-Reggiano)
½ cup chopped parsley
⅓ cup chopped basil

Invented in the seventies at New York's legendary Le Cirque restaurant, this "springtime pasta" traditionally showcases delicate spring vegetables in all their glory. In our version, we get a big flavor boost from sun-dried tomatoes. A little unorthodox, but wonderful!

1 Combine the boiling water and the tomato halves in a heatproof bowl; let stand until the tomatoes are softened, 6 minutes. Drain, discarding the water; when cool enough to handle, slice the tomatoes into thin strips.

2 Cook the farfalle according to package directions; drain and keep warm.

3 Heat a large nonstick skillet over medium heat. Swirl in the oil, then add the garlic. Sauté until fragrant, 30 seconds. Add the fennel, asparagus, and onion; cook, stirring occasionally, 5 minutes. Stir in the peas, wine, salt, and pepper; reduce the heat to medium-low, cover, and simmer 2 minutes. Remove from the heat and stir in the farfalle; toss to coat. Add the cheese, parsley, and basil; toss and serve immediately or at room temperature.

PER SERVING (generous 1 cup): 278 Cal, 8 g Total Fat, 2 g Sat Fat, 6 mg Chol, 569 mg Sod, 40 g Carb, 5 g Fib, 12 g Prot, 175 mg Calc.
PointsPlus value: 7.

Substitute any quick-cooking vegetables you have on hand in this versatile recipe. Ones to try: Thinly sliced red or yellow bell peppers, zucchini, or yellow squash, or small broccoli florets.

orechiette with broccoli rabe, garlic, and red pepper flakes

SERVES 4

Vegetarian

1 pound broccoli rabe, trimmed of tough stalks and chopped
1¼ teaspoons salt
1⅓ cups orechiette
5 teaspoons extra-virgin olive oil
6 garlic cloves, thinly sliced
¼ teaspoon crushed red pepper
¾ cup reduced-sodium vegetable broth
¼ cup freshly grated Parmesan cheese

We all fell in love with pasta in the eighties, but by the nineties we became more adventurous with pasta shapes. Orechiette ("little ears") are the classic shape for this dish. If they're not available, substitute small shells. And if you can't find broccoli rabe—broccoli's delightfully bitter Italian cousin—regular broccoli will work nicely.

1 Bring a large pot of water to a boil. Add the broccoli and 1 teaspoon of the salt; cook until bright green, 2 minutes, and remove with a slotted spoon. Rinse in a colander under cold running water to stop cooking; squeeze out the excess water and reserve.

2 Return the pot to a boil and cook the orechiette according to package directions. Drain and transfer to a large serving bowl; keep warm.

3 Heat a large nonstick skillet over medium heat. Swirl in the oil, then add the garlic and red pepper. Cook, stirring, until the garlic just begins to brown, 1 minute. Add the broth and continue cooking 1 minute. Stir in the broccoli rabe and heat through. Add to the bowl with the orechiette; stir in the cheese and the remaining ¼ teaspoon salt, tossing well to combine. Serve hot or at room temperature.

PER SERVING (1¼ cups): 330 Cal, 9 g Total Fat, 2 g Sat Fat, 5 mg Chol, 722 mg Sod, 50 g Carb, 4 g Fib, 13 g Prot, 140 mg Calc.
PointsPlus value: 9.

Lemon Risotto with Spring Vegetables

lemon risotto with spring vegetables

SERVES 8

Vegetarian

- 1 pound asparagus, trimmed and cut into 1-inch pieces
- 1 teaspoon salt
- 5½ cups reduced-sodium vegetable broth
- 1 tablespoon olive oil
- 2 leeks, cleaned and chopped
- 3 garlic cloves, minced
- 1 teaspoon chopped thyme
- 1½ cups Arborio rice
- ⅓ cup dry white wine
- 1 cup thawed frozen baby peas
- 1 teaspoon grated lemon zest
- 3 tablespoons fresh lemon juice
- ½ cup freshly grated Parmesan cheese
- ¼ teaspoon freshly ground pepper

A well-made risotto is creamy yet never mushy; it's probably the most sophisticated of comfort foods. We've flavored this one with delicate spring vegetables and fresh lemon.

1 Bring a large pot of water to a boil. Add the asparagus and salt, and cook 2 minutes to maintain bright green color. Drain and rinse the asparagus in a colander under cold running water to stop cooking; set aside.

2 Bring the broth to a gentle simmer in a large saucepan over medium-low heat; reduce the heat and keep at a simmer.

3 Heat the oil in a large nonstick skillet. Sauté the leeks, garlic, and thyme until the leeks begin to soften, about 3 minutes. Add the rice and cook, stirring, until the outer shell is translucent, about 1 minute. Stir in the wine and cook, stirring constantly, until it is absorbed. Add the hot broth 1 cup at a time, stirring until it is absorbed before adding more, until the rice is just tender. Add the asparagus, peas, lemon zest, and lemon juice with the last ½-cup addition of broth. The cooking time from the first addition of broth should be about 22 minutes. Stir in the cheese and pepper; serve immediately.

PER SERVING (1 cup): 221 Cal, 4 g Total Fat, 2 g Sat Fat, 5 mg Chol, 574 mg Sod, 36 g Carb, 2 g Fib, 9 g Prot, 135 mg Calc.
PointsPlus value: 6.

For the creamiest texture, be sure to use Arborio or another Italian medium-grain rice such as Carnaroli or Vialone Nano. They're available in better supermarkets and gourmet stores.

---

pad thai

SERVES 4

Vegetarian

8 ounces flat rice noodles or pad thai noodles
6 tablespoons ketchup
3 tablespoons reduced-sodium soy sauce
2 tablespoons packed dark brown sugar
1 teaspoon chili garlic paste
2 tablespoons peanut oil
2 eggs, lightly beaten
3 garlic cloves, minced
12 ounces reduced-fat firm tofu, pressed and cut into ½-inch cubes
4 scallions, cut into ½-inch pieces
2 tablespoons chopped unsalted peanuts
2 cups bean sprouts
4 lemon wedges

Pad Thai is a delectable mix of hot, sour, salty, and sweet flavors as well as chewy and crunchy textures. The surprising ingredient is all-American ketchup, which lends a sweet tomatoey flavor to the sauce.

1 Bring a large pot of water to a boil. Add the noodles and cook until tender, 6–8 minutes; drain in a colander under cold running water to stop cooking. Set aside.

2 Combine the ketchup, soy sauce, sugar, and chili paste in a small bowl; set aside.

3 Heat a large nonstick skillet over medium heat. Swirl in 1 tablespoon of the oil. Add the eggs and cook, stirring occasionally, 2 minutes. Transfer the eggs to a bowl; return the skillet to the heat, and swirl in the remaining 1 tablespoon oil. Add the garlic and sauté until fragrant, 30 seconds. Stir in the tofu; cook until hot, about 3 minutes. Add the scallions and the cooked eggs; cook, stirring, 1 minute. Add the reserved noodles and the ketchup mixture; cook, tossing, until just heated through, 3 minutes. Transfer to a serving platter. Sprinkle with the peanuts, and serve with the bean sprouts and lemon wedges.

PER SERVING (1½ cups): 404 Cal, 15 g Total Fat, 3 g Sat Fat, 106 mg Chol, 896 mg Sod, 15 g Carb, 4 g Fib, 18 g Prot, 98 mg Calc. *PointsPlus value: 7.*

To press the tofu, place it between two plates and weight the top with a heavy can. Let stand until some of the liquid is pressed out, 20 to 30 minutes. Drain off the liquid and pat tofu dry with a paper towel.

---

barley mushroom "risotto"

SERVES 6

Vegetarian

1 ounce dried porcini mushrooms
2 cups hot water
2 tablespoons extra-virgin olive oil
1 medium onion, chopped
8 ounces shiitake or oyster mushrooms (or a combination), stemmed and sliced
3 garlic cloves, minced
2 teaspoons chopped fresh thyme
2 teaspoons chopped fresh rosemary
1 cup pearl barley
4 cups reduced-sodium vegetable broth
½ teaspoon salt
¼ teaspoon freshly ground pepper
⅓ cup chopped parsley
⅓ cup freshly grated Parmesan cheese

In this delightful homage to risotto, we've used pearl barley instead of the traditional Arborio rice. It too becomes lusciously creamy when cooked, and offers a delightful chewy texture.

1 Rinse the porcini in several changes of water to remove any dirt or grit. Place in a heatproof bowl and cover with the hot water; let soak until softened, about 15 minutes. Remove the porcini from the liquid, squeeze them gently and coarsely chop.

2 Strain the porcini liquid into a small saucepan. Bring to a boil and cook until it is reduced to ½ cup, 8–10 minutes; set aside.

3 Heat a large saucepan over medium-high heat. Swirl in the oil, then add the onion. Cook, stirring often, until beginning to soften, 4–5 minutes. Add the fresh mushrooms and porcini; cook, stirring occasionally, until golden, about 8 minutes. Stir in the garlic, thyme, and rosemary and cook 1 minute. Add the barley and cook, stirring, 1 minute.

4 Pour in 3 cups of the broth, the reserved porcini liquid, the salt, and pepper. Bring to a boil, reduce the heat to medium, and simmer, covered, until the liquid is almost absorbed and the barley is almost tender, about 30 minutes. Add the remaining 1 cup broth and cook uncovered, stirring occasionally, until the barley is tender, 12–15 minutes. Remove from the heat, stir in the parsley and cheese, and serve at once.

PER SERVING (¾ cup): 232 Cal, 8 g Total Fat, 2 g Sat Fat, 4 mg Chol, 626 mg Sod, 32 g Carb, 6 g Fib, 10 g Prot, 109 mg Calc.
PointsPlus value: 6.

Porcini mushrooms, also called cèpes, are brown wild mushrooms with a robust, earthy flavor. Look for dried porcini in gourmet stores and better supermarkets; they're pricey but worth every penny, since their intense flavor goes a long way.

creamy polenta with mushroom ragu

SERVES 6

20 Min or Less
Vegetarian

1 tablespoon extra-virgin olive oil
2 shallots, chopped
8 ounces shiitake mushrooms, sliced (4 cups)
8 ounces cremini mushrooms, sliced (4 cups)
1 teaspoon chopped thyme
¼ cup dry sherry
½ cup reduced-sodium vegetable broth
1 tablespoon reduced-sodium soy sauce
3 cups low-fat (1%) milk
2 cups water
½ teaspoon salt
¼ teaspoon freshly ground pepper
1 cup instant polenta
½ cup freshly grated Parmesan cheese

Polenta, made from cornmeal, is Italian comfort food at its highest level. Served creamy or firm, polenta can be eaten plain or topped with any number of boldly flavored, chunky sauces such as this one. Experiment with different types of mushrooms, if you like, depending on what looks good in the produce aisle.

1 Heat a large skillet over medium-high heat. Swirl in the oil, then add the shallots. Cook, stirring occasionally, 1 minute. Add the shiitake and cremini mushrooms, and the thyme; cook, stirring occasionally, until the mushrooms soften, about 5 minutes. Add the sherry and continue cooking until it is just absorbed. Add the broth and soy sauce; cook until slightly thickened, 2–3 minutes. Remove from the heat and keep warm.

2 Combine the milk, water, salt, and pepper in a large saucepan over medium-high heat. Bring to a boil; then pour the polenta into the saucepan in a slow steady stream, whisking constantly, until smooth. Cook, stirring constantly, 5 minutes, until the polenta is thick and creamy. Stir in the cheese. Divide the polenta among 6 plates; top each with ⅓ cup of the mushroom sauce and serve immediately.

PER SERVING (⅔ cup polenta, with ⅓ cup sauce): 212 Cal, 7 g Total Fat, 3 g Sat Fat, 13 mg Chol, 733 mg Sod, 28 g Carb, 2 g Fib, 11 g Prot, 351 mg Calc.
PointsPlus value: 6.

Cremini mushrooms are brown Italian mushrooms, similar in size and shape to white mushrooms, with a slightly earthier flavor. If they're unavailable, substitute white mushrooms.

black bean and corn cakes

SERVES 6

Vegetarian

1 cup all-purpose flour
1 teaspoon baking powder
½ teaspoon ground cumin
½ teaspoon ground coriander
½ teaspoon salt
¼ teaspoon baking soda
⅛ teaspoon cayenne
3 large eggs
¾ cup low-fat buttermilk
1 tablespoon corn oil
1 cup cooked drained black beans
1 cup cooked or thawed frozen corn kernels
¾ cup salsa
6 tablespoons fat-free sour cream

These savory pancakes, with their southwestern flavorings, are a wonderful brunch treat. They're also the perfect accompaniment to grilled or roasted meat or poultry.

1 Combine the flour, baking powder, cumin, coriander, salt, baking soda, and cayenne in a large bowl.

2 Whisk together the eggs, buttermilk, and oil in a medium bowl; gently stir into the flour mixture until well combined. Fold in the beans and corn.

3 Spray a large nonstick skillet or griddle with nonstick spray; set over medium heat until a drop of water sizzles. Spoon the batter by ¼-cup measures into the skillet. Cook until the tops are just covered with bubbles and the edges of the cakes look cooked, 2–3 minutes. Flip and cook until lightly browned, about 1½ minutes more. Transfer to a warmed plate and repeat with the remaining batter. Serve with the salsa and sour cream.

PER SERVING (2 cakes with 2 tablespoons salsa and 1 tablespoon sour cream): 230 Cal, 6 g Total Fat,1 g Sat Fat, 108 mg Chol, 493 mg Sod, 35 g Carb, 4 g Fib, 11 g Prot, 170 mg Calc.
PointsPlus value: 6.

italian favorites

blue-ribbon pizza and pasta dishes

marinara sauce

SERVES 8

Vegetarian

1 (28-ounce) can whole Italian plum tomatoes
1 teaspoon olive oil
¼ medium onion, finely chopped
2 garlic cloves, minced
1 teaspoon sugar
½ teaspoon salt
¼ teaspoon ground pepper
2 tablespoons chopped basil

This quick and versatile recipe can be easily doubled if you'd like to keep some extra in the freezer. Serve it over pasta, use as a pizza sauce, or spoon it over grilled fish or chicken.

1 Pulse the tomatoes in a food processor or blender until coarsely chopped; set aside.

2 Heat a medium soup pot or Dutch oven. Swirl in the oil, then add the onion. Sauté until translucent, about 3 minutes. Add the garlic, and sauté until just fragrant, 30 seconds more.

3 Stir in the tomatoes, sugar, salt, and pepper; bring to a boil. Reduce the heat to low and simmer until thickened, at least 20 minutes and up to 1 hour. Stir in the basil during the last 5 minutes of cooking time.

PER SERVING (½ cup): 30 Cal, 1 g Total Fat, 0 g Sat Fat, 0 mg Chol, 307 mg Sod, 5 g Carb, 1 g Fib, 1 g Prot, 29 mg Calc.
PointsPlus value: 1.

Many chefs swear by canned San Marzano tomatoes for making the best marinara sauce. San Marzanos are a thick-fleshed, sweet-tasting variety of plum tomato grown in Italy in the shadows of Mount Vesuvius. Look for them in specialty food markets and large supermarkets.

---

basic pizza crust

SERVES 8
(TWO 12-INCH CRUSTS)

Vegetarian

3 cups all-purpose flour
2 teaspoons quick-rise yeast
1 teaspoon salt
1 cup warm (105°F–115°F) water
4 teaspoons olive oil
2 tablespoons cornmeal

This recipe uses quick-rise yeast, so there's hardly any kneading—and it's a cinch to whirl in your food processor. What's more, the recipe makes enough dough for two pizzas; enjoy one now and refrigerate the rest of the dough for up to two days—or freeze it for up to two months, so you're pizza-ready anytime.

1 Pulse the flour, yeast, and salt in a food processor 2 or 3 times to blend. With the machine running, add the water and oil through the feed tube; process until the mixture forms a ball, about 10 seconds. Turn the dough out onto a lightly floured work surface; knead a few minutes until it forms a smooth ball and is lightly coated with flour.

2 Spray a large bowl with nonstick spray; place the dough in the bowl. Cover lightly with plastic wrap and let rise in a warm place until it doubles in size, 45–60 minutes. Or let the dough rise in the refrigerator for at least 8 hours or overnight. (At this point, the dough can be frozen. To reuse, thaw overnight in the refrigerator.)

3 Turn the dough out onto a lightly floured work surface, divide it in half, and knead each half until it just forms a smooth ball and is lightly coated with flour. Spray 2 large bowls with nonstick spray; put a dough ball in each bowl. Cover lightly with plastic wrap and let rise in a warm spot until they puff up a little, 10–15 minutes.

4 To assemble the pizza(s), preheat the oven to 500°F. For each crust, lightly spray a 12-inch nonstick pizza pan with nonstick spray; dust each pan with one tablespoon of the cornmeal.

5 Turn the dough out onto a lightly floured work surface, and shape it into a round, flat disk; let it rest for a few minutes, then place it in the pizza pan. Pat and gently stretch it to the edge of the pizza pan. Sprinkle with toppings of your choice, and bake until the crust is crisp and golden brown, about 15 minutes.

PER SERVING (¼ pizza crust): 201 Cal, 3 g Total Fat, 0 g Sat Fat, 0 mg Chol, 292 mg Sod, 38 g Carb, 2 g Fib, 5 g Prot, 9 mg Calc.
PointsPlus value: 5.

rotelle with walnut-gorgonzola sauce

SERVES 4

20 Min or Less

2 cups rotelle
½ cup part-skim ricotta cheese
¼ cup reduced-sodium chicken broth
1 teaspoon grated lemon zest
½ cup coarsely chopped walnuts
¼ cup crumbled Gorgonzola cheese
2 tablespoons chopped flat-leaf parsley

Walnuts and Gorgonzola cheese were a winning combination in the popular bistro salads of the nineties, and they work brilliantly in this hearty pasta dish. We've chosen rotelle, a stubby, spiral-shaped pasta, because its twists capture and hold bits of cheese and nuts. But any ridged, chunky pasta, such as cavatappi or rigatoni, will also do nicely.

1 Cook the rotelle according to package directions. Drain and place in a warmed serving bowl.

2 Meanwhile, combine the ricotta, broth, and lemon zest in a medium bowl; mix until smooth. Spoon over the rotelle, then add the walnuts, Gorgonzola cheese, and parsley; toss to coat. Serve hot or at room temperature.

PER SERVING (1 cup): 339 Cal, 15 g Total Fat, 4 g Sat Fat, 17 mg Chol, 193 mg Sod, 38 g Carb, 2 g Fib, 13 g Prot, 152 mg Calc.
PointsPlus value: 9.

To make this dish ahead of time, just cover and refrigerate for up to a day. However, it doesn't reheat well; instead, take it out of the refrigerator about 30 minutes before serving time and enjoy it at room temperature. Do not freeze.

Rotelle with Walnut-Gorgonzola Sauce

farfalle with tomatoes, goat cheese, and basil

SERVES 4

20 Min or Less
Vegetarian

2 cups farfalle
4 teaspoons olive oil
1 garlic clove, bruised
6 medium plum tomatoes, peeled and chopped
¼ teaspoon salt
Freshly ground pepper
2 ounces herbed or plain goat cheese, crumbled
½ cup chopped basil

In the eighties and nineties, goat cheese and fresh basil were ubiquitous ingredients. Here, they're combined to bring out the best of summer's bounty. Farfalle, sometimes called bow-ties or butterflies, are particularly attractive shapes. But any pasta will show off these super garden flavors. Only fresh basil and fresh tomatoes will do for this recipe.

1 Cook the farfalle according to package directions. Drain and place in a warmed serving bowl.

2 Meanwhile, heat a large nonstick skillet. Swirl in the oil, then add the garlic. Sauté until fragrant, about 30 seconds; discard the garlic. Add the tomatoes, salt, and pepper. Cook, stirring occasionally, until the tomatoes have begun to release some of their juice, about 3 minutes.

3 Pour the tomatoes over the farfalle, then top with the cheese and basil. Toss to coat. Serve hot or at room temperature.

PER SERVING (1½ cups): 235 Cal, 8 g Total Fat, 3 g Sat Fat, 13 mg Chol, 202 mg Sod, 33 g Carb, 2 g Fib, 8 g Prot, 91 mg Calc.
PointsPlus value: 6.

The goat cheese (or any soft cheese) will be easier to crumble if you freeze it for about 5 minutes.

penne alla vodka

SERVES 4

20 Min or Less

2 cups penne
2 tablespoons butter
1 shallot, finely chopped
1 plum tomato, peeled and chopped
¼ cup reduced-sodium chicken broth
1 tablespoon tomato paste
¼ teaspoon crushed red pepper
¼ cup heavy cream
2 tablespoons vodka
¼ cup diced tomato
2 tablespoons freshly grated Parmesan cheese
2 tablespoons minced flat-leaf parsley

For many, this is the classic eighties pasta dish, and it still makes people swoon. With its creamy tomato sauce spiked with just a splash of vodka, it looks and tastes sinfully rich but isn't. Even if it's loaded with restaurant-style sophistication, it's incredibly easy to make. And, yes, that's real cream on the ingredients list. Weight Watchers has come a long way!

1 Cook the penne according to package directions; drain and keep warm.

2 Meanwhile, melt the butter in a medium nonstick skillet, then add the shallot and tomato. Sauté until softened, about 5 minutes. Add the broth, tomato paste, and pepper. Reduce the heat to low, then add the cream and vodka. Cook, stirring constantly, until just heated through (do not boil). Pour the sauce over the penne and toss to coat. Sprinkle with the diced tomato, cheese, and parsley and serve at once.

PER SERVING (¾ cup): 371 Cal, 13 g Total Fat, 7 g Sat Fat, 34 mg Chol, 401 mg Sod, 51 g Carb, 3 g Fib, 11 g Prot, 75 mg Calc.
PointsPlus value: 10.

Easy Homemade
Macaroni and Cheese

easy homemade macaroni and cheese

SERVES 4

Vegetarian

- 2 cups rotini pasta
- 1 tablespoon butter
- 1 tablespoon + 2 teaspoons all-purpose flour
- 1½ cups low-fat (1%) milk
- 1¼ cups shredded reduced-fat sharp cheddar cheese
- ½ teaspoon salt
- ⅛ teaspoon ground pepper
- 1 tablespoon plain dried bread crumbs
- 1 tablespoon grated Parmesan cheese

Our delicious mac 'n' cheese from scratch can be on your table in less than 30 minutes. It uses low-fat milk and reduced-fat cheddar, but doesn't skimp on flavor and richness: A little butter gives the sauce a silky texture, and a broiled topping of bread crumbs and Parmesan makes it a comfort classic.

1 Cook the rotini according to package directions. Drain and keep warm.

2 Meanwhile, melt the butter in a large ovenproof skillet over medium heat. Add the flour and cook, whisking constantly, for 1 minute. Gradually whisk in the milk. Increase the heat to medium-high and cook, whisking constantly, until the mixture comes to a boil and thickens slightly, about 5 minutes. Remove from the heat and add 1 cup of the cheddar cheese, the salt, and pepper, whisking until the cheese is melted. Add the rotini to the cheese sauce, stirring to coat.

3 Preheat the broiler.

4 Sprinkle the rotini with the remaining ¼ cup cheddar cheese. Stir together the bread crumbs and Parmesan cheese in a small bowl, then sprinkle over the rotini. Broil 5 inches from the heat, until the cheese melts and the crumbs are browned, about 1 minute.

PER SERVING (about 1 cup): 433 Cal, 11 g Total Fat, 6 g Sat Fat, 28 mg Chol, 834 mg Sod, 58 g Carb, 3 g Fib, 23 g Prot, 399 mg Calc.
PointsPlus value: 11.

spinach and roasted red pepper ravioli casserole

SERVES 6

Vegetarian

1 (9-ounce) package refrigerated low-fat cheese ravioli
1 (24-ounce) jar fat-free marinara sauce
2 (10-ounce) packages frozen chopped spinach, thawed and squeezed dry
1 (12-ounce) jar roasted red peppers (not oil-packed), drained and thinly sliced
1 cup shredded part-skim mozzarella cheese
2 tablespoons grated Parmesan cheese

This easy baked pasta recipe is a great example of how satisfying meals on the Weight Watchers plan can be. Sure, it sounds like a decadent dinner (and it tastes like one, too!), but making smart ingredient choices like low-fat ravioli instead of a full-fat variety and opting for part-skim mozzarella really pays off. Enjoy!

1 Preheat the oven to 375°F.

2 Cook the ravioli according to package directions.

3 Spray a 2-quart baking dish with nonstick spray. Spread half the marinara sauce in the dish. Add half of the ravioli, then top with half of the spinach, half of the peppers, and half of the mozzarella. Repeat layering once. Sprinkle with the Parmesan. Cover with foil and bake until bubbling, about 20 minutes. Uncover and bake until the cheese is melted and slightly golden, 6–8 minutes longer.

PER SERVING (1⁄6 of casserole): 232 Cal, 8 g Total Fat, 4 g Sat Fat, 31 mg Chol, 922 mg Sod, 31 g Carb, 5 g Fib, 14 g Prot, 309 mg Calc.
PointsPlus value: 6.

While the casserole bakes, toss together a classic Caesar Salad, page 53, to serve alongside. Make the salad with pre-washed romaine lettuce to speed up prep.

---

linguine with red clam sauce

SERVES 4

12 medium clams
1/4 cup dry white wine or reduced-sodium vegetable broth
1 tablespoon fresh thyme leaves, or 1 teaspoon dried
1 tablespoon chopped fresh oregano, or 1 teaspoon dried
3 large garlic cloves, minced
1/4 teaspoon crushed red pepper
6 ounces linguine
4 teaspoons olive oil
8 plum tomatoes, chopped
2 tablespoons chopped basil
3 tablespoons finely chopped flat-leaf parsley
1/2 teaspoon anchovy paste

Forty years ago, this classic combination was a staple on Italian restaurant menus. Today, it remains a favorite, despite all the competition from exotic pasta shapes, risottos, and polentas. Thank goodness, it's easy to make at home, too!

1 Scrub the clams well with a vegetable brush under cold running water. Place them in a large pot of cold water; let them soak a few minutes to release any residual grit, then drain. Repeat for several changes of water until no sand falls to the bottom of the pot.

2 Combine the clams, wine or broth, thyme, oregano, garlic, and pepper in a large saucepan. Cover and cook over medium heat until the clams open, about 5 minutes. Discard any clams that don't open. As soon as they are cool enough to handle, remove the clams from their shells, coarsely chop them, cover, and set aside. Reserve a few of the shells for garnish; reserve the cooking liquid (including the garlic and herbs) separately.

3 Cook the linguine according to package directions. Drain and place in a warmed serving bowl; keep warm.

4 Meanwhile, heat a medium nonstick skillet. Swirl in the oil, then add the tomatoes, basil, 2 tablespoons of the parsley, and the anchovy paste. Sauté over medium heat 5 minutes, then add the reserved clam cooking liquid; reduce the heat and simmer until thickened. Stir the clams into the sauce and heat just to serving temperature. Pour over the linguine, toss to coat, and garnish with the reserved clam shells. Sprinkle with the remaining 1 tablespoon parsley and serve at once.

PER SERVING (1 cup): 298 Cal, 6 g Total Fat, 1 g Sat Fat, 13 mg Chol, 488 mg Sod, 44 g Carb, 4 g Fib, 15 g Prot, 50 mg Calc.
PointsPlus value: 7.

vegetable ragu with tagliatelle

SERVES 8

Vegetarian

2 tablespoons olive oil
1 onion, finely chopped
1 small (5-ounce) zucchini, finely chopped
1 celery stalk, finely chopped
1 frying pepper, seeded and finely chopped
1 carrot, peeled and finely chopped
5 mushrooms, finely chopped
1 (28-ounce) can whole plum tomatoes, pureed, with juice
½ cup chopped flat-leaf parsley
¼ cup chopped basil
1 tablespoon chopped oregano
1 garlic clove, minced
1 bay leaf
½ teaspoon salt
Freshly ground pepper
6 ounces tagliatelle
¼ cup freshly grated Parmesan cheese

Once you've prepared this savory, vegetable-packed sauce, you'll find it as versatile as the famous Weight Watchers Garden Vegetable Soup recipe (page 33). It's great on any type of pasta (we like thin, ribbonlike tagliatelle), spread onto a whole wheat pizza crust, or atop omelettes, chicken, or fish. While you're at it, make a double batch of the sauce and freeze it.

1 Heat a large nonstick saucepan. Swirl in the oil, then add the onion. Sauté over medium heat until translucent, about 8 minutes. Add the zucchini and celery and sauté until softened. Add the frying pepper, carrot, and mushrooms; cook, stirring frequently, until the mushrooms have released and reabsorbed their juices and the carrots are softened, about 10 minutes.

2 Add the tomatoes, parsley, basil, oregano, garlic, bay leaf, salt, and ground pepper. Cover and simmer, stirring occasionally, until the vegetables are tender and the sauce has thickened, about 30 minutes.

3 Cook the tagliatelle according to package directions. Drain and place in a warmed serving bowl. Pour the sauce over the tagliatelle and toss to coat. Sprinkle with the cheese and serve.

PER SERVING (1½ cups): 159 Cal, 6 g Total Fat, 1 g Sat Fat, 21 mg Chol, 381 mg Sod, 23 g Carb, 3 g Fib, 6 g Prot, 97 mg Calc.
PointsPlus value: 4.

Frying peppers, sometimes labeled "Italian" or "Cubanelle" peppers, are similar to bell peppers, with the same color spectrum and a more slender, tapered shape. Their flesh is thinner than that of bells, with slightly sweeter flavor. If unavailable, substitute ½ to 1 large green bell pepper.

Vegetable Ragu with Tagliatelle

capellini with seafood

SERVES 4

12 medium clams
12 medium mussels
¼ cup dry white wine or reduced-sodium vegetable broth
2 garlic cloves, minced
2 teaspoons olive oil
½ pound bay scallops, rinsed and patted dry
¼ pound medium shrimp, peeled and deveined
2 tablespoons chopped parsley
1 tablespoon thyme leaves
1 tablespoon minced oregano
6 ounces capellini
Freshly ground pepper
Parsley, thyme, and/or oregano sprigs (optional)

Capellini are thin, delicate strands of pasta that are sometimes aptly called angel hair. Best served in soups rather than topped with a sauce, they shine in this simple combination of clams, mussels, scallops, shrimp, and fresh herbs in a briny, light broth.

1 Scrub the clams and mussels well with a vegetable brush under cold running water. Pull off the hairy beards that may be attached to some of the mussels; if difficult, use a small knife. Place the clams and mussels in a large pot of cold water; let them soak a few minutes to release any residual grit, then drain. Repeat for several changes of water, until no sand falls to the bottom of the pot.

2 Combine the clams, mussels, wine or broth, and garlic in a large saucepan; cover and cook over medium heat until the shells open, about 8 minutes; discard any that don't open. Set the clams and mussels aside with their cooking liquid.

3 Heat a large nonstick skillet. Swirl in the oil, then add the scallops, shrimp, parsley, thyme, and oregano. Sauté until the shrimp are pink and the scallops are just opaque, 5–10 minutes. Remove from the heat, and add the clams and mussels with their cooking liquid.

4 Meanwhile, cook the capellini according to package directions; drain and place in a warmed serving bowl. Top with the seafood, sprinkle with the pepper, and toss to combine. Garnish with the herb sprigs, if using, and serve at once.

PER SERVING (1 cup): 354 Cal, 5 g Total Fat, 1 g Sat Fat, 71 mg Chol, 560 mg Sod, 44 g Carb, 2 g Fib, 31 g Prot, 77 mg Calc.
PointsPlus value: 9.

spaghetti carbonara

SERVES 4

20 Min or Less

6 ounces spaghetti
1 tablespoon + 1 teaspoon unsalted butter
4 (1-ounce) slices Canadian bacon, trimmed of all visible fat and cut into matchstick-size pieces
1 shallot, finely chopped
2 garlic cloves, bruised
⅔ cup fat-free egg substitute
¼ cup freshly grated Romano cheese
1 tablespoon finely chopped flat-leaf parsley
Freshly ground pepper

Even with egg substitute and Canadian-style bacon replacing the usual whole eggs and pancetta (Italian-style unsmoked bacon), this is a great-tasting dish. Timing is everything in this recipe: The sauce ingredients should be ready just as the spaghetti finishes cooking; then, the hot pasta cooks the sauce as you toss it.

1 Cook the spaghetti according to package directions.

2 Meanwhile, melt the butter in a large nonstick skillet, then add the bacon, shallot, and garlic. Sauté until the bacon and shallot are browned and the garlic is golden, about 5 minutes, then discard the garlic. (If the spaghetti is not quite done at this point, remove the skillet from the heat.)

3 Drain the spaghetti and immediately add it to the skillet; set the skillet over low heat. Add the egg substitute and cheese; toss to coat. Cook, stirring constantly, until the egg is just cooked through, about 2 minutes. Sprinkle with the parsley and pepper and serve at once.

PER SERVING (¾ cup): 288 Cal, 8 g Total Fat, 4 g Sat Fat, 29 mg Chol, 475 mg Sod, 36 g Carb, 2 g Fib, 16 g Prot, 78 mg Calc. ***PointsPlus value: 7.***

Bruising garlic helps release its flavor. Here's how to do it: Place a peeled clove on a cutting board and flatten it slightly with the side of a large knife.

Baked Ziti with Meatballs

baked ziti with meatballs

SERVES 8

1 tablespoon olive oil
1 onion, finely chopped
1 (28-ounce) can diced plum tomatoes in juice, drained (reserve the juice)
1 garlic clove, minced
½ pound lean ground beef (7% or less fat)
¼ pound lean ground pork
¼ cup freshly grated Parmesan cheese
1 cup chopped flat-leaf parsley
½ cup plain dried bread crumbs
3 egg whites, or ¼ cup fat-free egg substitute
1 tablespoon chopped basil, or 1 teaspoon dried
1 teaspoon chopped oregano or marjoram, or ½ teaspoon dried
1 teaspoon chopped thyme, or ¼ teaspoon dried
¼ teaspoon salt
Freshly ground pepper
4 cups ziti
¼ cup shredded part-skim mozzarella cheese

Here's an Italian-American all-time favorite, straight from many a Sunday dinner and minus the usual fat and calories. It's a little time-consuming to prepare, but the results are definitely worth it and much can be done ahead of time. If you prefer, substitute lean ground turkey for all or part of the meat.

1 Heat a large nonstick saucepan. Swirl in the oil, then add the onion. Sauté until translucent, about 5–8 minutes. Stir in the tomatoes and garlic. Reduce the heat to medium-low; cook, stirring occasionally, until bubbling.

2 Meanwhile, combine the beef, pork, Parmesan cheese, ½ cup of the parsley, the bread crumbs, egg whites, basil, oregano, thyme, salt, and pepper in a large bowl. Form the mixture into 40 walnut-size meatballs, then drop them gently and carefully into the bubbling sauce (watch for splashing).

3 Reduce the heat to low; simmer, without stirring, until the meatballs are resistant to gentle pressure from a wooden spoon, about 15 minutes. Stir in the remaining ½ cup parsley. Continue cooking, stirring occasionally and adding the reserved tomato juice ¼ cup at a time, until the meatballs are tender and the sauce has thickened, about 20 minutes.

4 Cook the ziti according to package directions. Drain well, then toss with the sauce and meatballs in a large bowl. (The dish may be made up to a day ahead at this point; just cover and refrigerate until ready to bake.)

5 Preheat the oven to 400°F. Spray a 9 × 13-inch baking dish with nonstick spray. Place the ziti mixture in the baking dish, and sprinkle evenly with the mozzarella. Cover with foil and bake until heated through, 15–20 minutes (if the mixture has been refrigerated, it will take 5–10 minutes longer). Uncover; bake until bubbling and golden on top, 5–10 minutes more.

PER SERVING (1 cup ziti with 5 meatballs): 345 Cal, 8 g Total Fat, 3 g Sat Fat, 29 mg Chol, 554 mg Sod, 47 g Carb, 4 g Fib, 21 g Prot, 139 mg Calc.
PointsPlus value: 8.

shells with spinach, ricotta, and raisins

SERVES 4

Vegetarian

¼ cup golden raisins
1 tablespoon olive oil
1 onion, chopped
1 (10-ounce) box frozen chopped spinach, thawed and squeezed dry
¼ teaspoon salt
2 cups medium pasta shells
¼ cup part-skim ricotta
¼ cup freshly grated Parmesan cheese
Freshly ground white pepper

In southern Italy, spinach, ricotta, and raisins are a popular trio and a perfect combination of taste and texture. This is a foolproof pasta for company; you can assemble it ahead of time, refrigerate it, and bring it to room temperature for 30 minutes before serving.

1 Put the raisins in a small bowl of hot water until plump and soft, about 10 minutes; drain and set aside.

2 Heat a medium nonstick skillet. Swirl in the oil, then add the onion. Sauté until translucent, about 8 minutes; reduce the heat to low. Stir in the spinach and salt; cook, stirring, until heated through. Set aside and keep warm.

3 In a large pot of boiling water, cook the shells according to package directions. Drain and place in warmed serving bowl. Add the spinach mixture, the raisins, ricotta, and Parmesan cheese; toss to coat. Sprinkle with the pepper and serve at once.

PER SERVING (1¼ cups): 298 Cal, 7 g Total Fat, 3 g Sat Fat, 10 mg Chol, 325 mg Sod, 47 g Carb, 4 g Fib, 12 g Prot, 217 mg Calc.
PointsPlus value: 8.

Instead of the spinach, other greens like broccolini, broccoli, broccoli rabe, or Swiss chard would also work beautifully in this recipe. Steam them until tender but still bright green, about 10 minutes.

rigatoni with meat sauce

SERVES 4

2 teaspoons olive oil
1 onion, finely chopped
1 celery stalk, finely chopped
1 carrot, peeled and finely chopped
1 garlic clove, peeled and minced
8 ounces lean ground beef (7% or less fat)
1 (28-ounce) can diced tomatoes in juice
¼ cup finely chopped flat-leaf parsley
¼ cup dry red wine or reduced-sodium beef broth
1 rosemary sprig
1 bay leaf
¼ teaspoon salt
Freshly ground pepper
2 cups rigatoni
¼ cup freshly grated Parmesan cheese

Pasta with meat sauce is a staple in any Italian kitchen—yesterday, today, forever! This recipe calls for rigatoni, which have a thick tubular shape, but any thick pasta, such as shells, penne, or ziti, works just as well. Make a double, triple, or quadruple batch of sauce and freeze it for up to three months.

1 Heat a large nonstick saucepan. Swirl in the oil, then add the onion. Sauté until translucent, about 8 minutes. Add the celery, carrot, and garlic; sauté until wilted, 5 minutes more.

2 Add the ground meat and brown, breaking it apart with a spoon, until it is no longer pink. Add the tomatoes, parsley, wine or broth, rosemary, bay leaf, salt, and pepper, and cook, stirring occasionally, until the sauce is bubbling. Immediately lower the heat and simmer, uncovered, stirring occasionally, until thickened, about 45 minutes. Discard the rosemary and bay leaf.

3 Cook the rigatoni according to package directions. Drain and place in a warmed serving bowl. Pour the tomato sauce over the rigatoni and toss. Sprinkle with the cheese and serve at once.

PER SERVING (1½ cups): 428 Cal, 9 g Total Fat, 3 g Sat Fat, 37 mg Chol, 809 mg Sod, 61 g Carb, 6 g Fib, 25 g Prot, 183 mg Calc.
PointsPlus value: 11.

vegetable lasagna

SERVES 4

Vegetarian

1 medium (1 pound) eggplant, peeled and sliced ¼-inch thick
1 medium (8-ounce) zucchini, sliced ¼-inch thick
¼ teaspoon salt
Freshly ground pepper
1 tablespoon olive oil
1 garlic clove, minced
1 (28-ounce) can whole tomatoes, chopped, with their juice
1 (10-ounce) package mushrooms, sliced
2 frying peppers (or 1 large green bell pepper), finely chopped
½ cup chopped flat-leaf parsley
5 (6½ × 7-inch) sheets or 10 (3½ × 6½-inch) sheets no-boil lasagna noodles
¼ cup freshly grated Parmesan cheese

No-boil lasagna noodles hit supermarket shelves in the nineties, raising lasagna's status from a labor-intensive special-occasion dish to a convenience food. Here, we've created a chock-full-of-veggies version that's easy to prepare—especially if you roast the vegetables and prepare the sauce ahead of time.

1 Preheat the oven to 400°F. Spray 2 baking sheets and an 8-inch-square baking dish with nonstick spray. Arrange the eggplant and zucchini slices on the baking sheets, overlapping a few slices, if necessary. Spray the tops with nonstick spray, sprinkle with the salt and pepper, and bake until tender, 15 minutes. Set aside (leave the oven on).

2 Heat a large nonstick skillet. Swirl in the oil, then add the garlic. Sauté until fragrant, about 30 seconds. Add the tomatoes, mushrooms, frying peppers, parsley, and another grinding of the pepper; cook over medium-low heat until the sauce is bubbling but not yet thickened. Remove from the heat. (The sauce can be made up to 3 days ahead at this point; just transfer to an airtight container and refrigerate.)

3 Spread ½ cup of the sauce evenly over the bottom of the baking dish. Cover with 1 or 2 lasagna noodles (depending on the size you are using); top with one-fourth of the eggplant and zucchini slices, then top with another ½ cup of the sauce. Sprinkle with 1 tablespoon of the Parmesan cheese. Repeat the procedure to make 4 more layers, ending with a layer of noodles topped with sauce. If any sauce remains, pour it on the top and around the edges of the lasagna. Be sure to use all the sauce (it's needed to cook the noodles). Press down gently on the lasagna with a spatula to help the noodles absorb the sauce; the lasagna will compact as it cooks.

4 Cover with foil and bake until bubbling, about 35 minutes. Remove the foil and continue baking until all the sauce has been absorbed, about 10–15 minutes.

PER SERVING (2 cups): 365 Cal, 8 g Total Fat, 2 g Sat Fat, 5 mg Chol, 599 mg Sod, 62 g Carb, 9 g Fib, 15 g Prot, 182 mg Calc.
PointsPlus value: 9.

Vegetable Lasagna

cheese ravioli with butternut squash sauce

SERVES 4

4 teaspoons olive oil
3 shallots, peeled and chopped
1 garlic clove, chopped
1 (1¼–1½ pound) butternut squash, peeled, seeded, and coarsely chopped
3 cups reduced-sodium chicken broth
1 tablespoon minced thyme, or 1 teaspoon dried
1 tablespoon minced sage, or 1 teaspoon dried
½ teaspoon ground pepper
⅛ teaspoon nutmeg
½ cup part-skim ricotta
5 tablespoons freshly grated Parmesan cheese
2 tablespoons minced flat-leaf parsley
1 large egg white
24 wonton wrappers (one 12-ounce package)
Fresh whole sage leaves (optional)

Thanks to ready-made wonton wrappers, available in most supermarkets, homemade cheese ravioli is a fairly simple task—and even more fun if you have your family (or dinner guests) help assemble them. The butternut squash sauce topping is an especially rich and delicious treat.

1 Heat a large nonstick skillet. Swirl in the oil, then add the shallots and garlic. Sauté until fragrant, about 1 minute. Add the squash, broth, thyme, sage, ¼ teaspoon of the pepper, and the nutmeg; cook, stirring frequently, until the squash is very tender and the liquid has evaporated, about 15 minutes. Remove from the heat and let cool 15 minutes.

2 Meanwhile, combine the ricotta, 3 tablespoons of the Parmesan cheese, the parsley, egg white, and the remaining ¼ teaspoon pepper in a medium bowl.

3 To assemble the ravioli, lightly dust a work surface with flour. Lay out 12 wonton wrappers and put 1½ teaspoons of the cheese mixture in the center of each. Wet the area around the filling with a pastry brush dipped lightly in water, then place another wrapper on top of each, pressing the air out as you seal the edges. Cover lightly with a damp towel and set aside.

4 Meanwhile, puree the squash mixture in a food processor. If it is too thick for a sauce, add 1 tablespoon of water at a time until it reaches a smooth, thick consistency. Place it in a saucepan and bring to a gentle simmer, stirring frequently; keep warm.

5 Cook the ravioli, half a batch at a time, in gently boiling water until they are tender and float to the surface, about 4 minutes. Transfer them with a slotted spoon to a colander, drain well, and place in a warmed serving bowl. Cover the ravioli generously with the sauce, sprinkle with the remaining 2 tablespoons Parmesan cheese, and garnish with the sage leaves, if using.

PER SERVING (3 ravioli with ½ cup sauce): 358 Cal, 11 g Total Fat, 4 g Sat Fat, 40 mg Chol, 598 mg Sod, 48 g Carb, 6 g Fib, 17 g Prot, 281 mg Calc.
PointsPlus value: 9.

state-of-the-art subs

How things change . . . often for the better! In years past, shoppers rarely paused to read the ingredient labels on the foods they bought (it wasn't until 1994 that the Food and Drug Administration began requiring most packaged foods to carry nutritional facts). Today, we have more information than ever about our foods. While there are no "forbidden foods" on the Program, there are many healthier choices available.

Old School	New Thinking	Why?
Artificial smoke flavor	**Smoked paprika or naturally smoked sea salt**	Gives chemicals the boot and uses a natural flavor alternative
Artificial sweeteners	**Fruits, fruit juices, honey, and maple syrup**	Taste better, and the jury's still out on the long-term health effects of many artificial sweeteners
Bouillon cubes	**Reduced-sodium broths**	Less sodium and better flavor
Canned beans, tomatoes	**No-salt or low-salt canned options**	Reduces the sodium in your recipes
Salt	**Fresh herbs, citrus juice, and other seasonings**	Replaces at least some of the added salt and lowers sodium without compromising flavor
Imitation bacon bits	**Chopped crisp-cooked turkey bacon**	Natural flavor and less sodium
Margarine	**Butter or olive oil**	Little or no trans fats and better flavor so you can usually use less
Pork sausage	**Turkey and chicken sausage**	Generally lower in fat and still packed with flavor
Sugary jams and jellies	**Pure fruit preserves**	More flavor and nutrients, and less sugar
Vegetable oil	**Olive, canola, safflower, or sunflower oil**	More heart-healthy fats
White flour	**Whole wheat flour**	More fiber and nutrients; most recipes will work fine with a half and half mix of flours
White pasta	**Whole-grain pasta**	More fiber and protein

pizza margherita

SERVES 4

Vegetarian

Dough for 1 pizza [see Basic Pizza Crust, page 209], or 1 prebaked thin pizza crust
¾ cup prepared fat-free tomato sauce
¼ cup shredded part-skim mozzarella cheese
2 teaspoons olive oil
1 tablespoon chopped flat-leaf parsley
½ tablespoon chopped oregano, or ½ teaspoon dried
½ tablespoon chopped basil, or ½ teaspoon dried
¼ teaspoon salt
⅛ teaspoon crushed red pepper

This is the world's favorite pizza from time immemorial, perhaps for its simplicity of toppings: tomato sauce, mozzarella cheese, and herbs (representing, not unintentionally, the red, white, and green colors of the Italian flag).

1 Preheat the oven according to the directions for the crust you are using.

2 Spread the tomato sauce evenly over the crust; sprinkle with the cheese. Drizzle with the oil, then sprinkle with the parsley, oregano, basil, salt, and pepper. Bake until the cheese is bubbling, 10–15 minutes. Serve at once.

PER SERVING (¼ pizza): 256 Cal, 6 g Total Fat, 1 g Sat Fat, 4 mg Chol, 681 mg Sod, 41 g Carb, 2 g Fib, 8 g Prot, 76 mg Calc.
PointsPlus value: 7.

Shape and stretch the dough like a pro: Place one hand over the dough; with your other hand, gently pull on one side as far as it will stretch without breaking. Turn the dough a quarter turn and repeat until it has reached the desired size. If it tears, let it rest 10 minutes. This relaxes the proteins and makes it easier to stretch.

---

broccoli-cheddar-mushroom pizza

SERVES 4

Vegetarian

Dough for 1 pizza [see Basic Pizza Crust, page 209], or 1 prebaked thin pizza crust
1 cup shredded reduced-fat cheddar cheese
1 (10-ounce) box frozen chopped broccoli, thawed and squeezed dry
1 (10-ounce) package mushrooms, sliced
¼ teaspoon salt
Freshly ground pepper

Sometimes a little break with tradition can be fun and delicious. This veggie pizza was inspired by the tasty toppings at a salad bar.

1 Preheat the oven according to the directions for the crust you are using.

2 Sprinkle the cheese evenly over crust; top with the broccoli, mushrooms, salt, and pepper. Bake until the crust is golden, the cheese is bubbling, and the mushrooms are cooked through, 10–15 minutes. Serve at once.

PER SERVING (¼ pizza): 318 Cal, 8 g Total Fat, 4 g Sat Fat, 15 mg Chol, 606 mg Sod, 46 g Carb, 5 g Fib, 17 g Prot, 254 mg Calc.
PointsPlus value: 8.

For an even quicker pizza, use broccoli florets and sliced mushrooms from the salad bar of your supermarket. Give the broccoli a quick steam in the microwave before using.

Pizza all'Insalata

pizza all'insalata

SERVES 4

Vegetarian

Dough for 1 pizza [see Basic Pizza Crust, page 209], or 1 prebaked thin pizza crust
6 medium plum tomatoes, sliced
3 tablespoons dry white or red wine, or vegetable broth
4 teaspoons olive oil
1 tablespoon red-wine vinegar, white-wine vinegar, or cider vinegar
1 teaspoon balsamic vinegar
1 garlic clove, bruised
¼ teaspoon dried oregano, marjoram, or basil
¼ teaspoon salt
Freshly ground pepper
1 medium bunch arugula, trimmed
2 cups trimmed and torn romaine or Bibb lettuce leaves
1 Belgian endive, sliced
2 medium carrots, peeled and shredded
1 cup chopped seeded peeled cucumber
2 tablespoons shaved Parmesan cheese

This unusual pizza started appearing on restaurant tables in the Italo-centric eighties. Insalata, Italian for salad, makes for a deliciously healthy, fresh pizza topping—no gooey cheese needed!

1 Preheat the oven according to the directions for the crust you are using.

2 Arrange the sliced tomatoes on the crust; spray with nonstick spray. Bake until the crust is golden and the tomatoes are cooked through, 10–15 minutes.

3 Meanwhile, combine the wine or broth, oil, wine or cider vinegar, balsamic vinegar, garlic, oregano, salt, and pepper in a large bowl; let stand 10 minutes. Whisk vigorously to blend; discard the garlic. Add the arugula, lettuce, endive, carrots, and cucumber to the bowl and toss with the dressing.

4 When the pizza crust is done, remove it from the oven and top with the salad. Sprinkle with the cheese and serve at once.

PER SERVING (¼ pizza): 311 Cal, 9 g Total Fat, 2 g Sat Fat, 2 mg Chol, 540 mg Sod, 48 g Carb, 5 g Fib, 9 g Prot, 123 mg Calc.
PointsPlus value: 8.

seafood pizza

SERVES 4

12 littleneck clams
1 pound medium mussels
Dough for 1 pizza [see Basic Pizza Crust, page 209], or 1 prebaked thin pizza crust
½ pound medium shrimp, peeled and deveined
½ cup dry white wine or vegetable broth
¼ cup chopped flat-leaf parsley
2 tablespoons chopped basil
1 tablespoon chopped thyme
3 garlic cloves, minced
¼ teaspoon crushed red pepper
1 (14-ounce) can diced tomatoes in juice, drained

This pizza calls for the crust to bake separately while the shellfish are steaming. Don't skimp on the seafood; only the freshest will do. For an especially dramatic presentation, serve a few of the clams and mussels in their shells.

1 Scrub the clams and mussels well with a vegetable brush under cold running water. Pull off the hairy beards that may be attached to some of the mussel shells; if it's difficult, use a small knife. Place the clams and mussels in a large pot of cold water; let them soak a few minutes to release any residual grit, then drain. Repeat for several changes of water until no sand falls to the bottom of the pot.

2 Preheat the oven to 500°F. Bake the pizza crust until crispy but still pale, about 8 minutes. Remove from the oven, but leave it on.

3 Meanwhile, combine the clams, mussels, shrimp, wine or broth, parsley, basil, thyme, garlic, and pepper in a large saucepan; cover and cook over medium heat until the clams and mussels open and the shrimp turn pink, 7–8 minutes (do not overcook). Discard any clams or mussels that don't open. Transfer the clams and mussels to a large bowl with a slotted spoon; set them aside until they are cool enough to handle, then remove them from their shells. Reserve ¼ cup of their cooking liquid, and a few shells, if desired, for garnish.

4 Combine the tomatoes and the reserved cooking liquid in a medium nonstick skillet; cook over medium heat until thickened, about 5 minutes.

5 Spread the tomato sauce over the crust. Place a few mussels and clams in the reserved shells, if using, then distribute all the shellfish evenly over the tomato sauce. Return the pizza to the oven and bake until heated through and the crust is golden, 4–5 minutes. Serve at once.

PER SERVING (¼ pizza): 316 Cal, 4 g Total Fat, 1 g Sat Fat, 79 mg Chol, 826 mg Sod, 45 g Carb, 3 g Fib, 23 g Prot, 95 mg Calc.
PointsPlus value: 8.

tex-mex pizza

SERVES 4

Vegetarian

Dough for 1 pizza [see Basic Pizza Crust, page 209], or 1 prebaked thin pizza crust
½ cup salsa
1 (15-ounce) can black beans, rinsed and drained
½ cup shredded reduced-fat cheddar cheese
½ onion, chopped
½ teaspoon chili powder
½ cup fat-free sour cream (optional)

The Tex-Mex craze of the eighties led to some wild, and sometimes forgettable, experimentation. But here's one combination that worked nicely: Pizza meets quesadilla.

1 Preheat the oven according to the directions for the crust you are using.

2 Spread the salsa over the crust. Top with the beans, cheese, and onion; sprinkle with the chili powder. Bake until the crust is golden, the cheese is bubbling, and the onion has started to brown, 10–15 minutes.

3 Top with dollops of the sour cream, if using, and serve at once.

PER SERVING (¼ pizza): 360 Cal, 6 g Total Fat, 2 g Sat Fat, 8 mg Chol, 631 mg Sod, 61 g Carb, 8 g Fib, 16 g Prot, 183 mg Calc.
PointsPlus value: 9.

This pizza is particularly freezer-friendly, so why not make two and freeze one before baking it. Just allow 5 to 10 minutes extra baking time when you put a frozen pizza in the oven, and add the sour cream, if using, just before serving.

---

ham, pepper, and onion calzones

SERVES 4

1 tablespoon olive oil
1 medium onion, sliced
1 green bell pepper, seeded and cut into thin strips
1 red bell pepper, seeded and cut into thin strips
2 garlic cloves, minced
1 teaspoon dried oregano
4 ounces deli-thin-sliced lean ham, cut crosswise into thin strips
1 pound refrigerated or thawed frozen pizza dough
1 cup shredded part-skim mozzarella

A calzone is a pizza that is folded in half to form a closed, filled pocket—sort of the Neapolitan version of an empanada. When making calzones, use fresh or frozen pizza dough from your supermarket, or a full (8-serving) recipe of Basic Pizza Crust [page 209].

1 Preheat the oven to 400°F. Spray a baking sheet with nonstick spray.

2 Heat a large nonstick skillet over medium-high heat. Swirl in the oil, then add the onion, bell peppers, garlic, and oregano; cook, stirring occasionally, until softened, 5–7 minutes. Stir in the ham and cook 3 minutes; remove from the heat and let cool slightly.

3 Turn out the dough onto a lightly floured work surface and divide it in half. Stretch or roll each dough half into a 10-inch circle. Spread half of the ham mixture over one-half of each circle, leaving a 1-inch border, then top each with half of the cheese. Fold the dough over, making a half circle, and firmly pinch the edges together to seal. Using a spatula, transfer the calzones to the baking sheet. Bake until tops are golden brown, about 20 minutes. Cool 5 minutes, then cut each calzone in half, crosswise, to make 4 portions.

PER SERVING (½ calzone): 494 Cal, 15 g Total Fat, 5 g Sat Fat, 30 mg Chol, 979 mg Sod, 67 g Carb, 4 g Fib, 23 g Prot, 237 mg Calc. *PointsPlus value: 13.*

Ham, Pepper, and Onion Calzones

white pizza

SERVES 4

Vegetarian

Dough for 1 pizza [see Basic Pizza Crust, page 209], or 1 prebaked thin pizza crust
1 cup shredded part-skim mozzarella cheese
1 large Vidalia onion, sliced and separated into rings
¼ teaspoon salt
Freshly ground white pepper

In the United States, so-called white pizza (or pizza bianca) may have any number of toppings, from feta cheese to clams; the only essential is a pale color. In our version, gooey mozzarella cheese and sweet, crunchy Vidalia onion rings play the starring roles.

1 Preheat the oven according to the directions for the crust you are using.

2 Sprinkle the cheese and onion rings evenly over the crust. Spray lightly with nonstick spray; sprinkle with the salt and pepper. Bake until the crust is golden, the cheese is melted, and the onions are tender and starting to brown, about 15 minutes. Serve at once.

PER SERVING (¼ pizza): 295 Cal, 8 g Total Fat, 3 g Sat Fat, 15 mg Chol, 588 mg Sod, 42 g Carb, 2 g Fib, 14 g Prot, 224 mg Calc. ***PointsPlus value: 8.***

Vidalia onions are only available in the spring, but don't let that stop you from trying this satisfyingly delicious pizza. You can substitute for Maui, Texas Sweets, or Walla Walla onions at other times of the year.

greek pizza

SERVES 4

20 Min or Less
Vegetarian

- 1 (10-ounce) pre-baked thin pizza crust
- 1 cup fat-free pasta sauce
- 2 plum tomatoes, thinly sliced
- 1 cup sliced fresh white mushrooms
- 2 scallions, chopped
- ½ cup crumbled feta cheese
- 4 kalamata olives, pitted and thinly sliced

Sharp-tasting feta cheese is a dieter's dream—just a few crumbles can flavor an entire dish. If you typically use it only on salads, try it on this fantastic quick-to-make pizza. Using a pre-baked crust and purchased pasta sauce make it faster than calling for pizza delivery.

1 Preheat the oven to 450°F.

2 Meanwhile, place the pizza crust on a baking sheet and top with the pasta sauce, leaving a ½-inch border around the edge. Top with the tomatoes, mushrooms, scallions, cheese, and olives. Bake until the cheese melts slightly and the crust is crisp, about 10 minutes.

PER SERVING (¼ of pizza): 308 Cal, 10 g Total Fat, 4 g Sat Fat, 17 mg Chol, 750 mg Sod, 42 g Carb, 2 g Fib, 12 g Prot, 211 mg Calc. *PointsPlus value: 8.*

side stories

celebrated veggies and sides

cauliflower casserole, pizza-style

SERVES 6

Vegetarian

1 medium (2-pound) cauliflower head, trimmed and separated into florets
2 cups low-fat marinara sauce
¼ cup seasoned dried bread crumbs
1 cup shredded part-skim mozzarella cheese
2 tablespoons freshly grated Parmesan cheese

In the distant Weight Watchers past, occasionally a "pizza" was made using cauliflower as the "crust" and cooked-down tomato juice as the "sauce." Today's version packs a lot more flavor and cheesy goodness but still keeps the inspiration. Use marinara sauce from a jar, or try our easy recipe *[see page 208].*

1 Preheat the oven to 350°F.

2 Fill a medium saucepan two-thirds full with water and bring to a boil; add the cauliflower. Reduce the heat and simmer until the cauliflower is tender-crisp, 8–10 minutes; drain.

3 Spread 1 cup of the sauce in the bottom of an 8-inch-square baking dish or 9-inch pie plate. Add the cauliflower, then sprinkle with the bread crumbs. Pour the remaining sauce evenly over, then sprinkle with the mozzarella and Parmesan cheeses. Cover with foil and bake until the cauliflower is soft and the cheese is melted, about 30 minutes.

PER SERVING (¾ cup): 139 Cal, 6 g Total Fat, 3 g Sat Fat, 12 mg Chol, 566 mg Sod, 14 g Carb, 3 g Fib, 9 g Prot, 217 mg Calc.
PointsPlus value: 4.

cheese sauce

SERVES 6

Vegetarian

½ cup evaporated fat-free milk
3 tablespoons all-purpose flour
¾ cup low-fat (1%) milk
2 teaspoons Dijon mustard
½ teaspoon salt
½ cup shredded reduced-fat sharp cheddar cheese
¼ teaspoon ground pepper

Even the earliest Weight Watchers Cookbook *included a recipe for cheese sauce; then, as now, it was a great way to top vegetables deliciously. Try this rich, creamy version on cauliflower, broccoli, or asparagus. It just may get you to eat more vegetables!*

1 Whisk together the evaporated milk and flour in a small saucepan until smooth. Whisk in the low-fat milk, mustard, and salt. Bring to a simmer and cook, stirring frequently, until the sauce is slightly thickened, 4 minutes.

2 Stir in the cheddar cheese and pepper. Remove from the heat and stir until the cheese has just melted and the sauce is smooth. Serve at once.

PER SERVING (3 tablespoons): 72 Cal, 2 g Total Fat, 1 g Sat Fat, 7 mg Chol, 305 mg Sod, 7 g Carb, 0 g Fib, 6 g Prot, 171 mg Calc.
PointsPlus value: 2.

Today, it's easy to find reduced-fat cheeses in the supermarket dairy section. To get the most flavor, look for sharp cheddar, with the fat reduced by 50 percent (cheddar with a greater fat reduction tends to be rubbery when melted). You can also find reduced-fat cheddar preshredded and sold in plastic bags.

Green Bean Casserole

green bean casserole

SERVES 4

4 cups frozen cut green beans
1 medium onion, chopped
1 teaspoon sugar
1 (10¾-ounce) can reduced-fat condensed cream of mushroom soup
¾ cup reduced-fat shredded sharp cheddar cheese
1 teaspoon Worcestershire sauce
½ teaspoon garlic powder
½ cup French-fried onions

This beloved dish comes straight out of the fifties: Made with canned and/or frozen ingredients, it epitomizes that era's penchant for convenience food in all forms. Yet it still finds a place on our tables today, especially around the holidays. We've found a way to capture that same convenience without sacrificing flavor.

1 Preheat the oven to 350°F. Spray an 8-inch-square baking pan with nonstick spray.

2 Cook the green beans according to package directions on the stovetop or in the microwave. Drain and transfer to a large bowl.

3 Spray a small nonstick skillet with nonstick spray and set over medium-high heat. Add the onion and sugar; cook, stirring, until starting to brown, 5–6 minutes. Transfer the onion to the bowl with the green beans. Stir in the soup, cheese, Worcestershire sauce, and garlic powder. Pour into the baking pan.

4 Bake 25 minutes; sprinkle with the French-fried onions and bake until bubbly, 5 minutes longer.

PER SERVING (1 cup): 173 Cal, 8 g Total Fat, 3 g Sat Fat, 13 mg Chol, 514 mg Sod, 18 g Carb, 4 g Fib, 8 g Prot, 231 mg Calc. *PointsPlus value: 4.*

The topping for this classic casserole, canned French-fried onions, are just that—onions dipped in flour and seasonings and deep-fried. If you'd like a modern (and healthier) touch of crunch, try panko bread crumbs, crumbled whole grain snack crackers, or bran cereal.

---

tortilla-cheese casserole

SERVES 6

Vegetarian

4 (6-inch) corn tortillas
1 large sweet onion, chopped
1 green bell pepper, chopped
1½ teaspoons ground cumin
¾ teaspoon dried marjoram
1 (15-ounce) can creamed corn
2 large eggs
3 egg whites
⅔ cup shredded reduced-fat cheddar cheese
2 tablespoons chopped cilantro or parsley
2 tablespoons mild pepper sauce
¾ cup salsa

Corn lovers rejoiced when Weight Watchers removed this tasty vegetable from the "forbidden" list. Here, luxurious-tasting but fat-free creamed corn lends a touch of sweetness and creamy texture to this easy-to-make casserole. Don't worry about the pepper sauce; use a mild, flavorful type like Frank's Red Hot to add a spicy tang without a lot of heat.

1 Place the oven rack in the center of the oven; preheat the oven to 375°F. Spray a 1½-quart casserole dish with nonstick spray. Stack the tortillas and cut crosswise into 1-inch strips. Place the tortilla strips on a baking sheet in a single layer. Bake until lightly golden, 6 minutes.

2 Spray a large nonstick skillet with nonstick spray and set over medium heat. Add the onion and pepper and cook, stirring occasionally, until just tender, 12 minutes. Stir in the cumin and marjoram; remove from the heat and let cool in the pan.

3 Meanwhile, stir together the creamed corn, eggs, egg whites, ⅓ cup of the cheese, the cilantro or parsley, and the pepper sauce in a large bowl until blended. Stir in the cooled vegetable mixture. Spoon about half of the mixture into the prepared dish. Arrange half of the tortilla strips on top. Spoon on the remaining egg mixture and arrange the remaining strips on top. (You can stand a few rounded strips along the edges for a scalloped effect, if you like.) Bake until golden and set in the center, 35–40 minutes. Serve with the salsa.

PER SERVING (⅙ of casserole with 2 tablespoons salsa): 186 Cal, 5 g Total Fat, 2 g Sat Fat, 78 mg Chol, 581 mg Sod, 27 g Carb, 4 g Fib, 11 g Prot, 162 mg Calc.
PointsPlus value: 5.

ratatouille au gratin

SERVES 4

Vegetarian

4 teaspoons olive oil
1 large onion, chopped
2 garlic cloves, minced
1 yellow bell pepper, cut into ½-inch strips
1 green bell pepper, cut into ½-inch strips
1 cup water
1 medium (1¼-pound) eggplant, peeled and chopped
1 medium (8-ounce) zucchini, chopped
1 (14-ounce) can diced tomatoes, with juice
1 cup tomato juice
1 tablespoon chopped basil, or 1 teaspoon dried
1 tablespoon chopped oregano, or 1 teaspoon dried
1 tablespoon chopped thyme, or 1 teaspoon dried
¼ teaspoon salt
Freshly ground pepper
¼ cup freshly grated Parmesan cheese
¼ cup plain dried bread crumbs
Fresh parsley (optional)

Anyone who says she doesn't like vegetables has probably never tasted a good ratatouille. A staple in the south of France (and in the kitchens of seventies gourmet cooks), this medley of Mediterranean vegetables is a tasty addition to just about any meal. Here, we've topped it with a crunchy Parmesan crust for extra impact. Got leftovers? They're even more delicious the next day.

1 Heat a large nonstick skillet over medium heat. Swirl in the oil, then add the onion and garlic. Cook, stirring occasionally, until fragrant, about 2 minutes.

2 Add the yellow and green peppers and ½ cup of the water; cook, stirring frequently, until the liquid has evaporated and the peppers are wilted. Add the eggplant, zucchini, and the remaining ½ cup water; cook, stirring frequently, until the liquid has evaporated and the eggplant and zucchini are wilted. Add the tomatoes, tomato juice, basil, oregano, thyme, salt, and pepper. Cook, stirring occasionally, until the liquid has evaporated and the vegetables are tender, 15–20 minutes.

3 Meanwhile, preheat the broiler. Spray a 2-quart shallow flameproof casserole dish with nonstick spray.

4 Transfer the ratatouille to the casserole dish. Combine the cheese and bread crumbs in a small bowl; sprinkle the mixture over the ratatouille. Broil 5 inches from the heat, watching carefully, until the top is golden brown, about 2 minutes. Sprinkle with the parsley, if using.

PER SERVING (1 cup): 191 Cal, 8 g Total Fat, 2 g Sat Fat, 5 mg Chol, 708 mg Sod, 27 g Carb, 6 g Fib, 7 g Prot, 170 mg Calc.
PointsPlus value: 5.

Ratatouille is a perfect way to use up all those summer veggies from your garden or the farmers' market. Alter this versatile recipe based on what you've got a bumper crop of—use more eggplant and skip the zucchini, add an extra pepper or two, and if you've got fresh tomatoes, use those instead of canned.

asparagus en papillote

SERVES 4

Vegetarian

1 (1-pound) bunch asparagus, trimmed
2 teaspoons olive oil
2 teaspoons fresh lemon juice
¼ teaspoon salt
Freshly ground pepper

When choosing asparagus, look for bunches with straight, firm stalks and with tips tightly closed. To trim, bend the stalks near the base and the woody part of the stalk will snap off.

1 Preheat oven to 400°F. Cut a 24-inch sheet of heavy-duty foil.

2 Place the asparagus in the center of the foil; fold the foil into a packet, rolling and crimping the foil on all sides to make a tight seal. Bake until the asparagus is tender but still bright green, 20–30 minutes (watch for escaping steam as you open the foil to check).

3 Carefully open the packet, avoiding the steam, and transfer the asparagus with tongs to a serving platter. Drizzle with the oil and lemon juice, then sprinkle with the salt and pepper. Serve hot, cold, or at room temperature.

PER SERVING (4–6 spears): 37 Cal, 3 g Total Fat, 0 g Sat Fat, 0 mg Chol, 148 mg Sod, 3 g Carb, 1 g Fib, 2 g Prot, 15 mg Calc. ***PointsPlus value: 1.***

Don't just think of this low *PointsPlus* value recipe as a side dish—have it as a snack, too. Bake extra packets, cool, and refrigerate up to 3 days. Enjoy the asparagus cold with a dip made with 2 tablespoons plain fat-free yogurt and ½ teaspoon grated lemon zest.

broccoli rabe with lemon and garlic

SERVES 4

20 Min or Less

1 bunch broccoli rabe, trimmed of tough stalks, and coarsely chopped
4 teaspoons olive oil
½ cup reduced-sodium chicken broth
4 garlic cloves, minced
¼ teaspoon salt
¼ teaspoon crushed red pepper
2 tablespoons fresh lemon juice
4 lemon wedges (optional)

The first Weight Watchers Cookbook *included a recipe for Lemon Broccoli—cooked broccoli tossed with a little lemon juice and sugar substitute. We've improved on the original by adding a holy trio that makes any green vegetable taste better: lemon, garlic, and a little olive oil. Try this recipe with broccolini, Swiss chard, spinach, or just plain broccoli.*

1 Put the broccoli in a steamer basket; set it in a saucepan over 1 inch of boiling water. Cover tightly and steam until barely tender, 3–5 minutes.

2 Heat a large nonstick skillet. Swirl in the oil, then add the broccoli. Cook, stirring, 1 minute; add the broth, garlic, salt, and pepper. Cook, stirring frequently, until the broccoli is tender but still bright green and the liquid has evaporated, about 5 minutes. Add the lemon juice and toss to coat. Serve with the lemon wedges, if using.

PER SERVING (½ cup): 80 Cal, 5 g Total Fat, 1 g Sat Fat, 0 mg Chol, 236 mg Sod, 7 g Carb, 3 g Fib, 4 g Prot, 58 mg Calc.
PointsPlus value: 2.

brussels sprouts with dried cranberries and lemon

SERVES 4

20 Min or Less
Vegetarian

1 (10-ounce) package Brussels sprouts
½ cup dried cranberries
2 tablespoons fresh lemon juice
4 teaspoons olive oil
¼ teaspoon salt
¼ teaspoon ground pepper

Brussels sprouts used to be counted as a "limited" vegetable in the Weight Watchers program, to be eaten sparingly and only at dinner. To some, that may not have been much of a hardship—but then they hadn't tasted this colorful sweet-and-sour side dish. It pairs perfectly with roasted meat or fowl; try it at Thanksgiving.

1 Trim the tough outer leaves from the Brussels sprouts; slice off the stem end and cut a small × in the bottom of each sprout.

2 Put the sprouts in a steamer basket; set it in a saucepan over 2 inches of boiling water. Cover tightly and steam until the sprouts are tender but still bright green, 10–15 minutes.

3 Combine the cranberries, lemon juice, oil, salt, and pepper in a medium bowl. Add the Brussels sprouts and toss to coat. Serve hot or at room temperature.

PER SERVING (¾ cup): 118 Cal, 5 g Total Fat, 1 g Sat Fat, 0 mg Chol, 163 mg Sod, 19 g Carb, 4 g Fib, 3 g Prot, 19 mg Calc.
PointsPlus value: 3.

To make a roasted version, cut the Brussels sprouts in half, place in a baking pan, and toss with the olive oil, salt, and pepper. Roast at 400°F, stirring once, until browned and tender, about 25 minutes. Transfer to a bowl and stir in the cranberries and lemon juice.

cauliflower puree

SERVES 4

20 Min or Less
Vegetarian

1 medium (2-pound) cauliflower head, trimmed and separated into florets
⅓ cup fat-free half-and-half
½ teaspoon salt
⅛ teaspoon nutmeg
Pinch white pepper

Once upon a time, when potatoes were not allowed on the Weight Watchers Program, members were encouraged to whip up some Mock Mashed Potatoes—or pureed cooked cauliflower—whenever they wanted the real thing. Our update is creamier and more flavorful, but it's still a great substitute for mashed potatoes.

Fill a medium saucepan two-thirds full with water and bring to a boil; add the cauliflower. Reduce the heat and simmer until the cauliflower is soft, about 15 minutes; drain. Pulse the cauliflower in a food processor to a smooth puree. Add the half-and-half, salt, nutmeg, and pepper; pulse to blend. Serve at once.

PER SERVING (½ cup): 45 Cal, 0 g Total Fat, 0 g Sat Fat, 0 mg Chol, 345 mg Sod, 9 g Carb, 3 g Fib, 3 g Prot, 379 mg Calc.
PointsPlus value: 1.

You can also turn the puree into a creamy soup. Just thin it with a (14-ounce) can of reduced-sodium chicken broth to make four (1-cup) servings.

braised red cabbage with apples, onions, and raisins

SERVES 4

Vegetarian

2 teaspoons vegetable oil
1 large red onion, chopped
1 small red cabbage, coarsely chopped
1 cup hot water
1 apple, peeled, cored, and chopped
¼ cup raisins
3 tablespoons firmly packed dark brown sugar
3 tablespoons cider vinegar
½ teaspoon caraway seeds
¼ teaspoon salt
Freshly ground pepper
¼ cup chopped flat-leaf parsley (optional)

The sweet-and-sour tanginess of this side dish is a terrific partner for beef, ham, or pork. And try it on leftover-meat sandwiches, Reuben-style. It's best served a day or two after it's made.

1 Heat a large nonstick skillet. Swirl in the oil, then add the onion. Sauté over medium heat until golden, about 10 minutes.

2 Stir in the cabbage, water, apple, raisins, sugar, vinegar, caraway seeds, salt, and pepper. Reduce the heat to low; cook, covered, stirring occasionally, until the cabbage is tender but still crunchy, about 10 minutes. Uncover and cook, stirring occasionally, until the cabbage is very tender and the liquid has evaporated, about 10 minutes more. Sprinkle with the parsley, if using, or cover tightly and refrigerate until ready to serve.

PER SERVING (1 cup): 159 Cal, 3 g Total Fat, 0 g Sat Fat, 0 mg Chol, 178 mg Sod, 34 g Carb, 5 g Fib, 3 g Prot, 94 mg Calc.
PointsPlus value: 4.

Serve this autumnal side dish with Salisbury Steaks with Mushroom Gravy, page 116, Pork Loin Roast with Gingersnap Sauce, page 117, or Skillet Pork Chops with Onion Gravy, page 122.

---

coleslaw

SERVES 4

20 Min or Less
Vegetarian

- 1 tablespoon + 1 teaspoon reduced-fat mayonnaise
- ¼ cup + 2 tablespoons white wine or cider vinegar
- 3 tablespoons plain fat-free yogurt
- 1 tablespoon vegetable oil
- 1 teaspoon prepared mustard
- ½ teaspoon sugar
- ½ teaspoon celery seeds
- ¼ teaspoon salt
- Freshly ground pepper
- 1 small (1-pound) green cabbage, shredded (4 cups)
- 2 carrots, peeled and grated
- 1 small onion, minced (optional)

Were Weight Watchers members satisfied by the 1966 recipe for Coleslaw, in which shredded cabbage was tossed with a dressing that included mustard, nonfat dry-milk powder, and a little artificial sweetener? We may never know, but we're certain of how tangy and authentic-tasting our twenty-first-century version is.

Whisk the mayonnaise, vinegar, yogurt, oil, mustard, sugar, celery seeds, salt, and pepper in a large nonreactive bowl. Add the cabbage, carrots, and onion, if using, to the bowl; toss to coat evenly. Serve at once, or cover and refrigerate up to 3 hours (add the onion just before serving).

PER SERVING (1½ cups): 92 Cal, 5 g Total Fat, 1 g Sat Fat, 2 mg Chol, 254 mg Sod, 10 g Carb, 3 g Fib, 2 g Prot, 76 mg Calc.
PointsPlus value: 2.

Want to go green? Substitute 5 cups of packaged broccoli slaw mix for the cabbage and carrots.

stir-fried baby bok choy with snow peas, shiitake mushrooms, and ginger

SERVES 4

20 Min or Less
Vegetarian

1 tablespoon vegetable oil
4 (1/4-pound) heads baby bok choy, trimmed, and halved
1/2 cup reduced-sodium vegetable broth
1 onion, cut into 16 wedges
12 shiitake mushroom caps, sliced
1/4 pound snow peas, trimmed and thinly sliced on the diagonal
1 tablespoon reduced-sodium soy sauce
1 teaspoon sesame oil
1 teaspoon grated peeled fresh ginger
2 garlic cloves, finely chopped
1/2 teaspoon crushed red pepper

Stir-frying is the ideal cooking technique for vegetable lovers. Thanks to the larger cooking surface of a wok or large skillet and just a little oil, vegetables cook in a flash and retain their flavor and crunch.

Heat a large skillet or wok over high heat until a drop of water skitters. Pour in the vegetable oil; swirl to coat the pan. Add the bok choy and broth; cover and steam 1 minute. Uncover and stir in the onion and mushroom caps; stir-fry another 2–3 minutes. Add the snow peas, soy sauce, sesame oil, ginger, garlic, and pepper. Cook, stirring continuously, until the vegetables are tender-crisp and the liquid has evaporated, 3–4 minutes.

PER SERVING (1 cup): 100 Cal, 11 g Total Fat, 1 g Sat Fat, 0 mg Chol, 255 mg Sod, 11 g Carb, 3 g Fib, 5 g Prot, 135 mg Calc.
PointsPlus value: 4.

Freeze any leftover ginger in a zip-close freezer bag for up to three months. When you need some, just scrape off an inch or so of its tough brown outer skin and grate it in its frozen state.

Stir-Fried Baby Bok Choy with Snow Peas, Shiitake Mushrooms, and Ginger

steamed cauliflower with raisins and pine nuts

SERVES 4

20 Min or Less
Vegetarian

½ cup raisins
1 medium (2-pound) cauliflower head, trimmed and separated into florets
¼ cup pine nuts
4 teaspoons olive oil
¼ teaspoon salt
Freshly ground white pepper
4 lemon wedges

Here's a surprising trio! The cabbage-y taste and softness of the cauliflower are complemented by the sweet chewiness of the raisins and the crunch of pine nuts. Choose purple cauliflower or vibrant green broccoflower to give the dish some color. Or you could prepare this with broccoli, Brussels sprouts, or chopped sturdy greens like kale, cabbage, or collards instead of cauliflower.

1 Put the raisins in a small bowl of hot water until plump and soft, about 10 minutes; drain and set aside.

2 Put the cauliflower in a steamer basket; set it in a saucepan over 1 inch of boiling water. Cover tightly and steam until tender but not mushy, 6–8 minutes.

3 Meanwhile, toast the pine nuts in a small, dry nonstick skillet over medium-low heat; slide the pan gently back and forth over the heat so the nuts cook evenly. As soon as they begin to turn golden, remove the pan from the heat and transfer the nuts to a heatproof plate to cool.

4 Toss the cauliflower with the raisins, pine nuts, oil, salt, and pepper in a serving bowl. Serve with the lemon wedges.

PER SERVING (1¼ cups): 175 Cal, 9 g Total Fat, 1 g Sat Fat, 0 mg Chol, 191 mg Sod, 24 g Carb, 5 g Fib, 4 g Prot, 41 mg Calc.
PointsPlus value: 5.

the art of the cauliflower

Cauliflower has always been a favorite vegetable for Weight Watchers members because of its versatility: When pureed, its creamy texture mimics real cream and its mild flavor makes it adaptable to almost any dish—even macaroni and cheese! Try these retro recipes and see how versatile and delicious cauliflower can be.

baked macaroni, cheese, and cauliflower casserole circa 1980

SERVES 2

***PointsPlus* value: *12* per serving (1½ cups)**

2 tablespoons margarine
2 tablespoons all-purpose flour
1 cup fat-free milk
2 ounces shredded cheddar cheese
2 cups cooked cauliflower florets
1⅓ cups cooked macaroni
½ cup canned sliced mushrooms
Salt and white pepper to taste

Preheat the oven to 350°F. Spray a 1-quart baking dish with nonstick spray. Set aside.

Melt the margarine in a small saucepan set over medium heat. Add the flour and cook, stirring constantly, until the mixture comes to a boil. Slowly whisk in the milk. Cook, whisking constantly, until the mixture comes to a boil and thickens, about 5 minutes. Remove from the heat and add the cheddar, whisking until melted. Stir in the cauliflower, macaroni, mushrooms, salt, and pepper.

Spoon the mixture into the prepared baking dish and bake until bubbling, about 25 minutes.

"fried" cauliflower circa 1980

SERVES 2

***PointsPlus* value: *5* per serving (1 cup)**

1 large egg
3 tablespoons plain dried bread crumbs
2 cups cauliflower florets, cooked and cooled
1 tablespoon vegetable oil
⅛ teaspoon salt
Pinch black pepper

Place the egg in a shallow bowl and beat lightly. Place the bread crumbs in another shallow bowl. Dip the cauliflower in the egg, then in the bread crumbs; toss to coat.

Heat a medium nonstick skillet over medium heat. Swirl in the oil. Add the cauliflower and cook, turning often, until browned on all sides, 6–8 minutes. Transfer to a plate; sprinkle with the salt and pepper.

"cream" of cauliflower soup circa 1970

SERVES 6

***PointsPlus* value: *2* per serving (about ¾ cup)**

3 cups chopped cauliflower
2 cups reduced-sodium chicken broth
1 cup chopped celery
1 tablespoon dehydrated onion flakes
¼ teaspoon salt
Pinch white pepper
1½ cups fat-free evaporated milk

Combine the cauliflower, broth, celery, onion flakes, salt, and pepper in a large saucepan; cover and simmer until the vegetables are very soft, about 20 minutes. Uncover and let cool slightly.

Puree the cauliflower mixture in a blender. Return the puree to the saucepan and stir in the milk. Set over medium-low heat and cook, stirring often, until heated through (do not boil).

Note: All ***PointsPlus*** values were calculated using the Weight Watchers online recipe builder.

corn, zucchini, and green bean succotash

SERVES 4

20 Min or Less
Vegetarian

½ pound green beans, trimmed and cut into 1½-inch lengths
2 tablespoons unsalted butter
1 medium onion, chopped
1 garlic clove, minced
1 medium (8-ounce) zucchini, quartered lengthwise and cut into ½-inch pieces
2 plum tomatoes, seeded and chopped
2 cups cooked or thawed frozen corn kernels
½ teaspoon salt
⅛ teaspoon nutmeg
⅛ teaspoon cayenne

Succotash is a traditional Southern dish made from lima beans plus red or green bell peppers. In our version, we've given it a little more crunch with the addition of zucchini and green beans.

1 Bring a large pot of water to a boil. Add the beans; return to a boil and cook until just bright green, 3 minutes. Drain in a colander under cold water to stop cooking.

2 Melt the butter in a large skillet over medium-high heat. Stir in the onion and garlic; cook until starting to soften, 3 minutes. Add the zucchini and tomatoes, and sauté until softened, 3 minutes. Stir in the green beans, corn, salt, nutmeg, and cayenne; cook until heated through, about 3 minutes.

PER SERVING (1¼ cups): 151 Cal, 6 g Total Fat, 4 g Sat Fat, 16 mg Chol, 304 mg Sod, 24 g Carb, 5 g Fib, 4 g Prot, 43 mg Calc.
PointsPlus value: 4.

Succotash is the perfect summer side dish for—actually everything. Serve it with steak, BBQ ribs, roasted chicken, or grilled fish. Or, make it the centerpiece of a summer vegetable plate.

green beans with tomato and oregano

SERVES 4

Vegetarian

1 pound green beans, trimmed
4 teaspoons olive oil
1 onion, chopped
4 plum tomatoes, chopped
1 tablespoon chopped oregano, or 1 teaspoon dried
¼ teaspoon salt
Freshly ground pepper
Fresh oregano sprigs (optional)

Those who remember the old days of Weight Watchers fondly recall the recipe Cold String Bean Stew: frozen string beans, onions, and tomatoes cooked in chicken stock. After you've tried this twenty-first-century version—including fresh green beans with fresh oregano—it may become one of your family's new favorites.

1 Put the green beans in a steamer basket; set it in a saucepan over 1 inch of boiling water. Cover tightly and steam the beans until tender but still bright green, about 8 minutes. Rinse in a colander under cold water to stop the cooking; set aside.

2 Heat a large nonstick skillet. Swirl in the oil, then add the onion. Sauté until golden brown, 10–12 minutes. Add the tomatoes and sauté until they release some of their moisture, about 2 minutes.

3 Add the green beans, oregano, salt, and pepper to the skillet; cook over low heat, stirring occasionally, until heated through. Garnish with the oregano sprigs, if using, and serve at once.

PER SERVING (1½ cups): 89 Cal, 5 g Total Fat, 1 g Sat Fat, 0 mg Chol, 160 mg Sod, 11 g Carb, 4 g Fib, 2 g Prot, 59 mg Calc.
PointsPlus value: 2.

Got leftover oregano? Freeze the whole leaves (washed and thoroughly dried) in a zip-close freezer bag for up to three months. Once frozen, the oregano can be used (unthawed) in any recipe in which it is cooked.

baked vidalia onions balsamico

SERVES 4

Vegetarian

2 (8-ounce) Vidalia onions, peeled, trimmed, and sliced ¼-inch thick
¼ cup water
2 teaspoons olive oil
2 tablespoons balsamic vinegar
2 teaspoons sugar
½ tablespoon chopped thyme
¼ teaspoon salt
Freshly ground pepper
Fresh thyme sprigs (optional)

Two culinary discoveries of the eighties and nineties—sweet Vidalia onions and rich, caramel-like balsamic vinegar—combine to make a delightfully sweet side dish.

1 Prehcat the oven to 425°F. Spread the onions evenly in a 9 × 13-inch baking dish; pour in the water. Drizzle with the oil and vinegar; sprinkle with the sugar, thyme, salt, and pepper. Cover and bake until tender, about 30 minutes.

2 Uncover and continue baking, adding water ¼ cup at a time as needed to keep the onions moist, basting occasionally, until the onions are golden brown and caramelized, about 25 minutes. Garnish with the fresh thyme sprigs, if using.

PER SERVING (½ onion): 69 Cal, 3 g Total Fat, 0 g Sat Fat, 0 mg Chol, 149 mg Sod, 12 g Carb, 2 g Fib, 1 g Prot, 24 mg Calc.
PointsPlus value: 2.

oven-fried onion rings

SERVES 4

Vegetarian

2 tablespoons all-purpose flour
¼ teaspoon salt
Freshly ground pepper
⅓ cup plain dried bread crumbs
¼ cup fat-free egg substitute
2 large (8-ounce) onions, peeled, sliced ¼-inch thick, and separated into double rings

Through the years, Weight Watchers has learned many a thing about faux frying—and these crispy rings are proof. Though they're baked in the oven, they've got all the flavor and crunch of the rings served at your favorite steak house or pub, minus the greasiness. They're perfect for pairing with everything from burgers to steak.

1 Adjust the oven racks to divide the oven in half. Preheat the oven to 400°F. Spray a nonstick baking sheet with nonstick spray. On a sheet of waxed paper, combine the flour, salt, and pepper. Place the bread crumbs on another sheet of wax paper. Place the egg substitute in a shallow dish.

2 Coat each double onion ring on both sides with the flour mixture, shaking off the excess; dip into the egg substitute, then coat lightly with the bread crumbs. Arrange the rings on the baking sheet (save any broken or small inner rings or pieces for another use), and spray the tops with nonstick spray. Discard the excess flour mixture, egg, and bread crumbs.

3 Bake on the top oven rack until browned, 10 minutes. Turn carefully and bake until browned, 5 minutes. Serve at once.

PER SERVING (1 cup): 95 Cal, 1 g Total Fat, 0 g Sat Fat, 0 mg Chol, 245 mg Sod, 19 g Carb, 3 g Fib, 4 g Prot, 47 mg Calc.
PointsPlus value: 2.

Chop and freeze the unused parts of the onions in a zip-close freezer bag. Then you'll have them on hand when you need chopped onions in a recipe (don't bother thawing first).

cheddar corn pudding

SERVES 6

Vegetarian

1½ tablespoons all-purpose flour
1 cup low-fat (1%) milk
2 cups frozen corn kernels
2 scallions, chopped
2 teaspoons sugar
¼ teaspoon salt
¼ teaspoon poultry seasoning or dried thyme
¼ teaspoon ground pepper
1 large egg
1 egg white
½ cup shredded reduced-fat cheddar cheese

Ultra creamy and rich-tasting, you'll never believe this casserole doesn't contain a speck of cream— and knowing that corn used to be a "forbidden" food on the Weight Watchers program just makes it even more satisfying. The perfect side dish for a holiday meal!

1 Place the oven rack in the center of the oven; preheat the oven to 350°F. Spray a 1-quart baking dish with nonstick spray.

2 Place the flour in a medium saucepan. Gradually whisk in the milk. Add the corn, scallions, sugar, salt, poultry seasoning or thyme, and pepper. Bring to a simmer over medium heat, whisking frequently; cook until slightly thickened, 2 minutes.

3 Beat the egg and egg white in a small bowl. Gradually beat in some of the hot milk mixture, whisking constantly. Whisk the egg mixture back into the saucepan. Reserve 2 tablespoons of the cheese; stir the remaining cheese into the corn mixture. Spoon into the prepared baking dish and sprinkle the reserved cheese on top.

4 Pull the oven rack partly out. Place a large roasting pan on the rack; place the corn casserole inside it. Carefully pour enough hot water into the roasting pan to fill it one-third of the way up the side of the casserole. Bake until the pudding is just set in the center, about 35 minutes. Remove from the water bath and serve.

PER SERVING (⅙ of casserole): 115 Cal, 3 g Total Fat, 2 g Sat Fat, 42 mg Chol, 190 mg Sod, 16 g Carb, 2 g Fib, 7 g Prot, 130 mg Calc.
PointsPlus value: 3.

pureed peas with mint

SERVES 4

20 Min or Less
Vegetarian

- 1 (10-ounce package) frozen peas, or 1½ pounds fresh peas, shelled (about 2 cups)
- 2 tablespoons chopped mint
- 1 tablespoon unsalted butter
- ¼ teaspoon salt
- Freshly ground white pepper
- 2–3 tablespoons reduced-sodium vegetable broth, heated
- Mint leaves or small sprigs (optional)

"Delicious used as a stuffing for 1 cup baked mushroom caps," suggests the Weight Watchers Program Cookbook *(1972) for its Puree of Peas recipe—cooked frozen peas pureed with a little onion powder and chopped chives. We'd rather serve our updated version, with its fresh-mint flavor, as a side dish or sauce. It's especially good with lamb.*

1 Cook the peas according to package directions. (If using fresh peas, steam them over 1 inch of boiling water until just tender and bright green, 3–6 minutes, depending on their freshness.)

2 Puree the peas with the mint, butter, salt, and pepper in a food processor; add the broth, one tablespoon at a time, until the mixture has a thick, creamy consistency. Garnish with the mint leaves or sprigs, if using.

PER SERVING (¼ cup): 75 Cal, 3 g Total Fat, 2 g Sat Fat, 8 mg Chol, 63 mg Sod, 9 g Carb, 4 g Fib, 3 g Prot, 19 mg Calc.
PointsPlus value: 2.

creamed spinach

SERVES 4

20 Min or Less
Vegetarian

- 1 (1-pound) bag triple-washed fresh spinach, trimmed and torn
- 1 onion, minced
- ½ tablespoon all-purpose flour
- ¼ teaspoon salt
- Freshly ground white pepper
- Pinch ground nutmeg
- ¼ cup fat-free milk
- ¼ cup tub-style light cream cheese, softened

The second edition of Weight Watchers Program Cookbook *came up with a clever way of re-creating the creamy goodness of this classic steak house side dish, using a puree of braised onions, chicken broth, and nonfat dry-milk powder. Now that steak houses are enjoying a renaissance, we decided to revisit the dish—with creamier, tastier results!*

1 Put the spinach in a steamer basket; set it in a large pot over 1 inch of boiling water (the leaves will be tightly packed but will reduce as they start to wilt). Cover tightly and steam until just wilted, about 2 minutes. Drain in a colander; when cool enough to handle, squeeze out the excess moisture and coarsely chop.

2 Spray a medium nonstick skillet with nonstick spray and set over medium heat. Add the onion; sauté until translucent, 3–5 minutes.

3 Combine the flour, salt, pepper, and nutmeg in a small bowl; stir into the onion. Add the milk and cream cheese; cook one minute, stirring constantly with a whisk, until blended. Add the spinach; cook, stirring constantly, until just heated through.

PER SERVING (½ cup): 71 Cal, 2 g Total Fat, 1 g Sat Fat, 6 mg Chol, 300 mg Sod, 0 g Carb, 4 g Fib, 5 g Prot, 148 mg Calc.
PointsPlus value: 1.

If you buy bagged baby spinach in a microwavable bag, you can speed through Step 1: Following the directions on the spinach bag, microwave the spinach. Transfer the cooked greens to a colander. When cool enough to handle, squeeze out the excess moisture.

sautéed swiss chard and onion

SERVES 4

20 Min or Less
Vegetarian

4 teaspoons olive oil
1 onion, chopped
1 bunch Swiss chard, tough stems removed and leaves thinly sliced
¼ teaspoon salt
Freshly ground pepper
4 lemon wedges (optional)

The natural sweetness of onions is one reason why they were once considered a "limited" vegetable in the early days of Weight Watchers. Here, we've used that sweet onion flavor to tame the natural bitterness of earthy chard. This trick works for any leafy green, by the way.

Heat a large nonstick skillet. Swirl in the oil, then add the onion. Sauté until golden, 8–10 minutes. Stir in the chard and continue cooking until the chard is tender but still a vivid dark green, about 7 minutes. Remove from the heat and sprinkle with the salt and pepper. Serve hot or at room temperature with the lemon wedges, if using.

PER SERVING (½ cup): 68 Cal, 5 g Total Fat, 1 g Sat Fat, 0 mg Chol, 299 mg Sod, 6 g Carb, 2 g Fib, 2 g Prot, 56 mg Calc.
PointsPlus value: 2.

Here's a quick way to slice the chard: Stack a few leaves together, roll them up, and slice them.

roasted root vegetables

SERVES 4

Vegetarian

- 2 carrots, peeled and cut into chunks
- 2 medium (5-ounce) potatoes, peeled and cut into chunks
- 1 white turnip, peeled and cut into chunks
- 1 shallot, peeled and separated into cloves
- 4 teaspoons olive oil
- 1 tablespoon chopped fresh rosemary, or 1 teaspoon dried
- 1 tablespoon chopped fresh thyme, or 1 teaspoon dried
- ¼ teaspoon salt
- Freshly ground pepper

Everybody—especially health-conscious cooks—fell in love with their roasting pans in the nineties. What better tool to help turn humble vegetables into something glorious? In this very autumnal and colorful dish, carrots, potatoes, and turnip form a medley of roasted earthiness but any mix of root veggies will work. Serve alongside meat or poultry.

1 Preheat the oven to 400°F.

2 Combine the carrots, potatoes, turnip, and shallot in a large nonstick roasting pan; drizzle with the oil and sprinkle with the rosemary, thyme, salt, and pepper. Spread the vegetables evenly in the pan.

3 Roast, stirring occasionally, until the shallots are caramelized and the vegetables are browned and tender, about 40 minutes.

PER SERVING (½ cup): 119 Cal, 5 g Total Fat, 1 g Sat Fat, 0 mg Chol, 177 mg Sod, 19 g Carb, 3 g Fib, 2 g Prot, 32 mg Calc.
PointsPlus value: 3.

Almost any vegetable can be roasted. Some unusual options to try: Green beans, broccoli florets, okra pods, or scallions. Lightly spray them with cooking spray, season with salt and pepper and roast in a 400°F oven, stirring occasionally, until crisp-tender, 15 to 30 minutes.

carrot salad with sesame–ginger dressing

SERVES 4

Vegetarian

8 large carrots, peeled and thinly sliced on the diagonal (about 2 pounds)
½ cup water
2 tablespoons rice-wine or cider vinegar
1 tablespoon vegetable oil
1 teaspoon grated peeled fresh ginger
1 teaspoon sesame oil
½ teaspoon ground cumin
½ teaspoon sugar
¼ teaspoon salt
Freshly ground pepper
2 tablespoons sesame seeds
2 tablespoons chopped cilantro (optional)

A tasty and satisfying break from traditional green salads, this Asian-inspired combination is a great partner for shrimp, pork, or chicken. It's also a real crowd pleaser at a buffet supper.

1 Put the carrots in a steamer basket; set it in a saucepan over 2 inches of boiling water. Cover tightly and steam until tender, about 10 minutes. Set aside to cool to room temperature.

2 To prepare the dressing, puree ½ cup of the carrots, the water, vinegar, vegetable oil, ginger, sesame oil, cumin, sugar, salt, and pepper in a food processor.

3 To toast the sesame seeds, place them in a small nonstick skillet over medium-low heat; slide the pan constantly and gently back and forth over the heat so the seeds move around. As soon as they begin to turn golden, remove the pan from the heat and transfer to a heatproof plate to cool.

4 Toss the remaining carrots with the dressing and the sesame seeds in a large bowl. Sprinkle with the cilantro, if using, and serve at once.

PER SERVING (1 cup): 164 Cal, 7 g Total Fat, 1 g Sat Fat, 0 mg Chol, 225 mg Sod, 24 g Carb, 7 g Fib, 3 g Prot, 70 mg Calc.
PointsPlus value: 4.

You can make this salad up to four days in advance—just cover and refrigerate—but wait until serving time to sprinkle on the cilantro.

Oven-Fried Onion Rings, page 261, and Idaho Fries with Vinegar

idaho fries with vinegar

SERVES 4

Vegetarian

4 (5-ounce) Idaho potatoes, scrubbed
1 tablespoon olive or vegetable oil
¼ teaspoon salt
¼ teaspoon freshly ground pepper
2 tablespoons malt or white vinegar

Who can resist fries? This version allows you to indulge in one of the most adored foods in America. A fairly hot oven, with the rack near the hot oven bottom, guarantees a crisp potato. Eat them hot, with a splash of malt vinegar instead of ketchup, as the Brits do.

1 Adjust the oven rack to the lowest position in the oven. Preheat the oven to 450°F.

2 Cut the potatoes lengthwise into eighths to form wedges. Toss the potatoes with the oil on a heavy baking sheet or jelly-roll pan, and arrange them flat in a single layer. Bake the potatoes without turning, until the bottoms are deep golden and crisp, 20 minutes; turn the potatoes to the opposite cut side. Bake 10 minutes more until crisp. Remove from the oven and immediately sprinkle with the salt and pepper, then the vinegar. (You can also serve the vinegar in a small bowl on the side, for dipping.)

PER SERVING (8 fries): 154 Cal, 3 g Total Fat, 0 g Sat Fat, 0 mg Chol, 155 mg Sod, 29 g Carb, 3 g Fib, 3 g Prot, 13 mg Calc.
PointsPlus value: 4.

A different flavored vinegar will give these crispy fries even more pizzazz. Try white wine or tarragon vinegar—or even a fruit-infused version, such as pear or raspberry vinegar.

greek-style twice-baked potatoes

SERVES 4

Vegetarian

4 (5-ounce) Idaho potatoes, scrubbed
⅓ cup crumbled feta cheese, room temperature
⅓ cup plain low-fat (1%) yogurt, room temperature
1 tablespoon melted butter
1 tablespoon snipped fresh chives

Twice-baked potatoes were the trendy dish of the eighties. Today we've updated them with a Greek twist. If you prefer a classic version, use shredded extra-sharp cheddar in place of the feta cheese.

1 Preheat the oven to 425°F. Bake the potatoes on the oven rack until a knife can easily pierce the center of each potato, about 45 minutes. Remove the potatoes and let cool slightly on a rack; reduce the oven heat to 375°F.

2 Split the potatoes in half horizontally (use oven mitts to protect your hands). Scoop out the flesh from each potato half, leaving a ¼-inch-thick layer still in the shell. Transfer the potato flesh to a medium bowl.

3 Add the feta, yogurt, butter, and chives to the potato flesh and mash well. Stuff the filling into the shells and arrange filling-side up on a baking sheet. Bake until the filling is hot in the center and the edges are lightly browned, about 12 minutes.

PER SERVING (2 potato halves): 194 Cal, 6 g Total Fat, 4 g Sat Fat, 20 mg Chol, 181 mg Sod, 31 g Carb, 3 g Fib, 6 g Prot, 113 mg Calc.
PointsPlus value: 5.

roasted-garlic mashed potatoes

SERVES 8

Vegetarian

1 head garlic, top third sliced off
3 pounds Yukon Gold potatoes, peeled and cut into 1-inch pieces
⅔ cup low-fat (1%) milk
¼ cup (½ stick) unsalted butter
1½ teaspoons salt
¼ teaspoon freshly ground pepper

The term "comfort food" was coined in the eighties, and we can think of no better homage to these words than mashed potatoes. We've chosen rich-tasting, yellow-fleshed Yukon Gold potatoes and added mellow, fat-free flavor with a whole head of sweet roasted garlic. No one will miss the cream!

1 Preheat the oven to 400°F. Wrap the garlic with foil and place directly on the oven rack; roast until soft, 50–60 minutes. Remove from the oven and let cool completely. Squeeze the pulp from each clove and reserve; discard the skins.

2 Combine the potatoes in a large pot with enough cold water to cover them by 3 inches. Bring to a boil over high heat; simmer until tender, about 20 minutes. Drain the potatoes and return them to the pot. Mash the potatoes with a potato masher until fairly smooth.

3 Meanwhile, combine the milk, the reserved garlic, the butter, salt, and pepper in a medium saucepan. Cook over medium heat, stirring occasionally, until the butter melts and the mixture is heated through. Stir into the potatoes and serve at once.

PER SERVING (¾ cup): 196 Cal, 6 g Total Fat, 4 g Sat Fat, 16 mg Chol, 455 mg Sod, 33 g Carb, 3 g Fib, 4 g Prot, 45 mg Calc.
PointsPlus value: 5.

german hot potato salad

SERVES 4

1½ pounds Yukon Gold potatoes, peeled
1 slice bacon
1 teaspoon olive oil
1 medium red onion, very thinly sliced
¼–½ teaspoon crushed red pepper
¼ cup reduced-sodium chicken broth
2 tablespoons grainy mustard
1 tablespoon sherry vinegar
1 teaspoon sugar

It's still a favorite after all these years, and we've lightened it up and upgraded the ingredients for twenty-first-century palates. We use Yukon Gold potatoes for their smooth flavor, as well as premium-quality grainy mustard and sherry vinegar.

1 Combine the potatoes and enough water to cover by 1 inch in a medium saucepan; bring to a boil and cook until fork-tender, about 20 minutes. Drain and let cool to just warm. Cut into bite-size chunks and place in a large bowl.

2 Meanwhile, cook the bacon in a medium nonstick skillet until crisp; pat dry with paper towels, and finely chop. Measure the pan drippings, and add enough oil to equal 2 teaspoons; return the skillet to the heat.

3 Add the onion and red pepper; sauté over medium heat until tender, 2 minutes. Stir in the broth, mustard, vinegar, and sugar; bring to a simmer. Pour over the potatoes; toss gently and let stand 2–3 minutes to absorb some of the dressing. Sprinkle with the chopped bacon.

PER SERVING (1 cup): 181 Cal, 4 g Total Fat, 1 g Sat Fat, 2 mg Chol, 162 mg Sod, 34 g Carb, 3 g Fib, 4 g Prot, 24 mg Calc.
PointsPlus value: 5.

You can make this dish with cold leftover cooked potatoes, too—just skip Step 1. Be sure to warm the potatoes in a microwave before pouring the hot dressing over them; the warmth helps them absorb the dressing.

potato salad with tarragon-chive dressing

SERVES 6

- 1¾ pounds Yukon Gold potatoes, peeled and quartered
- 2 tablespoons minced chives
- 2 tablespoons white-wine or cider vinegar
- 4 teaspoons olive oil
- 1 tablespoon chopped tarragon
- 1 tablespoon chopped parsley
- 1 tablespoon dry white wine or reduced-sodium chicken broth
- ¼ teaspoon salt
- Freshly ground pepper
- Small handful whole chives (optional)
- 2–3 tarragon sprigs (optional)
- 2–3 parsley sprigs (optional)

On a summer evening, this salad is the perfect accompaniment to anything grilled. It's best made ahead of time and left at room temperature, as it loses its fresh taste once refrigerated.

1 Combine the potatoes and enough water to cover by 1 inch in a medium saucepan; bring to a boil and cook until fork-tender, about 20 minutes. Drain and let cool to just warm. Cut into bite-size chunks.

2 Combine the chives, vinegar, oil, tarragon, parsley, wine or broth, salt, and pepper in a large bowl; add the still-warm potatoes and toss to coat evenly. Garnish with the whole chives, tarragon sprigs, and/or parsley sprigs, if using. Let stand at least 30 minutes, and up to 3 hours, before serving.

PER SERVING (½ cup): 132 Cal, 3 g Total Fat, 0 g Sat Fat, 0 mg Chol, 105 mg Sod, 24 g Carb, 3 g Fib, 2 g Prot, 13 mg Calc.
PointsPlus value: 3.

sweet potato fritters

SERVES 4

Vegetarian

2 (8-ounce) sweet potatoes
¼ cup low-fat (1%) milk
1 large egg, separated
4 teaspoons sugar
½ teaspoon grated fresh ginger
¼ teaspoon salt
⅛ teaspoon cinnamon
¼ cup all-purpose flour
½ teaspoon baking powder

Using the (very) Petite Potato Pancakes in the 1972 Weight Watchers Program Cookbook *as a starting point, we've updated the recipe with sweet potatoes, global flavors, and best of all, a satisfying portion size.*

1 Preheat oven to 425°F. Line a baking sheet with foil. Pierce the potatoes in several places with a fork and place on the baking sheet. Bake until a knife can pierce them easily, 40 minutes. When cool enough to handle, peel off and discard the skins.

2 Rice or mash the potatoes, using a potato ricer or potato masher, in a medium bowl. Whisk in the milk, egg yolk, sugar, ginger, salt, and cinnamon. Combine the flour and baking powder in a cup or small bowl.

3 With an electric mixer on medium speed, beat the egg white to soft peaks in a medium bowl. Gently fold into the potato mixture. Sprinkle the flour mixture over the top and fold in until smooth.

4 Spray a large nonstick skillet with nonstick spray; heat over medium heat. Drop the batter into the skillet by slightly rounded tablespoonfuls, flattening them slightly to form 6 (2-inch) patties. Cook until golden and set, about 1½ minutes per side. Transfer to a warmed plate, cover loosely with foil, and continue with the remaining potato mixture to make 24 fritters. Serve immediately.

PER SERVING (6 fritters): 147 Cal, 2 g Total Fat, 1 g Sat Fat, 54 mg Chol, 237 mg Sod, 28 g Carb, 2 g Fib, 4 g Prot, 80 mg Calc.
PointsPlus value: 4.

Serve these pleasantly sweet fritters alongside saucy dishes like chili and curry, or with roasted pork, beef, or turkey—even our Cajun Catfish [see page 158].

grits with cheese

SERVES 4

20 Min or Less
Vegetarian

1¾ cups water
3 scallions, chopped
¼ teaspoon salt
¼ teaspoon dried thyme
½ cup quick-cooking grits
½ cup shredded reduced-fat cheddar cheese
3 tablespoons freshly grated Parmesan cheese
¼ teaspoon ground pepper

Grits are made from ground hominy—dried corn kernels from which the hull and germ have been removed. They are no longer just a Southern secret. In our version, they're spiked with creamy cheeses and other flavorings to make an anything-but-boring side dish. Make sure to use the quick-cooking grits to save time.

Bring the water, scallions, salt, and thyme to a boil in a medium saucepan. Slowly stir in the grits and reduce the heat to medium-low. Cover and cook, stirring occasionally, until thickened, about 9 minutes. Remove from the heat and stir in the cheddar and Parmesan cheeses and the pepper. Serve hot.

PER SERVING (½ cup): 138 Cal, 4 g Total Fat, 2 g Sat Fat, 11 mg Chol, 310 mg Sod, 17 g Carb, 1 g Fib, 8 g Prot, 182 mg Calc. ***PointsPlus value: 4.***

fried rice

SERVES 6

Vegetarian

- 1 tablespoon peanut or vegetable oil
- ¼ pound snow peas, thinly sliced
- 1 large celery stalk, diced
- 1 large carrot, coarsely shredded
- 1 large shallot, finely chopped
- 2 teaspoons grated fresh ginger
- ¼ teaspoon crushed red pepper
- 2½ cups cold cooked rice
- 3 tablespoons reduced-sodium soy sauce
- 1 tablespoon rice vinegar
- 1 teaspoon sugar
- ⅓ cup sliced scallion, green part only

Fried rice was one of the first dishes to convert Westerners to the pleasures of Chinese take-out, and it's actually very easy to make at home. The key is to use cold cooked rice; make it at least an hour ahead to allow it to chill thoroughly. Or that leftover take-out white rice in your fridge from a few nights ago? Works perfectly.

1 Heat a large nonstick skillet over high heat; swirl in the oil and add the snow peas, celery, carrot, shallot, ginger, and red pepper. Stir-fry 2 minutes; add the rice, stirring well to remove any clumps, and stir-fry until hot, 3–4 minutes.

2 Combine the soy sauce, vinegar, and sugar in a small bowl; sprinkle over the rice, along with the scallion, and stir-fry just to heat through, 2 minutes more. Serve immediately.

PER SERVING (¾ cup): 135 Cal, 3 g Total Fat, 0 g Sat Fat, 0 mg Chol, 316 mg Sod, 25 g Carb, 2 g Fib, 3 g Prot, 31 mg Calc.
PointsPlus value: 4.

bulgur pilaf

SERVES 6

- 1 tablespoon olive oil
- 2 shallots, finely chopped
- 1 cup coarse bulgur
- 1 large garlic clove, finely chopped
- 1 teaspoon cumin seeds
- 1 (14-ounce) can reduced-sodium chicken broth
- ½ teaspoon salt
- ¼ teaspoon cinnamon
- 1 (15-ounce) can chickpeas, drained and rinsed
- 7 dried mission figs, cut into small pieces
- 3 tablespoons finely chopped cilantro

Because this dish is simmered, it works best with coarse bulgur, not the finer stuff used for tabbouleh. Look for coarse bulgur in health-food stores, but no worries if you can't find it. The recipe will work just as well with regular bulgur but will have a softer texture and cook 5 to 10 minutes faster.

Heat a medium saucepan over medium heat. Swirl in the oil, then add the shallot. Sauté until translucent, 3 minutes. Add the bulgur, garlic, and cumin; toast, stirring occasionally, 3 minutes. Stir in the broth, salt, and cinnamon; reduce the heat, cover, and simmer until the liquid is absorbed, 15–18 minutes. Remove from the heat and let stand 5 minutes. Add the chickpeas, figs, and cilantro, fluffing with a fork.

PER SERVING (¾ cup): 194 Cal, 4 g Total Fat, 0 g Sat Fat, 0 mg Chol, 548 mg Sod, 35 g Carb, 8 g Fib, 7 g Prot, 43 mg Calc.
PointsPlus value: 5.

Bulgur is one of the quickest cooking whole grains—and one of the healthiest, too. It is made from wheat kernels that are boiled, dried, and then cracked; the pre-cooking step is what makes the end product so quick to prepare. With 4 grams in just ½ cup, it's a great source of fiber.

---

quinoa pilaf

SERVES 4

- 1 tablespoon olive oil
- 1 medium fennel bulb, finely chopped
- 1 onion, finely chopped
- 1 celery stalk, finely chopped
- 1 carrot, finely chopped
- 2 garlic cloves, minced
- ½ teaspoon salt
- ¼ teaspoon lightly crushed fennel seeds
- ⅛ teaspoon freshly ground pepper
- 1 cup quinoa, well rinsed
- 1½ cups reduced-sodium chicken broth
- ¼ cup chopped parsley
- 1 tablespoon chopped tarragon

An ancient grain highly prized by the Incas and still a staple in South American cookery, quinoa was rediscovered by adventurous American cooks in the nineties. Pronounced "keen-wah," this protein-rich grain looks like millet; has a delightful nutty, slightly herbal flavor; and best of all, cooks in minutes. Look for it in natural food stores and better supermarkets.

1 Heat a large saucepan over medium heat. Swirl in the oil, then add the fennel, onion, celery, carrot, garlic, salt, fennel seeds, and pepper; cook, stirring occasionally, until softened, about 5 minutes.

2 Stir in the quinoa and cook, stirring, 2 minutes. Add the broth and bring to a boil; reduce the heat to medium-low, cover, and simmer until the liquid is absorbed, about 15 minutes. Remove from the heat, let stand 5 minutes. Fluff with a fork, and stir in the parsley and tarragon.

PER SERVING (1 cup): 246 Cal, 7 g Total Fat, 1 g Sat Fat, 0 mg Chol, 530 mg Sod, 39 g Carb, 6 g Fib, 9 g Prot, 87 mg Calc.
PointsPlus value: 6.

Quinoa should be rinsed well to remove a naturally occurring bitter-tasting residue on the grain. To do so, place it in a sieve set into a large pot; pour in enough cold water to cover. Swirl the grains, allowing any debris to rise to the top. Pour off the debris, then drain well. Repeat until the water is clear.

---

confetti rice salad

SERVES 4

Vegetarian

- 2 cups water
- 1 cup Wehani-japonica-brown-rice blend, or other brown rice
- 3 teaspoons olive oil
- 1 small red bell pepper, diced
- 1 small yellow bell pepper, diced
- ½ cup cooked shelled green soybeans (edamame)
- ⅓ red onion, finely chopped
- 1 tablespoon rice-wine vinegar
- 1 tablespoon fresh lime juice
- 1 teaspoon finely chopped cilantro
- ½ teaspoon sugar

The Rice Salad in the Weight Watchers International Cookbook *printed in 1977 made a little bit of rice go a long way, with tomatoes, radishes, scallions, and parsley. Our update takes it to a new level by using green soybeans (edamame) and a mixed brown-rice combination.*

1 Combine water, rice, and 1 teaspoon of the oil in a medium saucepan. Bring to a boil, cover, reduce the heat, and simmer until the liquid is absorbed, about 45 minutes. Remove from the heat and let stand, covered, 30 minutes. (This helps reduce starchiness, giving the rice grains a better texture for salad.) Fluff with a fork.

2 Combine the red bell pepper, yellow bell pepper, soybeans, onion, vinegar, lime juice, the remaining 2 teaspoons oil, the cilantro, and sugar in another bowl; add to the rice and toss.

PER SERVING (generous 1 cup): 237 Cal, 5 g Total Fat, 1 g Sat Fat, 0 mg Chol, 10 mg Sod, 41 g Carb, 5 g Fib, 6 g Prot, 36 mg Calc.
PointsPlus value: 6.

best-in-show

delicious desserts and sweet treats

ambrosia

SERVES 6

20 Min or Less
Vegetarian

3 tablespoons honey
2 navel oranges
¼ medium pineapple, trimmed, cored, and cubed (1½ cups)
1 tart green or red apple, cored and chopped
1 cup seedless red or green grapes, (halved, if large)
¼ cup sweetened shredded coconut
½ ounce pecan halves, toasted and finely chopped (about 2 tablespoons)

To make this timeless Southern favorite, feel free to vary the fruits to your liking. But to keep it authentically Southern, be sure to include the coconut and pecans. We're breaking tradition, however, by omitting the maraschino cherries.

1 Place the honey in a large bowl. Trim the rind and white pith from the oranges, then cut each orange in half lengthwise. Slice the orange halves crosswise into ¼-inch-thick half rounds; place in the bowl, along with any of the juices. Add the pineapple, apple, grapes, and coconut, tossing to combine. (The salad can be made ahead up to this point up to 1 day in advance, then covered and refrigerated.)

2 When ready to serve, toss the fruit mixture gently and place it in a serving dish. Sprinkle with the toasted pecans and serve at once.

PER SERVING (about ½ cup): 139 Cal, 3 g Total Fat, 1 g Sat Fat, 0 mg Chol, 12 mg Sod, 29 g Carb, 3 g Fib, 1 g Prot, 27 mg Calc.
PointsPlus value: 4.

To toast the pecans, place them in a dry skillet over medium heat. Cook, shaking the pan often to prevent burning, until they become fragrant and only slightly darkened (watch for burning), about 3 minutes.

baked apples

SERVES 4

Vegetarian

4 medium apples, peeled and cored
¼ cup raisins or dried cranberries
1 tablespoon maple syrup
1 tablespoon unsalted butter, softened
¼ teaspoon cinnamon
½ cup apple cider

Simply prepared baked apples are a perfect autumn dessert. For best results, choose apples that hold their shape during baking, such as McIntosh or Granny Smith.

1 Preheat the oven to 350°F. Place the apples in a small baking dish or pie plate. Trim the bottoms, if necessary, to stand the apples upright.

2 Combine the raisins or cranberries, syrup, butter, and cinnamon in a small bowl. Spoon 1 tablespoon of the butter mixture into each apple's cavity. Pour the cider over, cover with foil, and bake until the apples are soft, about 30 minutes. Serve with the cooking juices spooned over each baked apple.

PER SERVING (1 apple): 157 Cal, 3 g Total Fat, 2 g Sat Fat, 8 mg Chol, 3 mg Sod, 35 g Carb, 3 g Fib, 1 g Prot, 25 mg Calc.
PointsPlus value: 4.

spiced plum-and-port compote

SERVES 6

Vegetarian

2 cinnamon sticks
4 slices peeled fresh ginger
8 black peppercorns
5 whole cloves
½ cup packed brown sugar
½ cup ruby port
½ cup cranberry juice
1½ pounds fresh plums (about 9 medium), halved and pitted
1 tablespoon fresh lemon juice

If you have fond memories of stewed prunes—one of the most delightful, old-fashioned desserts ever—you'll love this modern version. It's made with fresh plums, ginger for zing, and a splash of ruby port. If you prefer an alcohol-free version, try substituting fresh orange juice for the port.

1 Place the cinnamon, ginger, peppercorns, and cloves in the center of a 5-inch square of cheesecloth. Gather up the edges of the cheesecloth and tie them together with kitchen string. Place in a medium saucepan, along with the sugar, port, and cranberry juice. Cover and bring to a simmer over medium heat; reduce the heat to low and simmer 10 minutes.

2 Meanwhile, slice each plum half into thirds. Add to the saucepan, return to a simmer and cook, covered, until the plums are soft, 10–12 minutes. Remove from the heat, stir in the lemon juice and let cool in the pan. Refrigerate for at least 2 hours or up to 5 days. Serve cool or at room temperature.

PER SERVING (scant ½ cup): 144 Cal, 0 g Total Fat, 0 g Sat Fat, 0 mg Chol, 7 mg Sod, 36 g Carb, 2 g Fib, 1 g Prot, 25 mg Calc.
PointsPlus value: 4.

You can use any variety of plums for this compote, or try a mix for more complex flavor. The Black Beauty variety are large deep purple plums, Italian Prune plums are oval plums with red-blushed purple skin, and Santa Rosa plums are red with yellow freckles.

Spiced Plum-and-Port Compote

cranberry-stuffed apples

SERVES 4

Vegetarian

⅓ cup packed light brown sugar
1 cup cranberry juice
4 large baking apples (1½ pounds), such as Jonagold, McIntosh, or Gala
½ cup fresh or frozen cranberries, coarsely chopped
¼ cup dried cranberries
¼ cup golden raisins or chopped mixed dried fruit
2 tablespoons chopped crystallized ginger
½ teaspoon ground cinnamon
¼ teaspoon ground allspice
3 tablespoons reduced-fat sour cream
1 tablespoon confectioners' sugar
½ teaspoon vanilla extract

Both fresh and dried cranberries—and a hint of ginger—give a spirited lift to this favorite comfort food. Since apple sizes vary considerably, you may have a little leftover filling. Add the leftover filling to the liquid in the pan before baking. You can serve it with the sauce or simply mound it on top of the baked apples.

1 Place the oven rack in the center of the oven; preheat the oven to 375°F. Reserve 2 tablespoons of the brown sugar for the filling. Combine the remaining brown sugar and the cranberry juice in the bottom of a 1½-quart baking dish.

2 Using a melon baller, cut out the cores of the apples without cutting all the way through to the bottom. Peel the top halves of the apples. Trim the bottoms, if necessary, to stand apples upright.

3 Combine the fresh and dried cranberries, the raisins, ginger, the reserved 2 tablespoons brown sugar, the cinnamon, and allspice in a small bowl. Pack the mixture into the cavities of the apples. Place the apples in the baking dish and cover loosely with foil. Bake, occasionally spooning the pan juices over the apples, until the apples are just tender when pierced with a knife, 40–45 minutes. Cool on a rack.

4 Meanwhile, stir together the sour cream, confectioners' sugar, and vanilla in a small bowl until smooth. Just before serving, baste the apples with the pan juices. Serve with the pan juices on the side and a dollop of the sour cream mixture.

PER SERVING (1 apple with 2½ tablespoons juices and 2 teaspoons cream): 323 Cal, 2 g Total Fat, 1 g Sat Fat, 4 mg Chol, 30 mg Sod, 80 g Carb, 6 g Fib, 1 g Prot, 56 mg Calc.
PointsPlus value: 9.

campari-poached grapefruit

SERVES 4

20 Min or Less
Vegetarian

1¼ cups water
½ cup sugar
5 (3-inch) strips orange zest
2 star anise or 4 whole cloves
3 medium pink grapefruit
3 tablespoons Campari or pomegranate juice

Campari, that oh-so-chic sixties aperitif, is the perfect match for grapefruit: Both have a similar flavoring of tart and sweet. Serve this fruit mixture in goblets or dessert dishes as a refreshing summer dessert or for an elegant brunch treat.

1 Combine the water, sugar, orange zest, and anise or cloves in a large skillet. Cover, bring to a simmer, and cook 10 minutes.

2 Meanwhile, trim off the rind and white pith from the grapefruit, then cut each grapefruit into 8 wedges. Add the grapefruit pieces to the simmering liquid, and remove from the heat. Stir in the Campari or pomegranate juice; transfer to a serving bowl, then set aside to cool. Cover and refrigerate up to 4 days. Serve chilled or at room temperature.

PER SERVING (about ¾ cup): 202 Cal, 0 g Total Fat, 0 g Sat Fat, 0 mg Chol, 4 mg Sod, 47 g Carb, 2 g Fib, 1 g Prot, 26 mg Calc.
PointsPlus value: 5.

Pomegranate juice, with its refreshingly tart sweetness, is a nice substitute for the Campari. Look for it in the produce aisle or the juice section of supermarkets.

Cranberry Holiday Mold

cranberry holiday mold

SERVES 8

2 cups boiling water
2 (3-ounce) packages cranberry-flavored gelatin
1½ cups cold mandarin orange–flavored sparkling water
1 tablespoon grated orange zest
10 strawberries, stemmed and halved
1 Granny Smith apple, peeled, cored, and cut into ½-inch cubes
⅓ cup walnuts, chopped

A retro-recipe collection simply has to include a gelatin-based fruit dessert. This one would look great on a Thanksgiving table, when traditional recipes are a must. For a more beautiful look, use a fancy 6-cup mold or kugelhopf pan, but any 6-cup bowl will do nicely. You can substitute strawberry or raspberry gelatin for the cranberry-flavored variety.

1 Spray a 6-cup bundt pan or bowl with nonstick spray.

2 Combine the boiling water and gelatin in a medium heatproof bowl, stirring until completely dissolved. Stir in the sparkling water and orange zest. Refrigerate until thickened but not set, 1½–2 hours.

3 Stir in the strawberries, apple, and walnuts. Transfer the mixture to the bundt pan or bowl and refrigerate until the mold has set, at least 4 hours or overnight.

4 To unmold, dip the pan or bowl in a large bowl of warm water for 15–20 seconds. Wet a spoon with water, then gently loosen the gelatin from the sides of the pan with the spoon. Place a serving plate on top of the pan, then invert. Shake slightly to help free the gelatin, and gently lift off the pan.

PER SERVING (¾ cup): 128 Cal, 3 g Total Fat, 0 g Sat Fat, 0 mg Chol, 64 mg Sod, 24 g Carb, 1 g Fib, 3 g Prot, 12 mg Calc.
PointsPlus value: 4.

grilled tropical fruit with lime syrup

SERVES 8

Vegetarian

¼ cup sugar
3 tablespoons water
3 tablespoons fresh lime juice
1 teaspoon grated lime zest
1 teaspoon grated orange zest
1 pineapple, trimmed, cored, and cut lengthwise into 16 (½-inch-thick) slices
2 mangoes, pitted, peeled, and cut into 8 (½-inch-thick) slices

Here's a glamorous dessert that won't leave you feeling stuffed; it's a perfect finish to an outdoor dinner party. When you grill the fruit, the sugars on the surface concentrate and caramelize, adding smoky-sweet depth to the flavors.

1 Combine the sugar and water in a small saucepan. Bring to a boil over medium-high heat; continue cooking until syrupy, 2 minutes more. Stir in the lime juice, lime zest, and orange zest; set aside.

2 Prepare the grill for a medium fire, or preheat the broiler.

3 Spray the pineapple and mango slices with nonstick spray on both sides. Grill or broil, turning once, until softened, about 4 minutes. Brush the slices with the lime syrup and turn the fruit over; grill or broil 1 minute more. Brush again with the syrup, turn, and grill or broil until the syrup has caramelized slightly, 1 minute longer. Transfer the fruit to a serving platter and brush with the remaining syrup. Serve warm, at room temperature, or chilled.

PER SERVING (2 pineapple slices and 1 mango slice): 88 Cal, 0 g Total Fat, 0 g Sat Fat, 0 mg Chol, 3 mg Sod, 24 g Carb, 2 g Fib, 1 g Prot, 10 mg Calc.
PointsPlus value: 3.

no-bake strawberry-rhubarb crisp

SERVES 6

Vegetarian

½ cup sugar
1½ tablespoons cornstarch
1½ cups sliced fresh or frozen rhubarb
½ cup water
1 teaspoon grated lemon zest
½ teaspoon ground ginger
2 cups trimmed and halved strawberries
3 almond biscotti (1½ ounces)
1 tablespoon packed light brown sugar
⅛ teaspoon cinnamon
1 tablespoon unsalted butter, melted

This fresh fruit dessert is perfect for the heat of early summer (who wants to turn on the oven?). For the crispy topping, we've used packaged biscotti. If you like the licorice-like sweetness of anise, you can substitute anisette sponge cookies.

1 Stir together the sugar and cornstarch in a medium saucepan. Add the rhubarb, water, lemon zest, and ginger. Cover and bring to a simmer over medium heat. Cook, stirring occasionally, until the rhubarb is tender and the sauce has thickened, 8 minutes. Stir in the strawberries and cook 2 minutes more. Pour into a 9-inch pie plate or serving dish.

2 Chop the biscotti into ¼-inch pieces; place in a medium bowl. Crumble in the brown sugar and cinnamon. Drizzle in the butter and stir to distribute evenly. Sprinkle biscotti mixture over the fruit right before serving. Serve warm or at room temperature.

PER SERVING (⅙ of crisp): 142 Cal, 3 g Total Fat, 1 g Sat Fat, 6 mg Chol, 28 mg Sod, 30 g Carb, 2 g Fib, 1 g Prot, 75 mg Calc.
PointsPlus value: 4.

Make this easy summer dessert even more of a treat by serving it with fat-free vanilla ice cream (½ cup fat-free vanilla ice cream will increase the per-serving *PointsPlus* value by *2*).

raspberry-peach cobbler

SERVES 6

Vegetarian

½ cup raspberry jam
⅓ cup peach nectar or cranberry juice
1 tablespoon cornstarch
½ teaspoon cinnamon
¼ teaspoon ground nutmeg or allspice
1½ pounds (about 5 medium) firm-ripe peaches or nectarines, peeled, if desired, halved, pitted, and thinly sliced
1 cup all-purpose flour
3 tablespoons sugar
1 teaspoon baking powder
¼ teaspoon baking soda
½ cup low-fat buttermilk
2 tablespoons melted unsalted butter or margarine

Bubbling sweetened fruit topped with crumbly biscuits—this old-fashioned dessert was retro before retro was cool! Make it at the height of peach season, and substitute apples or pears in winter. Though it's not necessary, you can peel the peaches if you like.

1 Place the oven rack in the center of the oven; preheat the oven to 375°F. Whisk together the jam, nectar or cranberry juice, cornstarch, cinnamon, and nutmeg or allspice in a 9-inch deep-dish microwavable pie plate or casserole dish until blended. Stir in the peaches or nectarines to coat well. Microwave on High, stirring occasionally, until the mixture begins to bubble, 6–7 minutes.

2 Meanwhile, whisk together the flour, 2 tablespoons of the sugar, the baking powder, and baking soda in a medium bowl; make a well in the center. Pour the buttermilk and melted butter into the center. Quickly combine the dry ingredients with the wet, stirring just until combined.

3 Drop the mixture onto the hot fruit by the tablespoonful. Sprinkle the remaining tablespoon of sugar over the topping. Bake until the biscuits are golden and fruit mixture is bubbly, 25 minutes. Serve warm.

PER SERVING (⅙ of cobbler): 247 Cal, 4 g Total Fat, 3 g Sat Fat, 11 mg Chol, 167 mg Sod, 51 g Carb, 3 g Fib, 4 g Prot, 85 mg Calc.
PointsPlus value: 7.

To peel the peaches, plunge them in boiling water just long enough to loosen their skins, about 1 to 3 minutes. Remove to a bowl of ice water; when cool enough to handle, peel off the skin with your fingers. You can also use a swivel-bladed apple peeler, but you'll lose some of the delicious peach flesh beneath.

Raspberry-Peach Cobbler

bread pudding with winter fruits

SERVES 8

Vegetarian

- ¾ cup mixed dried fruit, diced
- 3 tablespoons water
- 2 tablespoons bourbon (optional)
- 1 ripe pear, peeled, quartered, cored, and sliced crosswise
- 4 cups cubed day-old whole-grain bread (1-inch pieces)
- ½ cup granulated sugar
- ¾ teaspoon cinnamon
- ¼ teaspoon nutmeg
- 3 cups low-fat (1%) milk
- 2 large eggs
- 1 large egg white
- 2 teaspoons vanilla extract
- 1 teaspoon grated orange zest
- 2 tablespoons confectioners' sugar (optional)

Bread pudding, everyone's favorite nursery food, enjoyed a resurgence in the "cocooning" days of the new millennium. We bake ours in a water bath to insure a smooth and creamy pudding. If you like, feel free to substitute your favorite dried fruit, such as dried cranberries, cherries, apricots, or dates, for the mixed dried fruit. Teetotalers can substitute orange juice for the bourbon.

1 Combine the dried fruit, water, and bourbon, if using, in a small saucepan. Bring to a simmer over medium heat. Remove from the heat, stir in the pear, and let cool.

2 Spray an 9 × 11-inch baking dish with nonstick spray. Scatter the bread in an even layer in the pan. Spoon the soaked fruit evenly on top.

3 Whisk together the granulated sugar, cinnamon, and nutmeg in a medium bowl. Whisk in the milk, eggs, egg white, vanilla, and orange zest. Pour over the bread, pressing down the cubes to soak up the liquid. Cover with foil and let stand 30 minutes. (The pudding can be made ahead up to this point, then stored in the refrigerator overnight.)

4 Preheat the oven to 350°F. Pull the oven rack partly out. Place a large roasting pan on the rack; place the bread pudding inside it. Carefully pour enough hot water into the roasting pan to fill it halfway up the side of the baking dish. Bake, covered, 30 minutes. Uncover and continue baking until puffed and golden, 30 minutes more. Remove from the pan and let cool. Serve warm, sifting the confectioners' sugar on top, if you wish.

PER SERVING (⅛ pudding): 197 Cal, 3 g Total Fat, 1 g Sat Fat, 57 mg Chol, 161 mg Sod, 37 g Carb, 3 g Fib, 7 g Prot, 142 mg Calc.
PointsPlus value: 5.

bananas foster

SERVES 4

20 Min or Less
Vegetarian

- ⅓ cup packed light brown sugar
- 3 tablespoons unsalted light butter
- ½ teaspoon cinnamon
- 2 large ripe bananas, peeled and sliced ¼-inch thick
- 2 tablespoons dark rum
- 1 pint low-fat vanilla ice cream

Although Bananas Foster was a classic long before the eighties, that decade's interest in Creole cooking gave the dessert star billing nationwide. And no wonder: The combination of bananas flambéed in rum with vanilla ice cream is a match made in heaven. Even though this version is much lower in fat than the original, it hasn't lost any of its richness.

1 Combine the sugar, butter, and cinnamon in a large nonstick skillet over medium-low heat. Cook, stirring often, until the butter melts and the sugar dissolves. Add the banana slices and cook, tossing to coat, until the bananas begin to soften, 2–4 minutes. Increase the heat to medium and, off the heat, pour in the rum. Return the skillet to the heat and ignite the rum with a long wooden match (or, if you have a gas stove, tilt the skillet toward the flame to ignite); cook, shaking the pan, until the flame goes out, about 30 seconds. Cook 1 minute longer to thicken the sauce slightly; remove from the heat.

2 Place a ½-cup scoop of the ice cream into each of 4 wine glasses or serving dishes. Top each with ½ cup of the warm banana mixture. Serve at once.

PER SERVING (½ cup each ice cream and bananas): 309 Cal, 8 g Total Fat, 5 g Sat Fat, 31 mg Chol, 66 mg Sod, 56 g Carb, 2 g Fib, 4 g Prot, 145 mg Calc.
PointsPlus value: 9.

If you'd rather omit the rum, try substituting 1 teaspoon imitation rum extract—or add 2 tablespoons pineapple juice and a few drops of vanilla extract to the bananas, and cook 1 minute before serving.

mini cheesecake bites with blueberry topping

SERVES 12

Vegetarian

2 teaspoons honey
8 gingersnaps, crushed to fine crumbs (about ½ cup)
1 (8-ounce) package light cream cheese (Neufchâtel), room temperature
¼ cup sugar
1 large egg
1 teaspoon grated lemon zest
1 teaspoon vanilla extract
¼ cup all-fruit blueberry jam
1 cup blueberries

These mini cheesecakes with crisp gingersnap crusts offer up creamy goodness with little compromising. Bake the cheesecakes up to two days in advance and store them in the refrigerator; they taste even better with a day of chilling. The blueberry topping can be assembled in minutes.

1 Place the oven rack in the center of the oven; preheat the oven to 375°F. Line 24 mini-muffin cups with paper liners, then spray the liners with nonstick spray.

2 Place the honey in a medium microwavable bowl. Microwave on High for 10 seconds. Add the gingersnap crumbs to the bowl, stirring to form a crumbly mixture. Spoon a scant teaspoon of the crumbs into the bottom of each muffin cup liner.

3 With an electric mixer on high speed, beat the cream cheese, sugar, egg, lemon zest, and vanilla in a medium bowl until light and fluffy, 3 minutes. Spoon 1 level tablespoon of the mixture into each muffin cup. Bake until puffed and set in the center, 9 minutes. Cool in pans on a rack.

4 Place the jam in a medium microwavable bowl and microwave on High, just until the jam begins to bubble, 15 seconds. Gently stir in the blueberries until evenly coated with the jam. Spoon the berries over the cheesecakes (about 5–6 blueberries each). Refrigerate until ready to serve.

PER SERVING (2 cheesecake bites): 117 Cal, 5 g Total Fat, 3 g Sat Fat, 32 mg Chol, 108 mg Sod, 15 g Carb, 1 g Fib, 3 g Prot, 21 mg Calc.
PointsPlus value: 3.

To crush the gingersnaps, place them in a zip-close plastic bag, squeeze out the air, and seal. Use a rolling pin to flatten the snaps to fine crumbs.

---

lemon bars

SERVES 16

Vegetarian

- ⅔ cup + 2 tablespoons all-purpose flour
- ⅓ cup animal cracker crumbs or vanilla wafer crumbs
- 1 cup + 2 tablespoons sugar
- 3 tablespoons unsalted butter or margarine
- 2 large eggs
- 2 egg whites
- 2 teaspoons grated lemon zest
- ½ cup fresh lemon juice (from about 4 lemons)

Everybody's favorite on the cookie tray, lemon bars are traditionally made with a shortbread crust and a rich lemon-curd topping. With animal cracker crumbs, plenty of fresh lemon, and a lot of ingenuity, our updated version measures up in every way to the original.

1 Place the oven rack in the center of the oven; preheat the oven to 350°F. Line an 8-inch-square baking pan with heavy-duty foil, extending 2 inches beyond the sides. (This creates a "handle," so that the bars can easily be lifted out of the pan.) Spray the bottom and sides of the foil with nonstick spray.

2 To prepare the crust: Stir together ⅔ cup of the flour, the animal cracker crumbs, 2 tablespoons of the sugar, and the butter in a medium bowl until the consistency of wet sand. Pat evenly into the pan to form a crust. Bake until firm, 12 minutes.

3 Whisk together the remaining 1 cup sugar and the remaining 2 tablespoons of the flour in a medium bowl. Add the eggs, egg whites, lemon zest, and lemon juice, and whisk to thoroughly combine, about 1 minute. Pour over the hot crust, return to oven, and bake until golden and set in the center, about 30 minutes. Cool completely on a rack. Lift out the bars, holding on to the foil ends, and place on a cutting board. Cut into 16 squares.

PER SERVING (1 bar): 119 Cal, 3 g Total Fat, 2 g Sat Fat, 32 mg Chol, 2 mg Sod, 21 g Carb, 0 g Fib, 2 g Prot, 6 mg Calc.
PointsPlus value: 3.

Before you squeeze the lemons, why not trim off their zest to save for another use? Remove the zest with a vegetable peeler, being careful to avoid the bitter white pith beneath, and store the strips in a small airtight freezer container for up to a month.

Boston Cream Pie

boston cream pie

SERVES 8

Vegetarian

A retro favorite, Boston Cream Pie is actually a light sponge cake with a cream filling and dense chocolate icing. Our cake is quite easy to make, and unusually low in fat.

custard

⅓ cup sugar
3 tablespoons cornstarch
¼ teaspoon salt
1½ cups low-fat (1%) milk
1 large egg
1 tablespoon unsalted butter
2 teaspoons vanilla extract

cake

1 cup cake flour (not self-rising)
1½ teaspoons baking powder
¼ teaspoon salt
3 large eggs, at room temperature
¾ cup sugar
¼ cup hot water
2 tablespoons unsalted butter, melted
1 teaspoon vanilla extract

glaze

⅓ cup confectioners' sugar
3 tablespoons unsweetened Dutch-process cocoa powder
½ cup fat-free sweetened condensed milk
½ teaspoon instant coffee powder

1 Custard: Whisk together sugar, cornstarch, and salt in a medium saucepan. Whisk in milk and egg until blended. Cook over medium heat, stirring constantly, until just boiling, about 3 minutes. Cook 1 minute more, stirring until thickened; remove from heat. Stir in butter and vanilla. Press a piece of wax paper onto surface to keep a skin from forming on the custard; set aside to cool.

2 Cake: Place oven rack in the center of oven; preheat oven to 350°F. Spray two 9-inch cake pans with nonstick spray; line with wax paper rounds and spray with nonstick spray. Sift together the flour, baking powder, and salt onto a sheet of wax paper; set aside. With an electric mixer on high, beat eggs in a medium bowl until thickened, about 3 minutes. Gradually beat in sugar, until fluffy, 3 minutes. On low speed, beat in water, butter, and vanilla, until just blended. Beat in flour mixture, until just incorporated. Pour into the pans. Bake 25–30 minutes; cool completely on a rack. To remove cake from the pans, run a knife around the edge of the cake layers and invert onto the rack. Peel off wax paper.

3 Glaze (prepare just before assembling): Sift the confectioners' sugar and cocoa into a small saucepan. Add the condensed milk and coffee powder; stir to combine. Heat over low heat, stirring, until the mixture bubbles and thickens, about 2 minutes; cook 1 minute more. Remove from heat and set aside to cool in the pan for 10 minutes, or until thickened.

4 Cake assembly: Place 1 layer, bottom-side up, on serving plate. Vigorously stir custard until smooth. Spread on inverted cake layer in an even thickness, leaving a ½-inch border along the edge. Top with remaining cake layer, top-side up. Spread the chocolate glaze evenly on top. Use a serrated knife to cut the cake, and serve at room temperature or slightly chilled.

PER SERVING (⅛ of cake): 336 Cal, 8 g Total Fat, 5 g Sat Fat, 120 mg Chol, 318 mg Sod, 60 g Carb, 1 g Fib, 8 g Prot, 180 mg Calc. ***PointsPlus value: 9.***

citrus, date, and raisin baklava

SERVES 16

Vegetarian

glaze

1/3 cup sugar
2 tablespoons water
3 tablespoons honey
2 tablespoons fresh lemon juice
1 tablespoon fresh orange juice

baklava

2 cups pitted dates, chopped
1 cup golden raisins
1/2 cup + 2 tablespoons sugar
1 tablespoon freshly grated lemon zest
1 teaspoon freshly grated orange zest
1/2 teaspoon ground allspice
1/8 teaspoon anise seeds
1/8 teaspoon nutmeg
3 tablespoons fresh orange juice
2 tablespoons fresh lemon juice
1/2 cup finely chopped walnuts
12 sheets phyllo dough, thawed, if frozen
8 tablespoons light unsalted butter, melted

This classic Greek dessert takes a little time to make, but it's well worth the effort. We've cut fat substantially by substituting golden raisins and dates for most of the nuts traditionally used and by brushing the phyllo layers with light butter. And for good measure, we've freshened up the flavorings with a hint of lemon and orange. As with any baklava, a small portion is plenty!

1 Preheat the oven to 350°F. Spray an 8-inch-square baking dish with nonstick spray.

2 Glaze: Combine the sugar and water in a small saucepan; bring to a boil. Continue boiling, without stirring, until the sugar dissolves, 1 minute. Remove from the heat and stir in the honey, lemon juice, and orange juice; let cool and reserve.

3 Baklava filling: Combine the dates, raisins, 2 tablespoons of the sugar, the lemon and orange zests, allspice, anise seeds, and nutmeg in the work bowl of a food processor. Pulse until dates and raisins are finely minced. Add the orange and lemon juices; pulse until mixture forms a thick paste. Transfer to a bowl and stir in walnuts.

4 Place the phyllo sheets on a cutting board in a stack. Using the bottom of the prepared baking pan as a guide, cut out 2 (8-inch-square) stacks, to make 24 sheets (discard the dough trimmings). Cover the sheets with plastic wrap to keep them from drying out as you work. Place 1 sheet on the bottom of the baking dish, brush lightly with the melted butter, and sprinkle with 1 teaspoon of the sugar. Repeat with another 9 layers of phyllo, butter, and sugar. Spread with half of the date mixture, then top with 4 more layers of phyllo, butter, and sugar. Spread with the remaining half of the date mixture, then top with 10 more layers of phyllo, butter, and sugar. With a sharp knife, lightly cut the top of the baklava to indicate 16 squares, being careful not to cut all the way through.

5 Bake 30 minutes, until crisp and lightly golden. Cut the baklava into pieces along the scored lines. Drizzle the reserved glaze over the top, and cool completely before serving.

PER SERVING (1-inch-square piece): 249 Cal, 8 g Total Fat, 4 g Sat Fat, 16 mg Chol, 30 mg Sod, 45 g Carb, 2 g Fib, 2 g Prot, 20 mg Calc.
PointsPlus value: 7.

banana cream pie

SERVES 8

Vegetarian

Adding fat-free half-and-half to the cream filling gives this old-fashioned pie a wonderfully rich flavor and silky smooth texture. To make the crust, we've used chocolate-flavored graham crackers. Feel free to substitute plain or cinnamon grahams, if you prefer.

crust

9 chocolate-flavored graham crackers (5 × 2½-inches each)
2 tablespoons honey
1 tablespoon vegetable oil
1 tablespoon low-fat (1%) milk

filling

½ cup sugar
¼ cup cornstarch
1½ cups low-fat (1%) milk
1 large egg
⅛ teaspoon salt
¼ cup fat-free half-and-half
1 teaspoon vanilla extract
3 medium bananas, well ripened
½ tablespoon orange or lemon juice

1 To prepare the crust, place the oven rack in the center of the oven and preheat the oven to 375°F. Spray a 9-inch glass pie plate with nonstick spray. Break up the graham crackers into a food processor or blender, and process until finely ground. Add the honey, oil, and milk; process until well combined and evenly crumbly. Press evenly into the bottom and sides of the pie plate. Bake for 9 minutes; cool completely on a rack.

2 To prepare the filling, whisk together the sugar and cornstarch in a medium saucepan. Whisk in the milk, egg, and salt. Bring to a boil over medium heat, whisking constantly as the mixture begins to thicken; let boil 30 seconds, whisking constantly. Remove from the heat and gradually whisk in the half-and-half and vanilla. Place a sheet of wax paper on the surface to prevent a skin from forming; set aside to cool for 15 minutes.

3 Slice two of the bananas lengthwise in half; cut crosswise into slices. Place the slices in an even layer in the bottom of the baked pie shell. Spoon in the cooled filling and spread evenly. Place a sheet of wax paper on the surface to prevent a skin from forming, and chill thoroughly, at least 3 hours or overnight.

4 To serve, slice the remaining banana and toss with the juice in a small bowl. Arrange on top of the pie and serve.

PER SERVING (⅛ of pie): 234 Cal, 5 g Total Fat, 1 g Sat Fat, 29 mg Chol, 163 mg Sod, 46 g Carb, 1 g Fib, 4 g Prot, 80 mg Calc.
PointsPlus value: 7.

Bananas produce ethylene gas, which makes them ripen faster. That's why the trick of putting bananas in a paper bag helps them ripen—the bag holds in the ethylene gas.

key lime pie

SERVES 8

½ cup fresh lime juice
2 teaspoons unflavored gelatin
1 (14-ounce) can sweetened condensed milk
2 teaspoons grated lime zest
1½ cups fat-free whipped topping
1 (9-inch) reduced-fat graham cracker crust
1 small lime, thinly sliced

If you're old enough to fondly remember the popular lime-flavored gelatin-based Key Lime Pie recipe that circulated in the seventies, you'll love this update. After all, it uses fresh limes—and it's easier to find genuine key limes (from the Florida Keys) in better supermarkets. They are smaller, with golden-yellow flesh, and slightly more tart than the common Persian lime.

1 Pour the juice into a small bowl and sprinkle with the gelatin. Let stand until the gelatin is softened, 5 minutes. Transfer to a small saucepan and heat over low heat, stirring, until the gelatin dissolves.

2 Stir in the condensed milk and cook, stirring occasionally, 5 minutes longer (do not boil). Remove from the heat and let cool 10 minutes. Transfer to a large bowl and refrigerate 30 minutes, or until the mixture starts to set.

3 Whisk the thickened filling until creamy and smooth; stir in the lime zest. Using a rubber spatula, gently fold in the whipped topping until combined. Pour into the pie crust and refrigerate until firm, at least 3 hours or overnight. Garnish with the lime slices just before serving.

PER SERVING (⅛ of pie): 300 Cal, 9 g Total Fat, 6 g Sat Fat, 22 mg Chol, 163 mg Sod, 50 g Carb, 0 g Fib, 5 g Prot, 149 mg Calc.
PointsPlus value: 8.

You'll need about 3 or 4 Persian limes, or 10 to 12 key limes, to yield ½ cup fresh juice.

---

classic desserts

In the earliest days of Weight Watchers, dessert recipes used to rely on gelatin, nonfat dry milk, and artificial sweeteners for flavor and texture. These days, healthy cooks are more inclined to use fresh fruit and just a touch of real sugar when making sweet treats. Yet, if you're craving a bit of nostalgia, these desserts from years gone by are still delicious.

hawaiian mousse circa 1970

SERVES 6
***PointsPlus* value: *3* per serving (about ¾ cup)**

1½ cups water
2 (¼-ounce) envelopes unflavored gelatin
1½ cups no-sugar-added crushed pineapple
1½ cups fat-free evaporated milk
½ teaspoon rum extract
½ teaspoon coconut extract
¼ teaspoon vanilla extract
Sugar substitute to equal 4 teaspoons sugar

Pour 1 cup of the water into a medium saucepan and sprinkle with the gelatin. Let stand until the gelatin is softened, 5 minutes. Cook over low heat, stirring, until the gelatin dissolves. Transfer the gelatin mixture to a blender; add the remaining ½ cup water, pineapple, milk, extracts, and sweetener; puree. Pour into a 1½-quart gelatin mold. Cover and refrigerate until set, at least 4 hours or overnight.

Dip the mold into a large pan of warm water for 15–20 seconds. Place a serving plate on top of the mold, then invert. Shake slightly to help free the mousse, and lift off the mold.

crunchy peanut butter fudge circa 1980

SERVES 4
***PointsPlus* value: *6* per serving (2 squares)**

⅔ cup instant nonfat dry milk
¼ cup chunky peanut butter
3 tablespoons thawed frozen apple juice concentrate
2 tablespoons cold water
¾ ounce ready-to-eat oven-toasted rice cereal
¼ cup raisins, chopped
1 tablespoon shredded coconut

Spray an 8½ × 4½-inch loaf pan with nonstick spray.

Combine the dry milk and peanut butter in a medium bowl; stir until combined. Stir in the apple juice concentrate and water. Add the cereal and raisins; stir to coat. Press the mixture into the prepared pan. Sprinkle with the coconut, pressing to adhere. Cover and refrigerate until firm, about 2 hours. Cut into 8 squares.

pumpkin chiffon pie circa 1980

SERVES 8
***PointsPlus* value: *4* per serving (1 wedge)**

½ cup water
1 (¼-ounce) envelope unflavored gelatin
2 cups canned pumpkin puree
Sugar substitute to equal ¼ cup sugar
1 teaspoon vanilla extract
½ teaspoon each ground allspice and grated orange zest
Pinch of salt
1 cup nondairy whipped topping
1 (9-inch) reduced-fat prepared graham-cracker crust

Pour the water into a small saucepan and sprinkle with the gelatin. Let stand 5 minutes. Cook over medium heat, stirring, until gelatin is dissolved, 2 minutes. Stir together pumpkin, sugar substitute, vanilla, allspice, orange zest, and salt in a medium bowl; stir in gelatin mixture. Cover and refrigerate 1 hour. Using a rubber spatula, fold in the whipped topping until combined. Spoon into the crust. Cover and refrigerate until firm, at least 3 hours or overnight. Cut into 8 wedges.

Note: All ***PointsPlus*** values were calculated using the Weight Watchers online recipe builder.

baked alaska

SERVES 8

Vegetarian

1 pint strawberry sorbet, softened
1 pint low-fat vanilla ice cream, softened
6 (½-inch-thick) slices fat-free pound cake (about 10 ounces)
6 large egg whites from pasteurized shell eggs at room temperature
⅛ teaspoon cream of tartar
¾ cup sugar

This miraculous dish amazes diners as much today as it did in the sixties, but the real miracle is how easy it is to create. Just make sure the ice cream and cake are frozen solid before baking the meringue.

1 Spray a 6-cup bowl with nonstick spray and line with plastic wrap, letting the wrap come up over the rim. Spread the sorbet evenly into the bowl; freeze 20 minutes. Top evenly with the ice cream; freeze 20 minutes.

2 Cut the pound cake into wedges and make a pinwheel pattern on top of the ice cream layer, patching any gaps. Freeze until solid, 2–4 hours.

3 Preheat the oven to 450°F. Place the oven rack in the middle of the oven.

4 With an electric mixer on low speed, beat the egg whites and cream of tartar in a medium bowl until soft peaks form, about 4 minutes. Increase the speed to high and gradually beat in the sugar, until stiff and glossy, about 3 minutes more.

5 Remove the bowl from the freezer and invert the dessert onto a baking sheet. Remove the plastic wrap. Mound the meringue over the dessert, spreading to the edges. Bake until just golden brown on top, 3–4 minutes. Transfer to a serving plate. Serve at once.

PER SERVING (⅛ of dessert): 300 Cal, 1 g Total Fat, 0 g Sat Fat, 1 mg Chol, 206 mg Sod, 67 g Carb, 0 g Fib, 6 g Prot, 73 mg Calc.
PointsPlus value: 8.

Baked Alaska

sweet potato pie

SERVES 8

Vegetarian

crust

1 cup all-purpose flour
1 tablespoon confectioners' sugar
1 teaspoon salt
3 tablespoons unsalted butter, cut into small chunks
3 tablespoons cold water
½ teaspoon cider vinegar

filling

2 large sweet potatoes (about 1½ pounds), peeled
2 large eggs
3 egg whites
½ cup packed light brown sugar
¾ cup evaporated fat-free milk
1 tablespoon fresh lime juice
1 teaspoon pumpkin pie spice
¼ teaspoon ground nutmeg

A traditional Southern treat, this pie is the real thing—with a buttery crust and a silky sweet filling. Serve it for Thanksgiving instead of the usual pumpkin pie.

1 To prepare pie crust, combine the flour, sugar, and ½ teaspoon of the salt in a food processor. Add the butter; pulse until the mixture resembles coarse crumbs. Stir together the water and vinegar in a small bowl; pour mixture through the feed tube, pulsing until the mixture is just combined. Scrape dough with a spatula onto a sheet of plastic wrap, flatten into a disk, wrap airtight, and refrigerate until chilled, at least 1 hour.

2 Preheat the oven to 375°F. Roll out the chilled dough between floured sheets of wax paper to a 13-inch circle. Fit into a 9-inch pie plate, crimp the edges, and prick the bottom lightly with a fork. Line the inside of the crust with heavy-duty foil; fold the foil over to completely cover the edge of the crust. Bake for 12 minutes. Remove the foil, pierce any bubbles in the crust with the tip of a knife, and bake until very lightly browned, 8 minutes more.

3 To make the filling, place the potatoes in a medium saucepan with enough cold water to cover. Bring to a boil and simmer until fork-tender, 45 minutes. Drain, then add enough cold water to cover. When the potatoes are cool enough to handle, drain and mash with a potato masher in a large bowl until smooth. Measure out 1⅓ cups of the puree (save any extra for another use), and return it to the bowl.

4 Preheat the oven to 350°F. Add the eggs, egg whites, and brown sugar to the puree; whisk together until smooth. Whisk in the milk, lime juice, pie spice, the remaining ½ teaspoon salt, and the nutmeg until blended. Pour the mixture into the pie crust. Bake until the center is set, 35–40 minutes (the pie should still quiver like gelatin when the pan is nudged). Cool completely on a rack and refrigerate for at least 3 hours or overnight. Serve chilled or at room temperature.

PER SERVING (⅛ of pie): 227 Cal, 5 g Total Fat, 1 g Sat Fat, 48 mg Chol, 376 mg Sod, 38 g Carb, 2 g Fib, 8 g Prot, 107 mg Calc. ***PointsPlus value: 6.***

lattice-topped cherry-almond pie

SERVES 8

Vegetarian

crust

1½ cups pastry flour or all-purpose flour
1 tablespoon confectioners' sugar
¾ teaspoon salt
3 tablespoons vegetable shortening
2 tablespoons unsalted butter, cut into small chunks
4½ tablespoons cold water
¾ teaspoon cider vinegar

filling

2 (15-ounce) cans pitted dark cherries, packed in juice or lite syrup
½ cup packed light brown sugar
1 tablespoon fresh lemon juice
¼ teaspoon almond extract
3 tablespoons cornstarch

This pretty pie is the ultimate American classic. For a well-cooked bottom crust, start the cooking in a hot oven. Cover the decorative edge with foil during the baking to prevent overbrowning.

1 Crust: Pulse the flour, confectioners' sugar, and salt in a food processor. Add the shortening and butter; pulse until the mixture resembles coarse meal. Stir together the water and vinegar in small bowl. Add to flour mixture and pulse until just combined. Remove one-third of mixture (about ½ cup) onto a sheet of plastic wrap, flatten into an oval, and wrap airtight (this will be used for the lattice top). Repeat with the remaining dough (for bottom crust). Refrigerate doughs for 1 hour or up to 2 days.

2 Roll out the larger dough piece between floured sheets of wax paper to a 13-inch circle. Fit into a 9-inch pie plate. Leaving a 1-inch border, trim off any excess dough. Add trimmings to remaining dough piece, and roll it between floured sheets of wax paper to a 9½ × 7-inch rectangle. Cut lengthwise into ½-inch-wide strips. Place oven rack in the center of oven; preheat oven to 425°F.

3 Filling: Drain the cherries in a strainer set over a large bowl. Shake the strainer to remove any excess juices. Reserve ½ cup of cherry juice and place in a large bowl; discard the remaining juice. Stir in the brown sugar, lemon juice, and almond extract. Add the cornstarch and stir until smooth. Stir in the drained cherries, and spoon the mixture into the unbaked pie shell.

4 Weave the strips of dough into a lattice pattern on top of filling. Pinch the edges together to seal, and crimp decoratively. Cover the crimped edge with strips of foil to prevent overbrowning.

5 Place the pie on a baking sheet and bake 30 minutes. Reduce oven temperature to 350°F, and bake 30–40 minutes more, until crust is golden brown and the filling is bubbly. Cool on a rack for at least 3 hours. Serve pie slightly warm or at room temperature.

PER SERVING (⅛ of pie): 272 Cal, 9 g Total Fat, 3 g Sat Fat, 8 mg Chol, 225 mg Sod, 48 g Carb, 2 g Fib, 3 g Prot, 27 mg Calc.
PointsPlus value: 8.

chocolate angel food cake

SERVES 12

Vegetarian

1½ cups cake flour
½ cup unsweetened cocoa powder
½ teaspoon salt
12 large egg whites, at room temperature
1 teaspoon cream of tartar
1½ cups sugar
1 teaspoon vanilla extract
12 tablespoons chocolate syrup

The quality of an angel food cake has long been the test of a baker's mettle: Using no leavening or shortening, it should get its ethereal texture from a large quantity of properly whipped egg whites folded into a minimal amount of flour. Angel food cake is naturally low in fat and high in protein, making it an ever-popular choice for Weight Watchers members.

1 Place an oven rack in the lower third of the oven and preheat the oven to 375°F.

2 Sift together the flour, cocoa, and salt into a medium bowl; set aside. With an electric mixer on medium speed, beat the egg whites and cream of tartar in a large bowl until soft peaks form, about 3 minutes. Gradually beat in the sugar, until stiff and glossy, about 2 minutes more. Beat in the vanilla.

3 Sift the flour mixture, one-third at a time, over the beaten egg whites, gently folding it in with a rubber spatula just until the cocoa is no longer visible. (Be careful not to overmix.)

4 Scrape the batter into an ungreased 10-inch tube pan; spread evenly. Bake until the cake springs back when lightly pressed, 35–40 minutes. Invert the pan onto its legs or onto the neck of a bottle and let the cake cool completely. Run a thin knife around the edge of the cake to loosen it from the side and center tube of the pan. Serve with the chocolate syrup.

PER SERVING (1⁄12 of cake with 1 tablespoon chocolate syrup): 240 Cal, 1 g Total Fat, 0 g Sat Fat, 0 mg Chol, 169 mg Sod, 54 g Carb, 2 g Fib, 6 g Prot, 12 mg Calc.
PointsPlus value: 7.

To make a terrific topping for this, combine 4 cups of raspberries, 1 tablespoon sugar, and 1 tablespoon lemon juice in a bowl. Let stand, stirring occasionally, until the berries begin to give off juices, about 30 minutes. (⅓ cup of the berries will increase the per-serving *PointsPlus* value by *1*.)

tiramisu

SERVES 24

Vegetarian

½ cup boiling water
5 teaspoons instant espresso powder
1 cup + 1 tablespoon sugar
1 (13-ounce) fat-free pound cake, sliced ½-inch thick
2 (8-ounce) packages tub-style light cream cheese
1 teaspoon vanilla extract
1 (8-ounce) tub fat-free whipped topping
6 ounces semisweet chocolate, finely chopped

So popular on eighties dessert menus that it became a cliché, tiramisu—which translates loosely as "lift-me-up" in Italian—nonetheless never fails to live up to its name. One of the great things about this heavenly dessert is that it can be made up to three days ahead—and it only gets better as the flavors develop.

1 Combine the boiling water, espresso powder, and 1 tablespoon of the sugar in a medium heatproof bowl; stir until dissolved, and let cool slightly.

2 Spray a 9 × 13-inch glass baking dish with nonstick spray. Line the bottom of the dish with the cake slices, cutting some pieces as needed to fill any gaps. Brush with the espresso mixture to saturate the cake; set aside.

3 Combine the cream cheese, the remaining 1 cup sugar, and the vanilla in a food processor. Process just until smooth; transfer to a large bowl. Gently fold in the whipped topping and spread over the cake in the baking dish. Sprinkle the top evenly with the chopped chocolate. Wrap with plastic wrap, being careful not to let the wrap touch the surface of the tiramisu and refrigerate at least 4 hours, or up to 3 days.

PER SERVING (1⁄24 of tiramisu): 174 Cal, 6 g Total Fat, 4 g Sat Fat, 7 mg Chol, 168 mg Sod, 28 g Carb, 1 g Fib, 3 g Prot, 34 mg Calc.
PointsPlus value: 5.

Classic Red Velvet Cake

classic red velvet cake

SERVES 16

Vegetarian

cake

2 cups cake flour
3 tablespoons unsweetened cocoa powder
2 teaspoons baking powder
½ teaspoon baking soda
½ teaspoon salt
¾ cup low-fat buttermilk
¾ cup granulated sugar
3 tablespoons canola oil
1 large egg
2 teaspoons red food coloring

frosting

1 (8-ounce) package fat-free cream cheese, at room temperature
1¼ cups confectioners' sugar
½ cup fat-free Greek yogurt
¾ teaspoon vanilla extract
¼ cup chopped pecans

The original incarnation of this cake was most likely a devil's food cake that obtained a subtle reddish hue from the combination of cocoa powder and buttermilk. When food dyes became popular with home bakers in the 1930s and '40s, however, the cake got a scarlet boost from the addition of red food coloring. Today red velvet is enjoying a resurgence and is wildly popular.

1 Cake: Preheat the oven to 350°F. Spray an 8-inch round baking pan with nonstick spray.

2 Whisk together the flour, cocoa powder, baking powder, baking soda, and salt in a large bowl. Whisk together the buttermilk, granulated sugar, oil, egg, and food coloring in a medium bowl. Add the buttermilk mixture to the flour mixture and stir until well blended.

3 Scrape the batter into the pan. Bake until a toothpick inserted into the center comes out clean, 35–40 minutes. Let cool completely in the pan on a rack. Run a knife around the edge of the cake to loosen it from the pan. Invert onto the rack.

4 Frosting: With an electric mixer on high speed, beat the cream cheese, confectioners' sugar, yogurt, and vanilla in a medium bowl until smooth, about 1 minute.

5 Cake assembly: Split the cake layer in half with a long serrated knife. Place the bottom layer, cut side up, on a serving plate. Spread ½ cup of the frosting over the layer, leaving a ½-inch border. Place the remaining cake layer on top, rounded side up. Spread the remaining 1 cup frosting over the top and side of the cake. Sprinkle the pecans onto the side of the cake, pressing to adhere. Cover the cake and store in the refrigerator up to 2 days. Bring to room temperature before serving.

PER SERVING (1⁄16 of cake): 197 Cal, 5 g Total Fat, 1 g Sat Fat, 15 mg Chol, 274 mg Sod, 34 g Carb, 0 g Fib, 5 g Prot, 95 mg Calc.
PointsPlus value: 5.

panna cotta with raspberry sauce

SERVES 4

2 tablespoons water
1 teaspoon unflavored gelatin
6 tablespoons heavy cream
¼ cup + 1 tablespoon sugar
1 cup fat-free vanilla yogurt
½ teaspoon vanilla extract
Scant ¼ teaspoon almond extract
2 cups fresh or thawed
frozen raspberries
1 teaspoon grated orange zest
1 teaspoon fresh orange juice

After the tiramisu phenomenon of the eighties, chefs of the following decade became enamored of another Italian dessert import: panna cotta (literally, "cooked cream" in Italian). This silky, eggless custard is traditionally served cold with a fruit sauce, so it's a great do-ahead dish. You can freeze the leftover cream in an airtight container for up to two months.

1 Pour the water into a small bowl and sprinkle with the gelatin. Let stand until the gelatin is softened, 6 minutes.

2 Combine the cream and ¼ cup of the sugar in a medium saucepan. Cook over medium heat, stirring, until the sugar dissolves. Remove from the heat and add the gelatin mixture, stirring to dissolve. Stir in the yogurt, vanilla, and almond extract until smooth. Divide the mixture among 4 (½-cup) custard cups. Cover and chill 4 hours or overnight.

3 Meanwhile, to prepare the raspberry sauce, combine the raspberries, the remaining 1 tablespoon sugar, the orange zest, and orange juice in a blender; puree until smooth. Strain through a fine sieve, cover, and refrigerate until ready to use.

4 To unmold the custards, run a thin-bladed knife around the edge of each cup, then dip the cups in a bowl of hot water for about 15 seconds. Immediately invert the cups onto a plate. Top each with 1 tablespoon of the raspberry sauce.

PER SERVING (1 custard with 1 tablespoon sauce): 202 Cal, 7 g Total Fat, 4 g Sat Fat, 26 mg Chol, 35 mg Sod, 32 g Carb, 4 g Fib, 4 g Prot, 111 mg Calc.
PointsPlus value: 5.

chocolate-almond mousse

SERVES 16

Vegetarian

8 ounces bittersweet chocolate, chopped
3 tablespoons almond liqueur
2 tablespoons light corn syrup
¼ cup powdered egg whites
¾ cup warm water
½ cup sugar

One of the greatest gifts for health-conscious chocolate lovers was research that confirmed that dark chocolate was high in antioxidants, the disease-fighting compounds most often associated with fruits and vegetables. We can't think of a better way to celebrate the news than with a dish of this light-as-air mousse.

1 Bring 1 inch of water to a boil in a medium saucepan; reduce to a simmer. Place the chocolate in a medium heatproof bowl and set over the simmering water. Cook, stirring constantly, until the chocolate melts, about 5 minutes. Remove the bowl from the saucepan.

2 Transfer the chocolate to a large bowl. Stir in the liqueur and corn syrup.

3 Whisk together the powdered egg whites and water in a large bowl until dissolved. With an electric mixer on low speed, beat egg white mixture until foamy, about 1 minute. Increase the speed to medium-high and beat until soft peaks form, about 2 minutes. Gradually beat in the sugar, until stiff and glossy, about 3 minutes longer.

4 With a rubber spatula, stir about one-third of the egg white mixture into the chocolate mixture. Fold the remaining egg white mixture into the chocolate mixture in two batches just until the whites are no longer visible. Refrigerate until firm, at least 3 hours.

PER SERVING (1/16 of mousse): 124 Cal, 4 g Total Fat, 2 g Sat Fat, 0 mg Chol, 22 mg Sod, 18 g Carb, 2 g Fib, 2 g Prot, 6 mg Calc.
PointsPlus value: 3.

Powdered egg whites are egg whites that have been pasteurized and then dried to a powder. They reconstitute with water and whip up just like fresh egg whites. Look for them in the baking aisle of supermarkets or in the cake decorating section of discount stores such as Walmart, Target, or Kmart.

chocolate fondue

SERVES 12 (2½ CUPS)

20 Min or Less
Vegetarian

⅓ cup whole milk
½ cup evaporated fat-free milk
¾ cup unsweetened cocoa powder
6 ounces semisweet chocolate, chopped
1 cup sugar
¼ cup water
2 tablespoons light corn syrup
4 ounces angel food cake, cut into 1-inch cubes (about 5 cups)
12 strawberries, stemmed

Here's another reason to dust off that old fondue pot: Chocolate fondue is actually an easy dessert to serve at a party. Pair it with fresh fruit and fat-free angel food cake cubes—that you prepare ahead—and you've got a crowd pleaser.

1 Whisk together the whole milk, evaporated milk, and cocoa powder in a medium saucepan until the cocoa dissolves. Add the chocolate and cook over medium-low heat, stirring constantly, until the chocolate is melted and the mixture is smooth.

2 Stir in the sugar, water, and corn syrup. Cook, stirring constantly, until the mixture is smooth, 4–6 minutes. Transfer to a fondue pot and set over moderate heat. Serve at once, with the angel food cake cubes and the strawberries for dipping.

PER SERVING (about 3 tablespoons fondue with scant ½ cup cake and 1 strawberry): 198 Cal, 6 g Total Fat, 3 g Sat Fat, 2 mg Chol, 94 mg Sod, 40 g Carb, 3 g Fib, 4 g Prot, 54 mg Calc.
PointsPlus value: 6.

Chocolate Fondue

baked rice pudding with currants

SERVES 8

Vegetarian

2 cups fat-free milk
¼ cup sugar
1⅓ cups Arborio or other short-grain rice
2 large eggs
¼ cup dried currants
1 teaspoon grated orange zest
1 teaspoon vanilla extract
1 tablespoon butter

Weight Watchers has published many recipes for rice pudding over the years, and with good reason: Not only is it one of the most beloved of all comfort desserts, but most recipes are packed with calcium and protein, both things that help keep dieters feeling satisfied for longer.

1 Combine 1 cup of the milk and the sugar in a medium saucepan. Bring to a boil, then stir in the rice. Reduce the heat and simmer, covered, stirring occasionally, until the milk is almost absorbed, 30 minutes.

2 Preheat the oven to 325°F. Spray a 1½-quart baking dish with nonstick spray.

3 Whisk together the remaining 1 cup milk, the eggs, currants, orange zest, and vanilla in a medium bowl; stir in the rice mixture. Pour into the prepared baking dish; dot with the butter. Bake, stirring twice, 25 minutes.

PER SERVING (⅛ of pudding): 205 Cal, 3 g Total Fat, 1 g Sat Fat, 52 mg Chol, 55 mg Sod, 37 g Carb, 1 g Fib, 6 g Prot, 95 mg Calc.
PointsPlus value: 5.

crêpes suzette

SERVES 6

Vegetarian

½ cup all-purpose flour
4 tablespoons sugar
⅛ teaspoon salt
¾ cup low-fat (1%) milk
2 large eggs, lightly beaten
1 tablespoon grated orange zest
⅓ cup fresh orange juice
2 oranges, peeled and cut into segments (about 1½ cups)
2 tablespoons orange-flavored liqueur, such as Grand Marnier
3 tablespoons unsalted light butter

In classy restaurants of the sixties and seventies, this dish came to a flaming conclusion with much fanfare when flambéed tableside by a tuxedoed waiter. Our version skips the flames but keeps all that wonderful caramelized-orange flavor.

1 Combine the flour, 1 tablespoon of the sugar, and the salt in a medium bowl. Combine the milk, eggs, and orange zest in a separate bowl. Slowly whisk the milk mixture into the flour mixture until smooth. Let stand 15 minutes.

2 Spray a small nonstick skillet or crêpe pan with nonstick spray and set over medium heat. Stir the batter, then pour a scant ¼ cup of the batter into the skillet, tilting in all directions to form a thin, even layer. Cook until the top is set and the bottom is golden, 1–1½ minutes. Flip and cook until the second side is lightly browned, 15–20 seconds. Transfer to a plate and repeat with the remaining batter to make 6 crêpes. Cover loosely with plastic wrap and reserve.

3 Combine the orange juice, the orange segments and their juices, and the remaining 3 tablespoons sugar in a large skillet. Cook over medium heat, stirring occasionally, until the sugar dissolves. Working one at a time, dip 1 crêpe into the hot juice mixture. Fold the crêpe into quarters and transfer to a warmed serving platter. Repeat with the remaining crêpes. Add the liqueur to the skillet and bring to a boil; continue boiling 30 seconds. Remove from the heat and swirl in the butter until melted. Pour the hot sauce over the crêpes and serve at once.

PER SERVING (1 crêpe, with about ⅓ cup sauce): 164 Cal, 5 g Total Fat, 3 g Sat Fat, 71 mg Chol, 84 mg Sod, 26 g Carb, 1 g Fib, 5 g Prot, 70 mg Calc.
PointsPlus value: 5.

If you prefer to make this sauce without the alcohol, simply substitute 1 tablespoon of lemon juice for the orange liqueur and omit boiling the sauce. When you swirl in the butter, add 1 teaspoon of grated lemon zest.

fudgy brownie pudding cake

SERVES 9

Vegetarian

¾ cup all-purpose flour
¾ cup sugar
⅓ cup + 4 tablespoons unsweetened cocoa powder
1 teaspoon instant espresso powder or instant coffee powder
2 teaspoons baking powder
¼ teaspoon baking soda
¼ teaspoon salt
½ cup low-fat (1%) milk
1 tablespoon unsalted butter, melted
1½ teaspoons vanilla extract
⅓ cup packed light brown sugar
1⅔ cups boiling water

The ultimate dessert for a chocoholic, this chewy, gooey creation hearkens back to the "impossible" cakes of the seventies (remember that cake with the fudgy tunnel in the center?). This cake magically reverses itself as it bakes—forming a wonderfully sugar-crusted brownie-like topping over a soft pudding base.

1 Place the oven rack in the center of the oven; preheat the oven to 350°F. Spray a 9-inch baking pan with nonstick spray.

2 Stir together the flour, sugar, ⅓ cup of the cocoa, the espresso powder, baking powder, baking soda, and salt in a large bowl. Make a well in the center, and pour in the milk, butter, and vanilla. Stir together until just blended and spoon evenly into the pan, spreading level.

3 Stir together the brown sugar and the remaining 4 tablespoons cocoa in a small bowl. Sprinkle evenly over the batter. Gently pour the boiling water over the top; do not stir. Bake until the top of the pudding is set, 35 minutes. Cool in the pan on a rack for at least 30 minutes. Serve warm or at room temperature.

PER SERVING (⅑ of cake): 165 Cal, 2 g Total Fat, 1 g Sat Fat, 4 mg Chol, 220 mg Sod, 37 g Carb, 2 g Fib, 3 g Prot, 94 mg Calc.
PointsPlus value: 5.

mocha espresso granita

SERVES 4

Vegetarian

½ cup packed light brown sugar
⅓ cup Dutch-process unsweetened cocoa powder
2 cups strong brewed espresso coffee, hot
2 (3 × ½-inch) strips lemon zest
5 tablespoons hazelnut liqueur (such as Frangelico)

Granita is a flavored ice dessert with a slightly granular texture. Did we create this one as a homage to the coffee-crazed nineties, or to the many coffee-laced frozen desserts and shakes of past Weight Watchers cookbooks? Either way, it's a great way to satisfy an ice cream craving. Try serving the granita in hollowed-out lemon shells [see below for our easy method].

1 Stir together the sugar and cocoa in a medium saucepan. Add the coffee and lemon zest; bring to a boil, reduce the heat, and simmer 3 minutes. Remove from the heat and let cool to room temperature. Remove and discard the lemon rind. Stir in 3 tablespoons of the liqueur.

2 Pour into a 9-inch square metal pan. Freeze until the mixture is frozen around the edges but still slushy in the center, about 1½ hours. Stir with a fork, breaking up the ice crystals. Return to the freezer and freeze until just solid in the center and firmer around the edges, about 1½ hours. Place in an airtight container and freeze until firm, at least 4 hours or up to 1 month.

3 To serve, scrape the granita with a fork to lighten its texture. Spoon into serving glasses, and drizzle each serving with ½ tablespoon of the remaining liqueur.

PER SERVING (⅔ cup granita and ½ tablespoon liqueur): 173 Cal, 1 g Total Fat, 1 g Sat Fat, 0 mg Chol, 26 mg Sod, 37 g Carb, 2 g Fib, 2 g Prot, 35 mg Calc.
PointsPlus value: 5.

Scoop out the pulpy centers from juiced lemon halves, then trim a little off the rounded edges of the shells, so they can stand upright. Freeze in zip-close freezer bags for up to a month and use for serving granita, sorbet, or ice cream.

(clockwise from top) Mango-Soy Smoothie, page 21, Double-Chocolate Malt, and Orange Dreamsicle Shake

double-chocolate malt

SERVES 4

20 Min or Less
Vegetarian

1½ cups fat-free milk
1 cup low-fat chocolate ice cream
2 tablespoons lite chocolate syrup
2 tablespoons malt powder

Recipes for malteds took up a lot of room in old Weight Watchers cookbooks; they were a great way to satisfy desires for treats and snacks—and meet the required daily milk servings. Today's version delivers plenty of chocolate power with ice cream and chocolate syrup.

Whirl the milk and ice cream in a blender until smooth. Add the chocolate syrup and malt powder; puree until smooth and frothy.

PER SERVING (¾ cup): 168 Cal, 4 g Total Fat, 2 g Sat Fat, 13 mg Chol, 123 mg Sod, 29 g Carb, 0 g Fib, 7 g Prot, 227 mg Calc.
PointsPlus value: 5.

orange dreamsicle shake

SERVES 4

20 Min or Less
Vegetarian

1 cup ice cubes
1 cup orange sherbet
1 cup fat-free vanilla frozen yogurt
1 cup fat-free milk
2 tablespoons thawed frozen orange juice concentrate

This creamy refreshing shake tastes just like the frozen treat on a stick you enjoyed as a kid.

Crush the ice cubes in a blender (or place them in a zip-close freezer bag, crush them with the back of heavy skillet, and place in the blender). Add the sherbet, yogurt, milk, and orange juice concentrate; puree until smooth.

PER SERVING (1 cup): 142 Cal, 1 g Total Fat, 0 g Sat Fat, 3 mg Chol, 77 mg Sod, 29 g Carb, 1 g Fib, 5 g Prot, 178 mg Calc.
PointsPlus value: 4.

PointsPlus value *index*

0 *PointsPlus* value

Banana "Ice Cream," 91
Frozen Grapes, 91

1 *PointsPlus* value

Asparagus en Papillote, 248
Cauliflower Puree, 251
Cheese Ball, 83
Cheese Crisps, 86
Coffee Frappé, 91
Creamed Spinach, 264
Ham-and-Swiss Mini Quiches, 100
Kale Chips, 91
Marinara Sauce, 208
Mushroom "Peanuts," 93
Swingin' Sixties Cheese Dip, 91
The Classic Garden Vegetable Soup, 33

2 *PointsPlus* value

"Cream" of Cauliflower Soup, 257
Baked Vidalia Onions Balsamico, 260
Borscht with Sour Cream, 44
Broccoli Rabe with Lemon and Garlic, 249
Caesar Salad, 53
Cheese Sauce, 243
Chilled Zucchini-Basil Soup with Tomatoes, 46
Chipotle Chili Popcorn, 91
Coleslaw, 253
Creamy Onion Dip, 89
Deviled Eggs, 82
Green Beans with Tomato and Oregano, 259
Oven-Fried Onion Rings, 261
Pureed Peas with Mint, 263
Sautéed Swiss Chard and Onion, 265
Shrimp Salsa with Tortilla Chips, 101
Spinach-Mushroom-Bacon Salad with Warm Onion Dressing, 63
Stuffed Celery Redux, 91
Vegetable Soup, 33
Watermelon, Tomato, and Orange Salad, 67
White Bean-Tomato Dip with Grilled Peppers, 90

3 *PointsPlus* value

Arugula-Pear Salad with Gorgonzola Dressing, 48
Arugula, Radicchio, and Belgian Endive Salad with Creamy Garlic Dressing, 52
Black Bean "Caviar," 96
Brussels Sprouts with Dried Cranberries and Lemon, 250
Cheddar Corn Pudding, 262
Cheese Puffs, 85
Cheesy Pepperoni-Mushroom Flatbread, 99
Chilled Broccoli Soup with Lemon and Herbs, 45
Chocolate Yogurt Pudding, 91
Chocolate-Almond Mousse, 313
Crab with Homemade Cocktail Sauce, 167
French Toast, 18
Fruit Salad with Yogurt Mint Dressing, 66
Gazpacho with Cilantro Croutons, 41
Greek Salad with Oregano Dressing, 59
Grilled Duck Breasts with Orange-Balsamic Glaze, 154
Grilled Tropical Fruit with Lime Syrup, 290
Hawaiian Mousse, 303
Iceberg Salad with Blue Cheese Dressing, 58
Irish Soda Bread, 79
Lemon Bars, 297
Mango-Soy Smoothie, 21
Microwave Chickpea and Vegetable Soup, 33
Mini Cheesecake Bites with Blueberry Topping, 296
Mushroom-Barley Soup, 32
Omelettes for Two, 2
Pickled Beet and Onion Salad, 56
Piña Colada Smoothie, 21
Potato Salad with Tarragon-Chive Dressing, 273
Roasted Root Vegetables, 266
Spanakopita Triangles, 92
Spicy Grilled Shrimp and Scallops, 173
Spicy Roast Chickpeas, 91
Swiss Fondue, 88
Tandoori-Marinated Turkey Breast, 149
Tuscan Panzanella, 55
Veggie Cup Scramble, 20

4 *PointsPlus* value

Ambrosia, 282
Baked Apples, 283
Baked Halibut with Lemon and Capers, 156
Braised Red Cabbage with Apples, Onions, and Raisins, 252
Buffalo Chicken Wings, 94
Buttermilk Shake, 91
Carrot Salad with Sesame-Ginger Dressing, 267
Cauliflower Casserole, Pizza-Style, 242
Cheese Blintzes, 13
Chef's Salad with Russian Dressing, 62

Chicken Liver Crostini, 97
Chicken Satay with Peanut Sauce, 135
Corn, Zucchini, and Green Bean Succotash, 258
Cranberry Holiday Mold, 289
Crunchy Almond Cakes, 91
Curried Vegetable Stew, 189
Fennel, Orange, and Red Cabbage Salad with Citrus Vinaigrette, 49
Fried Rice, 276
Frozen Chocolate-Banana Pop, 91
Green Bean Casserole, 245
Grilled T-Bone with Steak House Spices, 108
Grits with Cheese, 275
Idaho Fries with Vinegar, 269
Lemon-Basil Three-Bean Salad, 60
Mediterranean Clam Chowder, 26
Multigrain Loaf with Flaxseeds, 73
Mushroom Sandwich Spread, 191
Mushroom-Swiss Omelettes, 3
No-Bake Strawberry-Rhubarb Crisp, 291
Nutty Apple Slices, 91
Orange Dreamsicle Shake, 321
Peanut Butter-Banana Smoothie, 22
Potato-Leek Soup, 43
Prosciutto-Wrapped Scallops, 175
Pumpkin Chiffon Pie, 303
Roast Chicken with Lemon and Herbs, 128
Southwestern Chicken-Vegetable Soup, 34
Spice-Rubbed Beer Can Chicken, 129
Spiced Plum-and-Port Compote, 284
Stir-fried Baby Bok Choy with Snow Peas, Shiitake Mushrooms, and Ginger, 254
Sweet Potato Fritters, 274
Swiss Cheese Strata, 8
Vegetable Ragu with Tagliatelle, 218
Vegetable Salad with Dijon Vinaigrette, 47
Warm Lentils with Escarole, 197

5 ***PointsPlus*** value

Asian Noodle Soup with Tofu and Shrimp, 25
Bacon-Egg Pita, 20
Baked Rice Pudding with Currants, 316
Barley Waldorf Salad, 57
Basic Pizza Crust, 209
Berry Quinoa, 20
Blackened Tilapia with Remoulade, 160
Bread Pudding with Winter Fruits, 294
Broccoli-and-Bacon Egg Cups, 9
Bulgur Pilaf, 277
Butternut Squash Soup with Sage, 42
California Rolls, 182
Campari-Poached Grapefruit, 287
Chicken with Lemon-Caper Sauce, 142
Classic Red Velvet Cake, 311
Cobb Salad with Green Goddess Dressing, 65
Crêpes Suzette, 317
"Danish" Pastry, 19
Double-Chocolate Malt, 321
Field Greens with Roasted Beets, Goat Cheese Croutons, and Dijon Vinaigrette, 50
"Fried" Cauliflower, 257
Fudgy Brownie Pudding Cake, 318
German Hot Potato Salad, 272
Greek-Style Twice-Baked Potatoes, 270
Ham-and-Mushroom Crêpes, 12
Lamb Kebabs, 126
Minestrone, 39
Mocha Espresso Granita, 319
Nachos Grande, 87
Orange Chicken, 141
Panna Cotta with Raspberry Sauce, 312
Pepper-Cheese Muffin, 20
Poached Chicken Breasts with Green Sauce, 138
Pumpkin Rolls, 75
Ratatouille au Gratin, 247
Roasted Beef Tenderloin with Mushroom Sauce, 105
Roasted Garlic Mashed Potatoes, 271
Salisbury Steaks with Mushroom Gravy, 116
Saucy Oven-Baked BBQ Chicken, 130
Sausage Focaccia, 77
Soy-Lime Marinated Flank Steak, 109
Soy-Sesame Grilled Tuna, 166
Steamed Cauliflower with Raisins and Pine Nuts, 256
Stuffed Pork Chops, 121
Tiramisu, 309
Tomato Scramble, 20
Tortilla-Cheese Casserole, 246
Zucchini Corn Bread, 78

6 ***PointsPlus*** value

A.M. Banana Split, 20
Barley Mushroom "Risotto," 203
Beef, Bean, and Zucchini Chili, 114
Black Bean and Corn Cakes, 205
Bubble Bread with Herbs and Sun-Dried Tomatoes, 74
Cajun Catfish, 158
Canadian Bacon-Cheddar Frittata, 6
Chicken Cacciatore, 134
Chicken with 40 Cloves of Garlic, 143
Chickpea Croquettes with Roasted Tomato Sauce, 192
Chocolate Fondue, 314
Confetti Rice Salad, 279
Creamy Fish Chowder, 27
Creamy Polenta with Mushroom Ragu, 204
Crunchy Peanut Butter Fudge, 303
Diner-Style Meatloaf, 151
Duck Stir-Fry with Sugar Snap Peas, 155
Farfalle with Tomatoes, Goat Cheese, and Basil, 212
Fish Tacos with Chipotle Cream, 165
Hash Browns, Egg, and Cheese Casserole, 5
Hearty Stovetop Beef Stew, 112
Lemon Risotto with Spring Vegetables, 201
Lentil Soup, 31
Marinated Mediterranean Chicken, 147
Multigrain Cereal, 20
Mushroom-Cheese Pâté, 191
Oven-Fried Fish and Chips, 162
Polenta Hotcakes, 20

Pork Loin Roast with Gingersnap Sauce, 117
Portobello Burgers, 72
Quinoa Pilaf, 278
Salmon Cakes with Red Pepper Sauce, 179
Shake-in-the-Bag Chicken, 146
Skillet Pork Chops with Onion Gravy, 122
Skillet-Braised Chicken with Roasted Vegetables, 131
Smoky Black Bean and Corn Soup, 40
Soyful Scalloped Potatoes, 190
Spinach and Roasted Red Pepper Ravioli Casserole, 216
Split Pea Soup with Ham and Cheese, 29
Strawberry Crêpe, 20
Sweet Potato Pie, 306
Tempeh-Vegetable Stir-Fry with Peanut Sauce, 185
Turkey Meatballs, 153
Vegetarian Stuffed Cabbage Rolls, 186

7 *PointsPlus* value

Banana Cream Pie, 301
Biscuit-Topped Chicken Potpie, 148
Black Bean and Soy Chili, 187
Chicken Cordon Bleu, 132
Chicken Parmigiana, 137
Chicken Salad Véronique, 136
Chocolate Angel Food Cake, 308
Citrus, Date, and Raisin Baklava, 300
Cornmeal-Crusted Shrimp with Grits and Greens, 177
Creamy White Bean-Parmesan Soup, 37
Grilled Chicken with Corn–Cherry Tomato Relish, 139
Huevos Rancheros in Tortilla Cups, 14
Individual Beef Wellingtons, 106
Lamb Chops with Mint Pesto, 125
Lamb Chops with Rosemary and Red Wine, 124
Linguine with Red Clam Sauce, 217
Mussels in White Wine with Garlic, 169
Pad Thai, 202
Paella Valenciana, 172
Pasta Primavera, 198
Pizza Margherita, 230
Pork Marsala, 119
Raspberry-Peach Cobbler, 292
Red Bean, Spinach, and Tomato Burritos, 193
Red Potato and Fontina Frittata, 4
Southern-Style Chicken and Dumplings, 144
Spaghetti Carbonara, 221
Spicy Sausage, White Bean, and Greens Soup, 36
Spinach, Caramelized Onion, and Tomato Quiche, 11
Tofu-Lentil Burgers, 184
Yankee Pot Roast, 111

8 *PointsPlus* value

Baked Alaska, 304
Baked Ziti with Meatballs, 223
Beef Fajitas, 113
Broccoli-Cheddar-Mushroom Pizza, 231
Crab Cakes with Tartar Sauce, 168
French Onion Soup Gratinée, 24
Fruit and Nut Granola, 17
Greek Pizza, 239
Gumbo, 30
Key Lime Pie, 302
Lattice-Topped Cherry-Almond Pie, 307
Pizza all'Insalata, 233
Seafood Pizza, 234
Shells with Spinach, Ricotta, and Raisins, 224
Tabbouleh Niçoise, 170
Tuna Noodle Casserole, 180
Turkey Tetrazzini Casserole, 152
Vegetarian Mushroom Patties, 191
White Pizza, 238

9 *PointsPlus* value

Bananas Foster, 295
Boston Cream Pie, 299
California Salad Sandwiches, 68
Capellini with Seafood, 220
Cheese Ravioli with Butternut Squash Sauce, 228
Cranberry-Stuffed Apples, 286
Mexican Chicken Wraps, 69
Orechiette with Broccoli Rabe, Garlic, and Red Pepper Flakes, 199
Rotelle with Walnut-Gorgonzola Sauce, 210
Salmon en Papillote, 161
Shrimp Scampi with Fresh Linguini, 178
Tex-Mex Pizza, 235
The Iconic Weight Watchers Burger, 104
The New Pork and Beans, 118
Turkey Sloppy Joes, 70
Vegetable Lasagna, 226

10 *PointsPlus* value

Italian Bean and Vegetable Stuffed Mushrooms, 196
Penne alla Vodka, 213
Vegetable Quesadillas, 194

11 *PointsPlus* value

Easy Homemade Macaroni and Cheese, 215
Moroccan Swordfish with Couscous, 157
Rigatoni with Meat Sauce, 225

12 *PointsPlus* value

Baked Macaroni, Cheese, and Cauliflower Casserole, 257
Irish Lamb Stew, 127

13 *PointsPlus* value

Ham, Pepper, and Onion Calzones, 236

index

a

almond(s):
- Cakes, Crunchy, 91
- -Cherry Pie, Lattice-Topped, 307
- -Chocolate Mousse, 313

A.M. Banana Split, 20
Ambrosia, 16, 282
appetizers, 11, 81-101
- Black Bean "Caviar," 96
- Buffalo Chicken Wings, 94, 95
- Cheese Ball, 83, 84
- Cheese Crisps, 84, 86
- Cheese Puffs, 84, 85
- Cheesy Pepperoni-Mushroom Flatbread, 98, 99
- Chicken Liver Crostini, 97
- Creamy Onion Dip, 89
- Deviled Eggs, 82, 84
- Ham-and-Swiss Mini Quiches, 100
- Mushroom "Peanuts," 93
- Nachos Grande, 87, 95
- Shrimp Salsa with Tortilla Chips, 101
- Spanakopita Triangles, 92
- Swiss Fondue, 88
- White Bean-Tomato Dip with Grilled Peppers, 90

apple(s):
- Baked, 283
- Braised Red Cabbage with Onions, Raisins, and, 120, 252
- Cranberry-Stuffed, 286
- Nutty, Slices, 91

arugula:
- -Pear Salad with Gorgonzola Dressing, 48
- Radicchio, and Belgian Endive Salad with Creamy Garlic Dressing, 52

Asian flavors:
- California Rolls, 182
- Carrot Salad with Toasted Sesame-Ginger Dressing, 267
- Chicken Satay with Peanut Sauce, 135
- Fried Rice, 276
- Noodle Soup with Tofu and Shrimp, 25
- Pad Thai, 202
- Soy-Sesame Grilled Tuna, 166
- Stir-Fried Baby Bok Choy with Snow Peas, Shiitake Mushrooms, and Ginger, 254, 255

asparagus:
- en Papillote, 174, 248
- fresh vs. frozen, 47

b

Baby Bok Choy, Stir-Fried with Snow Peas, Shiitake Mushrooms, and Ginger, 254, 255
bacon:
- -and-Broccoli Egg Cups, 9
- -Cheddar Frittata, Canadian, 6, 7
- -Egg Pita, 20
- -Spinach-Mushroom Salad with Warm Onion Dressing, 63

Baked Alaska, 304, 305
Baked Apples, 283
Baked Halibut with Lemon and Capers, 156
Baked Macaroni, Cheese, and Cauliflower Casserole Circa 1980, 257
Baked Rice Pudding with Currants, 316
Baked Vidalia Onions Balsamico, 260
Baked Ziti with Meatballs, 222, 223
baking essentials, 176
Baklava, Citrus, Date, and Raisin, 300
banana(s):
- A.M., Split, 20
- -Chocolate Pop, Frozen, 91
- Cream Pie, 301
- Foster, 295
- "Ice Cream," 91
- -Peanut Butter Smoothie, 22

barley:
- Mushroom "Risotto," 203
- -Mushroom Soup, 32

basil:
- -Lemon Three-Bean Salad, 60, 61
- Tomatoes, and Goat Cheese, Farfalle with, 212
- -Zucchini Soup with Tomatoes, Chilled, 46

bean(s):
- Beef, and Zucchini Chili, 114, 115
- Curried Vegetable Stew, 188, 189
- Lemon-Basil Three-Bean Salad, 60, 61
- in Minestrone, 38, 39
- The New Pork and, 118
- see also specific beans

beef:
- Baked Ziti with Meatballs, 222, 223
- Bean, and Zucchini Chili, 114, 115
- cooking of, xi
- Fajitas, 113
- Grilled T-Bone with Steak House Spices, 108
- Hearty Stovetop Beef Stew, 112
- The Iconic Weight Watchers Burger, 104
- Individual Wellingtons, 106, 107
- lean cuts of, xii
- Rigatoni with Meat Sauce, 225
- Roasted Tenderloin with Mushroom Sauce, 105
- Salisbury Steaks with Mushroom Gravy, 116
- Soy-Lime Marinated Flank Steak, 109
- Yankee Pot Roast, 110, 111

beet(s):
- Borscht with Sour Cream, 44
- Pickled, and Onion Salad, 56
- precooked, 56

beet(s) *(continued)*
Roasted, Goat Cheese Croutons, and Dijon Vinaigrette, Field Greens with, 50, 51
berry(ies), vii
Cranberry Holiday Mold, 288, 289
Cranberry-Stuffed Apples, 286
Mini Cheesecake Bites with Blueberry Topping, 296
No-Bake Strawberry-Rhubarb Crisp, 291
Panna Cotta with Raspberry Sauce, 312
Quinoa, 20
Raspberry-Peach Cobbler, 292, 293
Strawberry Crêpe, 20
black bean(s):
"Caviar," 96
and Corn Cakes, 205
Smoky, and Corn Soup, 40
and Soy Chili, 187
Blackened Tilapia with Remoulade, 160
Blintzes, Cheese, 13
Blueberry Topping, Mini Cheesecake Bites with, 296
Bok Choy, Baby, Stir-Fried with Snow Peas, Shiitake Mushrooms, and Ginger, 254, 255
Borscht with Sour Cream, 44
Boston Cream Pie, 298, 299
Braised Red Cabbage with Apples, Onions, and Raisins, 120, 252
bread(s):
Bacon-Egg Pita, 20
Bubble, with Herbs and Sun-Dried Tomatoes, 38, 74
Cheesy-Pepperoni-Mushroom Flatbread, 98, 99
Cilantro Croutons, 41
French Toast, 16, 18
hand kneading, 73
Irish Soda, 79
Multigrain Loaf with Flaxseeds, 73
Pepper-Cheese Muffin, 20
Pumpkin Rolls, 75
Sausage Focaccia, 76, 77
Tuscan Panzanella, 54, 55
Zucchini Corn, 78
Bread Pudding with Winter Fruits, 294
breakfast fare, 1-22
A.M. Banana Split, 20
Ambrosia, 16, 282
Berry Quinoa, 20
Cheese Blintzes, 13
"Danish" Pastry, 19
French Toast, 16, 18
Fruit-and-Nut Granola, 16, 17
Mango-Soy Smoothie, 21, 320
Multigrain Cereal, 20
Peanut Butter-Banana Smoothie, 22
Piña Colada Smoothie, 21
Polenta Hotcakes, 20
Strawberry Crêpe, 20
see also egg(s)
broccoli:
-and-Bacon Egg Cups, 9
-Cheddar-Mushroom Pizza, 231
Chilled Soup with Lemon and Herbs, 45
broccoli rabe:
with Lemon and Garlic, 249
Orechiette with Garlic, Red Pepper Flakes, and, 199
Brussels Sprouts with Dried Cranberries and Lemon, 250
Bubble Bread with Herbs and Sun-Dried Tomatoes, 38, 74
Buffalo Chicken Wings, 94, 95
bulgur, viii
Pilaf, 277
Tabbouleh Niçoise, 170, 171
burger(s):
The Iconic Weight Watchers, 104
Portobello, 72
Tofu-Lentil, 184
Burritos, Red Bean, Spinach, and Tomato, 193
Buttermilk Shake, 91
butternut squash:
Sauce, Cheese Ravioli with, 228
Soup with Sage, 42

C

cabbage:
in Borscht with Sour Cream, 44
Braised Red, with Apples, Onions, and Raisins, 120, 252
Coleslaw, 71, 253
Red, Fennel, and Orange Salad with Citrus Vinaigrette, 49
Rolls, Vegetarian Stuffed, 186
Caesar Salad, 53
Cajun Catfish, 158, 159
cake(s):
Baked Alaska, 304, 305
Boston Cream Pie, 298, 299
Chocolate Angel Food, 308
Classic Red Velvet, 310, 311
Crunchy Almond, 91
Fudgy Brownie Pudding, 318
Tiramisu, 309
California Rolls, 182
California Salad Sandwiches, 68
Calzones, Ham, Pepper, and Onion, 236, 237
Campari-Poached Grapefruit, 287
cannellini beans, *see* white kidney bean(s)
Capellini with Seafood, 220
caper(s):
Baked Halibut with Lemon and, 156
-Lemon Sauce, Chicken with, 142
Carrot Salad with Toasted Sesame-Ginger Dressing, 267
Catfish, Cajun, 158, 159
cauliflower:
Casserole, Pizza-Style, 242
Casserole Circa 1980, Baked Macaroni, Cheese, and, 257
"Fried," Circa 1980, 257
Puree, 251
Soup Circa 1970, "Cream" of, 257
Steamed, with Raisins and Pine Nuts, 256
Celery Redux, Stuffed, 91
cheddar cheese:
Baked Macaroni, and Cauliflower Casserole Circa 1980, 257
-Broccoli-Mushroom Pizza, 231
-Canadian Bacon Frittata, 6, 7
Cheese Ball, 83, 84
Cheese Puffs, 84, 85
Corn Pudding, 262
Easy Homemade Macaroni and, 214, 215
Grits with, 275
Sauce, 243
Split Pea Soup with Ham and, 28, 29
-Tortilla Casserole, 246
cheese:
Ball, 83, 84
Blintzes, 13
Crisps, 84, 86
French Onion Soup Gratinée, 24
Grits with, 275
Puffs, 84, 85

Ratatouille au Gratin, 247
Sauce, 243
Soyful Scalloped Potatoes, 190
Split Pea Soup with Ham and, 28, 29
-Tortilla Casserole, 246
see also specific cheeses
Cheesecake Mini Bites with Blueberry Topping, 296
Chef's Salad with Russian Dressing, 62
Cherry-Almond Pie, Lattice-Topped, 307
chicken:
blackening mix with, 160
Buffalo, Wings, 94, 95
Cacciatore, 134
cooking of, xi
Cordon Bleu, 132, 133
and Dumplings, Southern-Style, 144, 145
with 40 Cloves of Garlic, 143
Grilled, with Corn-Cherry Tomato Relish, 139
lean cuts of, viii, xii
with Lemon-Caper Sauce, 142
Liver Crostini, 97
Marinated Mediterranean, 147
Mexican Wraps, 69
Orange, 140, 141
Parmigiana, 137
Poached Breasts with Green Sauce, 138
Potpie, Biscuit-Topped, 148
Roast, with Lemon and Herbs, 128
Salad Véronique, 136
Satay with Peanut Sauce, 135
Saucy Oven-Baked BBQ, 130
Shake-in-the-Bag, 146
Skillet-Braised with Roasted Vegetables, 131
Spice-Rubbed Beer Can, 129
-Vegetable Soup, Southwestern, 34, 35
chickpea(s):
Croquettes with Roasted Tomato Sauce, 192
Spicy Roast, 91
and Vegetable Soup Circa 1990, Microwave, 33
chili(s):
Beef, Bean, and Zucchini, 114, 115
Black Bean and Soy, 187
Popcorn, 91
Chilled Broccoli Soup with Lemon and Herbs, 45
Chilled Zucchini-Basil Soup with Tomatoes, 46
Chive-Tarragon Dressing, Potato Salad with, 273
chocolate:
-Almond Mousse, 313
Angel Food Cake, 308
-Banana Pop, Frozen, 91
Boston Cream Pie, 298, 299
Double-, Malt, 320, 321
Fondue, 314, 315
Fudgy Brownie Pudding Cake, 318
Graham Crust, 301
Mocha Espresso Granita, 319
Tiramisu, 309
Yogurt Pudding, 91
Cilantro Croutons, Gazpacho with, 41
citrus fruit:
Date, and Raisin Baklava, 300
Vinaigrette, Fennel, Orange, and Red Cabbage Salad with, 49
zest of, 319
see also specific fruits
clam(s):
Mediterranean Chowder, 26
Red Sauce, Linguine with, 217
Classic Garden Vegetable Soup, The, 33
Cobb Salad with Green Goddess Dressing, 64, 65
Cocktail Sauce, Crab with Homemade, 167
Coleslaw, 71, 253
Confetti Rice Salad, 279
corn:
and Black Bean Cakes, 205
Cheddar Pudding, 262
-Cherry Tomato Relish, Grilled Chicken with, 139
Chili Popcorn, 91
Creamy Polenta with Mushroom Ragu, 204
Polenta Hotcakes, 20
Soup, Smoky Black Bean and, 40
Tortilla-Cheese Casserole, 246
Vegetable Quesadillas, 194, 195
Zucchini, and Green Bean Succotash, 258
Zucchini Bread, 78
Cornmeal-Crusted Shrimp with Grits and Greens, 177
cottage cheese:
Cheese Ball, 83
Cheese Blintzes, 13
Hash Browns, Egg, and Cheese Casserole, 5
Mushroom-Cheese Pâté 1986, 191
Pepper-Cheese Muffin, 20
Swingin' Sixties Cheese Dip, 91
Couscous, Moroccan Swordfish with, 157
crab:
Cakes with Tartar Sauce, 168
with Homemade Cocktail Sauce, 167
cranberry(ies):
Brussels Sprouts with Lemon and Dried, 250
-Stuffed Apples, 286
cream cheese:
Cheese Ball, 83
Cheese Blintzes, 13
Creamed Spinach, 150, 264
Mini Cheesecake Bites with Blueberry Topping, 296
Creamed Spinach, 150, 264
"Cream" of Cauliflower Soup Circa 1970, 257
Creamy Fish Chowder, 27
Creamy Onion Dip, 89
Creamy Polenta with Mushroom Ragu, 204
Creamy White Bean-Parmesan Soup, 37
Creole and Cajun flavors:
Bananas Foster, 295
Blackened Tilapia with Remoulade, 160
Cajun Catfish, 158, 159
Gumbo, 30
crêpes:
Ham-and-Mushroom, 12
Strawberry, 20
Suzette, 317
croutons:
Cilantro, Gazpacho with, 41
Goat Cheese, Roasted Beets, and Dijon Vinaigrette, Field Greens with, 50, 51
Crunchy Almond Cakes, 91
Currants, Baked Rice Pudding with, 316
Curried Vegetable Stew, 188, 189
cutting boards, ix

d

"Danish" Pastry, 19
desserts, 281-321
Ambrosia, 16, 282
Baked Alaska, 304, 305
Baked Apples, 283
Baked Rice Pudding with Currants, 316
Banana Cream Pie, 301
Bananas Foster, 295
Boston Cream Pie, 298, 299
Bread Pudding with Winter Fruits, 294
Campari-Poached Grapefruit, 287
Chocolate-Almond Mousse, 313
Chocolate Angel Food Cake, 308
Chocolate Fondue, 314, 315
Citrus, Date, and Raisin Baklava, 300
Classic Red Velvet Cake, 310, 311
Cranberry Holiday Mold, 288, 289
Cranberry-Stuffed Apples, 286
Crêpes Suzette, 317
Crunchy Peanut Butter Fudge Circa 1980, 303
Double-Chocolate Malt, 320, 321
Fudgy Brownie Pudding Cake, 318
Grilled Tropical Fruit with Lime Syrup, 290
Hawaiian Mousse Circa 1970, 303
Key Lime Pie, 302
Lattice-Topped Cherry-Almond Pie, 307
Lemon Bars, 297
Mango-Soy Smoothie, 21, 320
Mini Cheesecake Bites with Blueberry Topping, 296
Mocha Espresso Granita, 319
No-Bake Strawberry-Rhubarb Crisp, 291
Orange Dreamsicle Shake, 320, 321
Panna Cotta with Raspberry Sauce, 312
Pumpkin Chiffon Pie Circa 1980, 303
Raspberry-Peach Cobbler, 292, 293
Spiced Plum-and-Port Compote, 284, 285
Sweet Potato Pie, 306
Tiramisu, 309
Deviled Eggs, 82, 84
Diner-Style Meatloaf, 150, 151
Double-Chocolate Malt, 320, 321
dough:
Basic Pizza Crust, 209
phyllo, 92, 100, 106, 107, 300
shaping and stretching, 230
Dreamsicle Shake, Orange, 320, 321
duck:
fresh vs. frozen, 154
Grilled, Breasts with OrangeBalsamic Glaze, 154
Stir-Fry with Sugar Snap Peas, 155

e

Easy Homemade Macaroni with Cheese, 214, 215
egg(s):
-Bacon Pita, 20
Broccoli-and-Bacon Cups, 9
Canadian Bacon-Cheddar Frittata, 6, 7
cooking of, xi
Deviled, 82, 84
Ham-and-Swiss Mini Quiches, 100
Hash Browns, and Cheese Casserole, 5
Huevos Rancheros in Tortilla Cups, 14, 15
Mushroom-Swiss Omelettes, 3
Omelettes for Two, 2
Red Potato and Fontina Frittata, 4
Spinach, Caramelized Onion, and Tomato Quiche, 10, 11
Swiss Cheese Strata, 8
Tomato Scramble, 20
Veggie Cup Scramble, 20
entrées, 103-205
see also meatless entrées; under Italian flavors; specific meats, poultry, and seafood
Escarole, Warm Lentils with, 197

f

Farfalle with Tomatoes, Goat Cheese, and Basil, 212
Fennel, Orange, and Red Cabbage Salad with Citrus Vinaigrette, 49
Field Greens with Roasted Beets, Goat Cheese Croutons, and Dijon Vinaigrette, 50, 51
fish:
Baked Halibut with Lemon and Capers, 156
Blackened Tilapia with Remoulade, 160
Cajun Catfish, 158, 159
and Chips, Oven-Fried, 162, 163
cooking times for, 158
Creamy Chowder, 27
Moroccan Swordfish with Couscous, 157
Salmon Cakes with Red Pepper Sauce, 179
Salmon en Papillote, 161
Soy-Sesame Grilled Tuna, 166
Tacos with Chipotle Cream, 164, 165
Tuna Noodle Casserole, 180, 181
Fontina Frittata, Red Potato and, 4
freezer staples, 176
French flavors, 96, 97, 158
Asparagus en Papillote, 174, 248
Chicken Cordon Bleu, 132, 133
Chicken Salad Véronique, 136
Chicken with Lemon-Caper Sauce, 142
Ham-and-Mushroom Crêpes, 12
Onion Soup Gratinée, 24
Ratatouille au Gratin, 247
Salmon en Papillote, 161
Spinach, Caramelized Onion, and Tomato Quiche, 10, 11
Tabbouleh Niçoise, 170, 171
French Toast, 16, 18
"Fried" Cauliflower Circa 1980, 257
Fried Rice, 276
frittata(s):
Canadian Bacon-Cheddar, 6, 7
Red Potato and Fontina, 4
frozen dishes:
Baked Alaska, 304, 305
Chocolate-Banana Pop, 91
Grapes, 91
lemon zest for, 319
Mocha Espresso Granita, 319
see also shakes
fruit(s):
-and-Nut Granola, 16, 17
Salad with Yogurt-Mint Dressing, 66
Tropical, Grilled, with Lime Syrup, 290
Winter, Bread Pudding with, 294
see also specific fruits
Fudgy Brownie Pudding Cake, 318

g

garic, 202
- Broccoli Rabe with Lemon and, 249
- Chicken with 40 Cloves of, 143
- Creamy Dressing, 52
- how to bruise, 48, 221
- Mussels in White Wine with, 169
- Orechiette with Broccoli Rabe, Red Pepper Flakes, and, 199
- Roasted, Mashed Potatoes, 107, 271

Gazpacho with Cilantro Croutons, 41
German Hot Potato Salad, 272
ginger:
- freezing, 254
- Stir-Fried Baby Bok Choy with Snow Peas, Shiitake Mushrooms, and, 254, 255
- -Toasted Sesame Dressing, Carrot Salad with, 267

goat cheese:
- Croutons, Roasted Beets, and Dijon Vinaigrette, Field Greens with, 50, 51
- Farfalle with Tomatoes, Basil, and, 212

Gorgonzola cheese:
- Dressing, Arugula-Pear Salad with, 48
- -Walnut Sauce, Rotelle with, 210, 211

Granola, Fruit-and-Nut, 16, 17
Grapefruit, Campari-Poached, 287
grapes:
- Chicken Salad Véronique, 136
- Frozen, 91

graters, ix
Greek flavors:
- Citrus, Date, and Raisin Baklava, 300
- Lamb Kebabs, 126
- Pizza, 239
- Salad with Oregano Dressing, 59
- Spanakopita Triangles, 92
- Twice-Baked Potatoes, 270

green bean(s):
- Casserole, 244, 245
- Corn, and Zucchini Succotash, 258
- with Tomato and Oregano, 259

greens:
- Cornmeal-Crusted Shrimp with Grits and, 177
- Field, with Roasted Beets, Goat Cheese Croutons, and Dijon Vinaigrette, 50, 51
- Spicy Sausage, and White Bean Soup, 36
- as spinach substitutes, 224
- see also salad(s)

grilled foods:
- Chicken with Corn-Cherry Tomato Relish, 139
- Duck Breasts with Orange-Balsamic Glaze, 154
- fruitwoods for, 166
- Lamb Kebabs, 126
- Soy-Sesame Tuna, 166
- Spicy Shrimp and Scallops, 173
- T-Bone with Steak House Spices, 108
- Tropical Fruit with Lime Syrup, 290

grits:
- with Cheese, 275
- Cornmeal-Crusted Shrimp with Greens and, 177

Gumbo, 30

h

Halibut, Baked, with Lemon and Capers, 156
ham:
- cooking of, xi
- -and-Mushroom Crêpes, 12
- Pepper, and Onion Calzones, 236, 237
- Prosciutto-Wrapped Scallops, 174, 175
- Split Pea Soup with Cheese and, 28, 29
- -and-Swiss Mini Quiches, 100

Hash Browns, Egg, and Cheese Casserole, 5
Hawaiian Mousse Circa 1970, 303
Hearty Stovetop Beef Stew, 112
herbs, vii, ix, 229
- Bubble Bread with Sun-Dried Tomatoes and, 38, 74
- Chilled Broccoli Soup with Lemon and, 45
- Roast Chicken with Lemon and, 128
- see also specific herbs

Huevos Rancheros in Tortilla Cups, 14, 15

i

Iceberg Salad with Blue Cheese Dressing, 58
"Ice Cream," Banana, 91
Iconic Weight Watchers Burger, The, 104
Idaho Fries with Vinegar, 268, 269
Indian flavors:
- Curried Vegetable Stew, 188, 189
- Tandoori-Marinated Turkey Breast, 149

Individual Beef Wellingtons, 106, 107
ingredients, vii-viii
- better choices for, 229
- shopping for, viii

Irish Lamb Stew, 127
Irish Soda Bread, 79
Italian flavors, 207-28, 230-39
- Baked Ziti with Meatballs, 222, 223
- Basic Pizza Crust, 209
- Broccoli-Cheddar-Mushroom Pizza, 231
- Capellini with Seafood, 220
- Cheese Ravioli with Butternut Squash Sauce, 228
- Chicken Cacciatore, 134
- Chicken Parmigiana, 137
- Creamy Polenta with Mushroom Ragu, 204
- Easy Homemade Macaroni and Cheese, 214, 215
- Farfalle with Tomatoes, Goat Cheese, and Basil, 212
- Ham, Pepper, and Onion Calzones, 236, 237
- Italian Bean and Vegetable Stuffed Mushrooms, 196
- Lemon Risotto with Spring Vegetables, 200, 201
- Linguine with Red Clam Sauce, 217
- Marinara Sauce, 208
- Minestrone, 38, 39
- Mocha Espresso Granita, 319
- Orechiette with Broccoli Rabe, Garlic, and Red Pepper Flakes, 199
- Panna Cotta with Raspberry Sauce, 312
- Pasta Primavera, 198
- Penne alla Vodka, 213
- Pizza all'Insalata, 232, 233
- Pizza Margherita, 230

Italian flavors *(continued)*
Prosciutto-Wrapped Scallops, 174, 175
Rigatoni with Meat Sauce, 225
Rotelle with Walnut-Gorgonzola Sauce, 210, 211
Sausage Focaccia, 76, 77
Seafood Pizza, 234
Shells with Spinach, Ricotta, and Raisins, 224
Shrimp Scampi with Fresh Linguine, 178
Spaghetti Carbonara, 221
Tiramisu, 309
Tuscan Panzanella, 54, 55
Vegetable Lasagna, 226, 227
Vegetable Ragu with Tagliatelle, 218, 219

k

Key Lime Pie, 302
kitchen shears, x
knives, ix

l

lamb:
Chops with Mint Pesto, 125
Chops with Rosemary and Red Wine, 124
cooking of, xi
Kebabs, 126
lean cuts of, xii
Stew, Irish, 127
Lasagna, Vegetable, 226, 227
Lattice-Topped Cherry-Almond Pie, 307
Leek-Potato Soup, 43
lemon(s):
Baked Halibut with Capers and, 156
Bars, 297
-Basil Three-Bean Salad, 60, 61
Broccoli Rabe with Garlic and, 249
Brussels Sprouts with Dried Cranberries and, 250
-Caper Sauce, Chicken with, 142
Chilled Broccoli Soup with Herbs and, 45
Risotto with Spring Vegetables, 200, 201
Roast Chicken with Herbs and, 128
shells for frozen desserts, 319
lentil(s):
Soup, 31
-Tofu Burgers, 184
Warm, with Escarole, 197
lime(s):
Key, Pie, 302
-Soy Marinated Flank Steak, 109
Syrup, Grilled Tropical Fruit with, 290
linguine:
with Red Clam Sauce, 217
Shrimp Scampi with Fresh, 178
lunch recipes, 23-79
see also bread(s); salad(s); sandwiches; soup(s)

m

Mango-Soy Smoothie, 21, 320
Margherita Pizza, 230
Marinara Sauce, 208
Marinated Mediterranean Chicken, 147
Mashed Potatoes, Roasted-Garlic, 107, 271
measurements, measuring, viii-ix
dry and liquid, xiii
metric, xiv
meat, *see* beef; lamb; pork
meatballs:
Baked Ziti with, 222, 223
Turkey, 153
meatless entrées, 183-205
Barley Mushroom "Risotto," 203
Black Bean and Corn Cakes, 205
Black Bean and Soy Chili, 187
Chickpea Croquettes with Roasted Tomato Sauce, 192
Creamy Polenta with Mushroom Ragu, 204
Curried Vegetable Stew, 188, 189
Lemon Risotto with Spring Vegetables, 200, 201
Mushroom Patties Circa 1990, 191
Orechiette with Broccoli Rabe, Garlic, and Red Pepper Flakes, 199
Pad Thai, 202
Pasta Primavera, 198
Red Bean, Spinach, and Tomato Burritos, 193
Soyful Scalloped Potatoes, 190
Stuffed Cabbage Rolls, 186
Tempeh-Vegetable Stir-Fry with Peanut Sauce, 185
Tofu-Lentil Burgers, 184
Vegetable Quesadillas, 194, 195
Warm Lentils with Escarole, 197
Meatloaf, Diner-Style, 150, 151
Meat Sauce, Rigatoni with, 225
Mediterranean flavors:
Clam Chowder, 26
Marinated Chicken, 147
Moroccan Swordfish with Couscous, 157
see also Greek flavors
Mexican flavors, 165
Beef, Bean, and Zucchini Chili, 114, 115
Beef Fajitas, 113
Black Bean and Corn Cakes, 205
Chicken Wraps, 69
Huevos Rancheros in Tortilla Cups, 14, 15
Nachos Grande, 87, 95
Red Bean, Spinach, and Tomato Burritos, 193
Southwestern Chicken-Vegetable Soup, 34, 35
Tex-Mex Pizza, 235
Tortilla-Cheese Casserole, 246
Vegetable Quesadillas, 194, 195
Microwave Chickpea and Vegetable Soup Circa 1990, 33
Minestrone, 38, 39
Mini Cheesecake Bites with Blueberry Topping, 296
mint:
Pesto, Lamb Chops with, 125
Pureed Peas with, 263
-Yogurt Dressing, Fruit Salad with, 66
Mocha Espresso Granita, 319
Moroccan Swordfish with Couscous, 157
mozzarella cheese:
Cheese Crisps, 86
Cheesy Pepperoni-Mushroom Flatbread, 98, 99
Multigrain Cereal, 20
Multigrain Loaf with Flaxseeds, 73
mushroom(s):
Barley "Risotto," 203
-Barley Soup, 32
-Broccoli-Cheddar Pizza, 231
-Cheese Pâté 1986, 191

Gravy, Salisbury Steaks with, 116
-and-Ham Crêpes, 12
Italian Bean and Vegetable Stuffed, 196
Patties Circa 1990, Vegetarian, 191
"Peanuts," 93
-Pepperoni Flatbread, Cheesy, 98, 99
Portobello Burgers, 72
Ragu, Creamy Polenta with, 204
Sandwich Spread Circa 1970, 191
Sauce, Roasted Beef Tenderloin with, 105
Shiitake, Stir-Fried Baby Bok Choy with Snow Peas, Ginger, and, 254, 255
-Spinach-Bacon Salad with Warm Onion Dressing, 63
-Swiss Omelettes, 3
mussels:
farm-raised, 169
in White Wine with Garlic, 169

n

Nachos Grande, 87, 95
New Pork and Beans, The, 118
No-Bake Strawberry-Rhubarb Crisp, 291
nut(s):
-and-Fruit Granola, 16, 17
how to toast, 282
see also specific nuts

o

omelettes:
Mushroom-Swiss, 3
for Two, 2
onion(s):
Baked Vidalia Balsamico, 260
Braised Red Cabbage with Apples, Raisins and, 120, 252
Caramelized, Spinach, and Tomato Quiche, 10, 11
chopped and frozen, 261
Dip, Creamy, 89
Gravy, Skillet Pork Chops with, 122, 123
Ham, and Pepper Calzones, 236, 237
Oven-Fried Rings, 261, 268
and Pickled Beet Salad, 56
Sautéed Swiss Chard and, 265
Soup Gratinée, French, 24
Warm Dressing, Spinach-MushroomBacon Salad with, 63
orange(s):
-Balsamic Glaze, Grilled Duck Breasts with, 154
Chicken, 140, 141
Fennel, and Red Cabbage Salad with Citrus Vinaigrette, 49
Watermelon, and Tomato Salad, 67
Orechiette with Broccoli Rabe, Garlic, and Red Pepper Flakes, 199
oregano:
Dressing, Greek Salad with, 59
freezing, 259
Green Beans with Tomato and, 259
Oven-Fried Fish and Chips, 162, 163
Oven-Fried Onion Rings, 261, 268

p

Pad Thai, 202
Paella Valenciana, 172
Panna Cotta with Raspberry Sauce, 312
pantry staples, 176
Parmesan Cheese:
Cheese Puffs, 84, 85
Chicken Parmigiana, 137
Creamy White Bean-Parmesan Soup, 37
Hash Browns, and Cheese Casserole, 5
Ratatouille au Gratin, 247
pasta, viii, 229
Asian Noodle Soup with Tofu and Shrimp, 25
Baked Macaroni, Cheese, and Cauliflower Casserole Circa 1980, 257
Baked Ziti with Meatballs, 222, 223
Capellini with Seafood, 220
Cheese Ravioli with Butternut Squash Sauce, 228
Easy Homemade Macaroni and Cheese, 214, 215
Farfalle with Tomatoes, Goat Cheese, and Basil, 212
Linguine with Red Clam Sauce, 217
Orechiette with Broccoli Rabe, Garlic, and Red Pepper Flakes, 199
Pad Thai, 202
Penne alla Vodka, 213
Primavera, 198
Rigatoni with Meat Sauce, 225
Rotelle with Walnut-Gorgonzola Sauce, 210, 211
Shells with Spinach, Ricotta, and Raisins, 224
Shrimp Scampi with Fresh Linguine, 178
Spaghetti Carbonara, 221
Spinach and Roasted Red Pepper Ravioli Casserole, 216
Tuna Noodle Casserole, 180, 181
Turkey Tetrazzini Casserole, 152
Vegetable Lasagna, 226, 227
Vegetable Ragu with Tagliatelle, 218, 219
pea(s):
Pureed with Mint, 263
snow, see snow peas
Split, Soup with Ham and Cheese, 28, 29
Sugar Snap, Duck Stir-Fry with, 155
Peach-Raspberry Cobbler, 292, 293
peanuts, peanut butter:
-Banana Smoothie, 22
Chicken Satay with Peanut Sauce, 135
Fudge Circa 1980, Crunchy, 303
Mushroom, 93
Nutty Apple Slices, 91
Tempeh-Vegetable Stir-Fry with Peanut Sauce, 185
Pear-Arugula Salad with Gorgonzola Dressing, 48
Penne alla Vodka, 213
pepper(s):
-Cheese Muffin, 20
Fish Tacos with Chipotle Cream, 164, 165
frying, 218
Ravioli Casserole, Spinach, and Roasted Red, 216
Red, Flakes, Orechiette with Broccoli Rabe, Garlic and, 199
Sauce, Salmon Cakes with Red, 179
White Bean-Tomato Dip with Grilled, 90
Pepperoni-Mushroom Flatbread, Cheesy, 98, 99
Pickled Beet and Onion Salad, 56

pie crusts, 306
Basic Pizza, 209
Chocolate Graham, 301
Lattice-Topped, 307
pies:
Banana Cream, 301
Boston Cream, 298, 299
Key Lime, 302
Lattice-Topped Cherry-Almond, 307
Pumpkin Chiffon Circa 1980, 303
Sweet Potato, 306
pilafs:
Bulgur, 277
Quinoa, 278
Piña Colada Smoothie, 21
Pine Nuts, Steamed Cauliflower with Raisins and, 256
pizzas:
basic crust, 209
Broccoli-Cheddar-Mushroom, 231
frozen, 235
Greek, 239
Ham, Pepper, and Onion Calzones, 236, 237
handmade dough, 230
all'Insalata, 232, 233
Margherita, 230
Seafood, 234
Tex-Mex, 235
White, 238
Pizza-Style Cauliflower Casserole, 242
Plum-and-Port Compote, Spiced, 284, 285
Poached Chicken Breasts with Green Sauce, 138
polenta:
Creamy, with Mushroom Ragu, 204
Hotcakes, 20
Popcorn, Chili, 91
pork:
and Beans, The New, 118
blackening mix with, 160
Chops, Stuffed, 120, 121
Chops with Onion Gravy, Skillet, 122, 123
cooking of, xi
lean cuts of, xii
Loin Roast with Gingersnap Sauce, 117
Marsala, 119
Port-and-Plum Compote, Spiced, 284, 285
Portobello Burgers, 72
potato(es):
and Fontina Frittata, Red, 4
German Hot Salad, 272
Hash Browns, Egg, and Cheese Casserole, 5
Idaho Fries with Vinegar, 268, 269
-Leek Soup, 43
Oven-Fried Fish and Chips, 162, 163
Roasted-Garlic Mashed, 107, 271
Salad with Tarragon-Chive Dressing, 273
Soyful Scalloped, 190
Twice-Baked, Greek-Style, 270
poultry, *see* chicken; duck; turkey
Prosciutto-Wrapped Scallops, 174, 175
Pudding (savory), Cheddar Corn, 262
pudding(s) (sweet):
Baked Rice, with Currants, 316
Boston Cream Pie, 298, 299
Bread, with Winter Fruits, 294
Chocolate Yogurt, 91
Fudgy Brownie Cake, 318
pumpkin(s)
Chiffon Pie Circa 1980, 303
Rolls, 75
Pureed Peas with Mint, 263

q

Quesadillas, Vegetable, 194, 195
quiche(s):
Ham-and-Swiss Mini, 100
Spinach, Caramelized Onions, and Tomato, 10, 11
quinoa, viii
Berry, 20
Pilaf, 278

r

Radicchio, Arugula, and Belgian Endive Salad with Creamy Garlic Dressing, 52
raisin(s):
Braised Red Cabbage with Apples, Onions, and, 120, 252
Citrus, and Date Baklava, 300
Shells with Spinach, Ricotta, and, 224
Steamed Cauliflower with Pine Nuts and, 256
raspberry(ies):
-Peach Cobbler, 292, 293
Sauce, Panna Cotta with, 312
Ratatouille au Gratin, 247
ravioli:
Casserole, Spinach and Roasted Red Pepper, 216
Cheese, with Butternut Squash Sauce, 228
refrigerator staples, 176
Rhubarb-Strawberry Crisp, No-Bake, 291
rice:
Confetti Salad, 279
Fried, 276
Pudding with Currants, Baked, 316
Rigatoni with Meat Sauce, 225
risotto:
Barley Mushroom, 203
Lemon, with Spring Vegetables, 200, 201
Roast Chicken with Lemon and Herbs, 128
Roasted Beef Tenderloin with Mushroom Sauce, 105
Roasted-Garlic Mashed Potatoes, 107, 271
Root Vegetables, Roasted, 266
Rosemary, Lamb Chops with Red Wine and, 124
Rotelle with Walnut-Gorgonzola Sauce, 210, 211

s

saffron, 172
Sage, Butternut Squash Soup with, 42
salad(s):
Arugula, Radicchio, and Belgian Endive, with Creamy Garlic Dressing, 52
Arugula-Pear with Gorgonzola Dressing, 48
Barley Waldorf, 57
Caesar, 53
California Sandwiches, 68
Carrot, with Toasted Sesame-Ginger Dressing, 267
Chef's, with Russian Dressing, 62
Chicken Véronique, 136
Cobb, with Green Goddess Dressing, 64, 65

Coleslaw, 71, 253
Confetti Rice, 279
Corn, Zucchini, and Green Bean, 258
Fennel, Orange, and Red Cabbage, with Citrus Vinaigrette, 49
Field Greens with Roasted Beets, Goat Cheese, Croutons, and Dijon Vinaigrette, 50, 51
Fruit, with Yogurt-Mint Dressing, 66
German Hot Potato, 272
Greek, with Oregano Dressing, 59
Iceberg, with Blue Cheese Dressing, 58
Lemon-Basil Three-Bean, 60, 61
Pickled Beet and Onion, 56
Pizza all'Insalata, 232, 233
Potato, with Tarragon-Chive Dressing, 273
Spinach-Mushroom-Bacon, with Warm Onion Dressing, 63
Tuscan Panzanella, 54, 55
Vegetable, with Dijon Vinaigrette, 47
Watermelon, Tomato, and Orange, 67
salad dressings:
Blue Cheese, 58
Citrus Vinaigrette, 49
Creamy Garlic, 52
Dijon Vinaigrette, 47, 50
Gorgonzola, 48
Green Goddess, 65
Oregano, 59
Russian, 62
Tarragon-Chive, 273
Toasted Sesame-Ginger, 267
Warm Onion, 63
Yogurt-Mint, 66
Salisbury Steaks with Mushroom Gravy, 116
salmon:
Cakes with Red Pepper Sauce, 179
en Papillote, 161
Salsa with Tortilla Chips, Shrimp, 101
sandwiches:
California Salad, 68
Mexican Chicken Wraps, 69
Mushroom Spread Circa 1970, 191
Portobello Burgers, 72
Tofu-Lentil Burgers, 184
Turkey Sloppy Joes, 70, 71
sauces:
Blueberry Topping, 296
Butternut Squash, 228
Carbonara, 221
Cheese, 243
Gingersnap, 117
Green, 138
Homemade Cocktail, 167
Lemon-Caper, 142
Lime Syrup, 290
Marinara, 208
Meat, 225
Mushroom, 105, 116
Mushroom Ragu, 204
Onion, 122
Orange-Balsamic Glaze, 154
Peanut, 135, 185
Raspberry, 312
Red Clam, 217
Red Pepper, 179
Remoulade, 160
Roasted Tomato, 192
Tartar, 168
Vegetable Ragu, 218
Vodka, 213
Walnut-Gorgonzola, 210
see also salad dressings
Saucy Oven-Baked BBQ Chicken, 130
sausage(s):
Focaccia, 76, 77
White Bean, and Greens Soup, Spicy, 36
Sautéed Swiss Chard and Onion, 265
scallops:
Prosciutto-Wrapped, 174, 175
Spicy Grilled Shrimp and, 173
seafood, viii, x
Capellini with, 220
Pizza, 234
see also fish; specific kinds of shellfish
sesame:
-Ginger Dressing, Carrot Salad with, 267
-Soy Grilled Tuna, 166
Shake-in-the-Bag Chicken, 146
shakes:
Buttermilk, 91
Double-Chocolate Malt, 320, 321
Mango-Soy Smoothie, 21, 320
Orange Dreamsicle, 320, 321
Peanut Butter-Banana Smoothie, 22
Piña Colada Smoothie, 21
shelf staples, 176
Shells with Spinach, Ricotta, and Raisins, 224
Shiitake Mushrooms, Stir-Fried Baby Bok Choy with Snow Peas, Ginger, and, 254, 255
shrimp:
Asian Noodle Soup with Tofu and, 25
blackening mix with, 160
Cornmeal-Crusted, with Grits and Greens, 177
Salsa with Tortilla Chips, 101
Scampi with Fresh Linguine, 178
Spicy Grilled Scallops and, 173
side dishes, 241-79
see also salad(s); specific vegetables and vegetable dishes
Sloppy Joes, Turkey, 70, 71
Smoky Black Bean and Corn Soup, 40
smoothies, *see under* shakes
Snow Peas, Stir-Fried Baby Bok Choy with Shiitake Mushrooms, Ginger, and, 254, 255
soup(s):
Asian Noodle, with Tofu and Shrimp, 25
Borscht with Sour Cream, 44
Butternut Squash, with Sage, 42
Cauliflower, 251
Chilled Broccoli, with Lemon and Herbs, 45
Chilled Zucchini-Basil, with Tomatoes, 46
"Cream" of Cauliflower Circa 1970, 257
Creamy Fish Chowder, 27
French Onion Gratinée, 24
Gazpacho with Cilantro Croutons, 41
Gumbo, 30
leftover cooking liquids used in, 42
Lentil, 31
Mediterranean Clam Chowder, 26
Minestrone, 38, 39
Mushroom Barley, 32
Potato-Leek, 43
Smoky Black Bean and Corn, 40

soup(s) *(continued)*
Spicy Sausage, White Bean, and Greens, 36
Split Pea, with Ham and Cheese, 28, 29
storage of, 31
see also vegetable soup(s)
Sour Cream, Borscht with, 44
Southwestern Chicken-Vegetable Soup, 34, 35
soy:
Chili, Black Bean and, 187
-Lemon Marinated Flank Steak, 109
-Mango Smoothie, 21, 320
-Sesame Grilled Tuna, 166
Soyful Scalloped Potatoes, 190
spaghetti:
Carbonara, 221
Turkey Tetrazzini Casserole, 152
Spanakopita Triangles, 92
Spanish flavors:
Chickpea Croquettes with Roasted Tomato Sauce, 192
Gazpacho with Cilantro Croutons, 41
Paella Valenciana, 95
Spiced Plum-and-Port Compote, 284, 285
Spice-Rubbed Beer Can Chicken, 129
Spicy Grilled Shrimp and Scallops, 173
Spicy Roast Chickpeas, 91
Spicy Sausage, White Bean, and Greens Soup, 36
spinach:
Caramelized Onion, and Tomato Quiche, 10, 11
Creamed, 150, 264
how to wash, 63
-Mushroom-Bacon Salad with Warm Onion Dressing, 63
Red Bean, and Tomato Burritos, 193
and Roasted Red Pepper Ravioli Casserole, 216
Shells with Ricotta, Raisins, and, 224
Split Pea Soup with Ham and Cheese, 28, 29
spring-loaded tongs, ix
Spring Vegetables, Lemon Risotto with, 200, 201
Steamed Cauliflower with Raisins and Pine Nuts, 256
stews:
Curried Vegetable, 188, 189
Hearty Stovetop Beef, 112
Irish Lamb, 127
leftover cooking liquid used in, 42
Paella Valenciana, 172
Ratatouille au Gratin, 247
Stir-Fried Baby Bok Choy with Snow Peas, Shiitake Mushrooms, and Ginger, 254, 255
Stir-Fry with Sugar Snap Peas, Duck, 155
strawberry(ies):
Crêpe, 20
-Rhubarb No-Bake Crisp, 291
Stuffed Celery Redux, 91
Stuffed Pork Chops, 120, 121
Succotash, Corn, Zucchini, and Green Bean, 258
Sugar Snap Peas, Duck Stir-Fry with, 155
sweet potato:
Fritters, 159, 274
Pie, 306
Swingin' Sixties Cheese Dip, 91
Swiss Chard, Sautéed Onion and, 265
Swiss cheese:
-and-Ham Mini Quiches, 100
-Mushroom Omelettes, 3
Strata, 8
Swiss Fondue, 88
Swordfish with Couscous, Moroccan, 157

t

Tabbouleh Niçoise, 170, 171
Tacos, Fish, with Chipotle Cream, 164, 165
Tagliatelle, Vegetable Ragu with, 218, 219
Tandoori-Marinated Turkey Breast, 149
tapenade, 96
Tarragon-Chive Dressing, Potato Salad with, 273
Tartar Sauce, Crab Cakes with, 168
Tempeh-Vegetable Stir-Fry with Peanut Sauce, 185
Tetrazzini Turkey Casserole, 152
Tex-Mex Pizza, 235
thermometers, x-xi
Three-Bean Salad, Lemon-Basil, 60, 61
Tilapia, Blackened, with Remoulade, 160
Tiramisu, 309
Toasted Sesame-Ginger Dressing, Carrot Salad with, 267
tofu:
Asian Noodle Soup with Shrimp and, 25
how to press, 202
-Lentil Burgers, 184
Pad Thai, 202
Soyful Scalloped Potatoes, 190
tomato(es):
Baked Ziti with Meatballs, 222, 223
Burritos, Red Bean, Spinach, and, 193
Chilled Zucchini-Basil Soup with, 46
Cobb Salad with Green Goddess Dressing, 64, 65
Curried Vegetable Stew, 188, 189
Farfalle with Goat Cheese, Basil, and, 212
Gazpacho with Cilantro Croutons, 41
Green Beans with Oregano and, 259
how to peel, 41
how to seed, 101
Huevos Rancheros in Tortilla Cups, 14, 15
in Lentil Soup, 31
Linguine with Red Clam Sauce, 217
Marinara Sauce, 208
Mediterranean Clam Chowder, 26
in Minestrone, 38, 39
Moroccan Swordfish with Couscous, 157
Pizza all'Insalata, 232, 233
Ratatouille au Gratin, 247
Relish, Grilled Chicken with Corn-Cherry, 139
Rigatoni with Meat Sauce, 225
Roasted, Sauce, Chickpea Croquettes with, 192
Scramble, 20
Seafood Pizza, 234
Spinach, and Caramelized Onion Quiche, 10, 11

Sun-Dried, Bubble Bread with Herbs and, 38, 74
Tagliatelle with Vegetable Ragu, 218, 219
Turkey Meatballs, 153
Vegetable Lasagna, 226, 227
Watermelon, and Orange Salad, 67
-White Bean Dip with Grilled Peppers, 90
tortilla(s):
-Cheese Casserole, 246
Chips, Shrimp Salsa with, 101
Cups, Huevos Rancheros in, 14, 15
Tropical Fruit, Grilled, with Lime Syrup, 290
tuna:
Noodle Casserole, 180, 181
Soy-Sesame Grilled, 166
Tabbouleh Niçoise, 170, 171
turkey, viii, 229
Chef's Salad with Russian Dressing, 62
cooking of, xi
Diner-Style Meatloaf, 150, 151
lean cuts of, xii
Meatballs, 153
Nachos Grande, 87, 95
Paella Valenciana, 172
Sloppy Joes, 70, 71
Tandoori-Marinated Breast, 149
Tetrazzini Casserole, 152
see also under sausage(s)
turkey bacon:
Broccoli-and-Bacon Egg Cups, 9
in Cobb Salad with Green Goddess Dressing, 64, 65
in Hash Browns, Egg, and Cheese Casserole, 5
Tuscan Panzanella, 54, 55

v

vegetable(s), vii-ix, xv
Cheese Sauce for, 243
Lasagna, 226, 227
Ragu with Tagliatelle, 218, 219
Ratatouille au Gratin, 247
Roasted Root, 266
Skillet-Braised Chicken with Roasted, 131
Veggie Cup Scramble, 20
see also meatless entrées; under salad(s); specific vegetables
vegetable soup(s):
The Classic Garden, 33
Microwave Chickpea and, Circa 1990, 33
Minestrone, 38, 39
1984, 33
Southwestern Chicken-, 33
vinaigrettes:
Citrus, 49
Dijon, 47, 50
vinegar(s):
balsamic, 154, 260
Idaho Fries with, 268, 269
Vodka, Penne alla, 213

w

Waldorf Salad, Barley, 57
walnut(s):
Chicken Salad Véronique, 136
Citrus, Date, and Raisin Baklava, 300
Cranberry Holiday Mold, 288, 289
-Gorgonzola Sauce, Rotelle with, 210, 211
Warm Lentils with Escarole, 197
Warm Onion Dressing, Spinach-Mushroom-Bacon Salad with, 63
Watermelon, Tomato, and Orange Salad, 67
white beans:
in California Salad Sandwiches, 68
Lemon-Basil Three-Bean Salad, 60, 61
white kidney bean(s) (cannellini):
in Minestrone, 38, 39
-Parmesan Soup, Creamy, 37
Spicy Sausage, and Greens Soup, 36
in Swiss Fondue, 88
-Tomato Dip with Grilled Peppers, 90
White Pizza, 238
wines:
alcohol-free substitutes for, 119
Madeira, 106, 132
Marsala, 119
Red, Lamb Chops with Rosemary and, 124
Spiced Plum-and-Port Compote, 284, 285
White, Mussels with Garlic in, 169
Winter Fruits, Bread Pudding with, 294
Wraps, Mexican Chicken, 69

y

Yankee Pot Roast, 110, 111
yogurt:
A.M. Banana Split, 20
Barley Waldorf Salad, 57
Chicken Salad Véronique, 136
Coleslaw, 253
Creamy Garlic Dressing, 52
Green Goddess Dressing, 64, 65
-Mint Dressing, Fruit Salad with, 66
Pudding, Chocolate, 91
Tandoori-Marinated Turkey Breast, 149

z

Ziti with Meatballs, Baked, 222, 223
zucchini:
-Basil Soup with Tomatoes, Chilled, 46
Beef, and Bean Chili, 114, 115
Corn, and Green Bean Succotash, 258
Corn Bread, 78
Curried Vegetable Stew, 188, 189
in Minestrone, 38, 39
Ratatouille au Gratin, 247
Tagliatelle with Vegetable Ragu, 218, 219
Turkey Meatballs, 153
Vegetable Lasagna, 226, 227